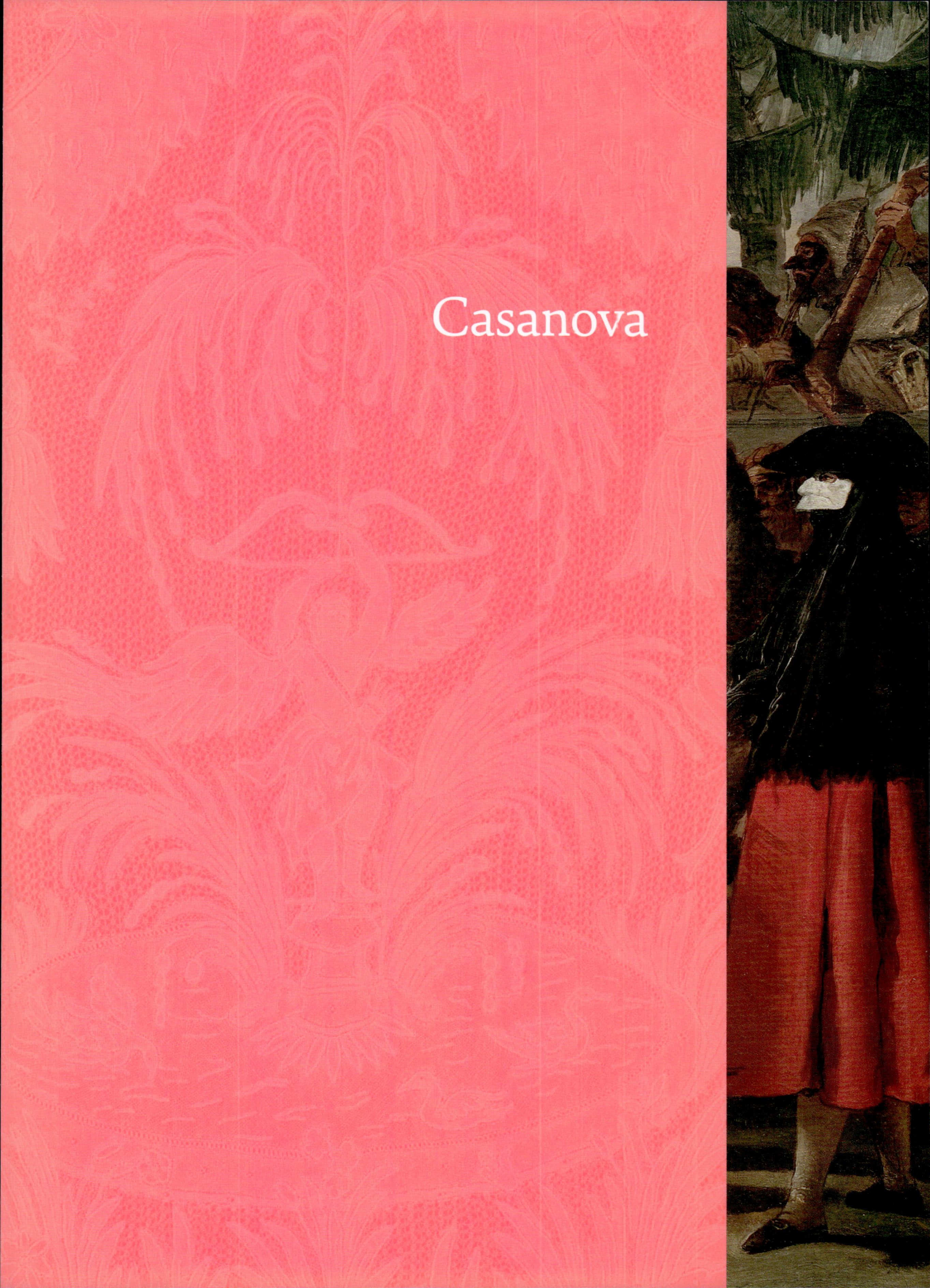

Casanova

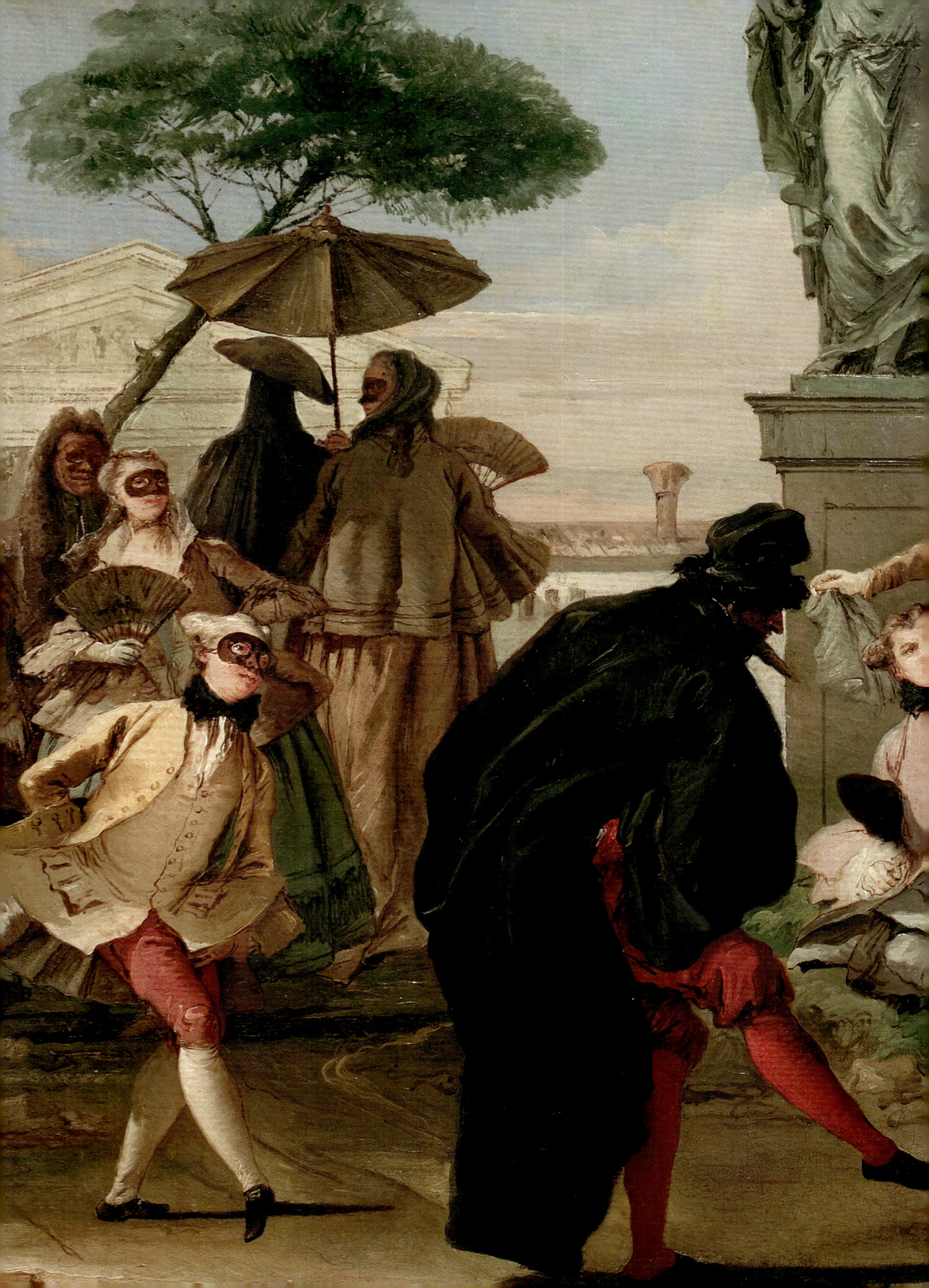

Casanova
The Seduction of Europe

Edited by Frederick Ilchman,
Thomas Michie, C. D. Dickerson III,
and Esther Bell

With contributions by Meredith Chilton, Jeffrey Collins,
Nina L. Dubin, Courtney Leigh Harris, James H. Johnson,
Pamela A. Parmal, Malina Stefanovska, Susan M. Wager,
and Michael Yonan

MFA PUBLICATIONS MUSEUM OF FINE ARTS, BOSTON

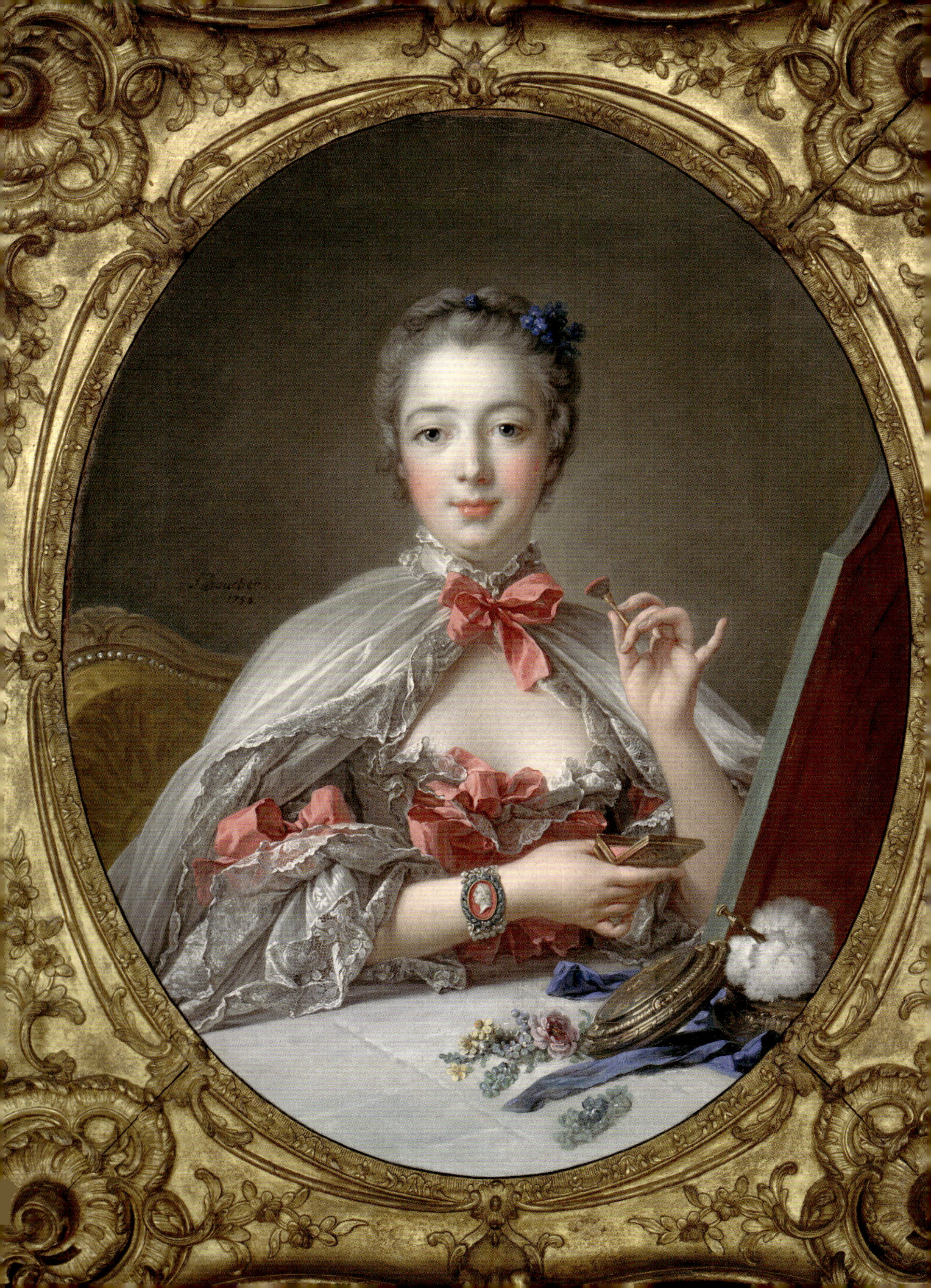

The Art of Display

The Art of Display

C. D. DICKERSON III

Venice is one of the shiftiest cities in the world. Built on unstable marshland in a lagoon, it appears to ride the waves surrounding it, bobbing up and down as the ground beneath it moves. The effect is magically captured in the cityscapes of the great eighteenth-century painter Canaletto, where the scurrying people and swaying ships reinforce the city's unsettled nature (figs. 1, 2). Venice is also shifty by reputation, a place where men and women have traditionally enjoyed disguising their identities and engaging in activities of dubious morality. No figure in Venice's history has contributed more to that reputation than its most famous native son, Giacomo Casanova, born in 1725 (fig. 3). Any reader of his memoirs, *History of My Life* (*Histoire de ma vie* in the original French), can understand why. They recount in excruciating detail his many exploits as a serial womanizer, inveterate cheat, and committed hedonist. He was apparently resigned to his fate as the stereotypical reprobate and unscrupulous lover, admitting in the original preface, "I allow them to call me a pig."[1] If the comment bears more than a hint of frustration, it is because he had spent his life trying to forge a different identity for himself. When he set down his memoirs during the final years of his long life, in the remote Bohemian town of Dux (now Duchcov), where he died in 1798, he hoped his reader would focus on the more edifying sides of his existence: conversations with monarchs and popes, far-flung adventures in all corners of Europe, debates with the great thinkers of his age including Voltaire and Rousseau, feats of audacious cleverness such as the founding of the French national lottery, and

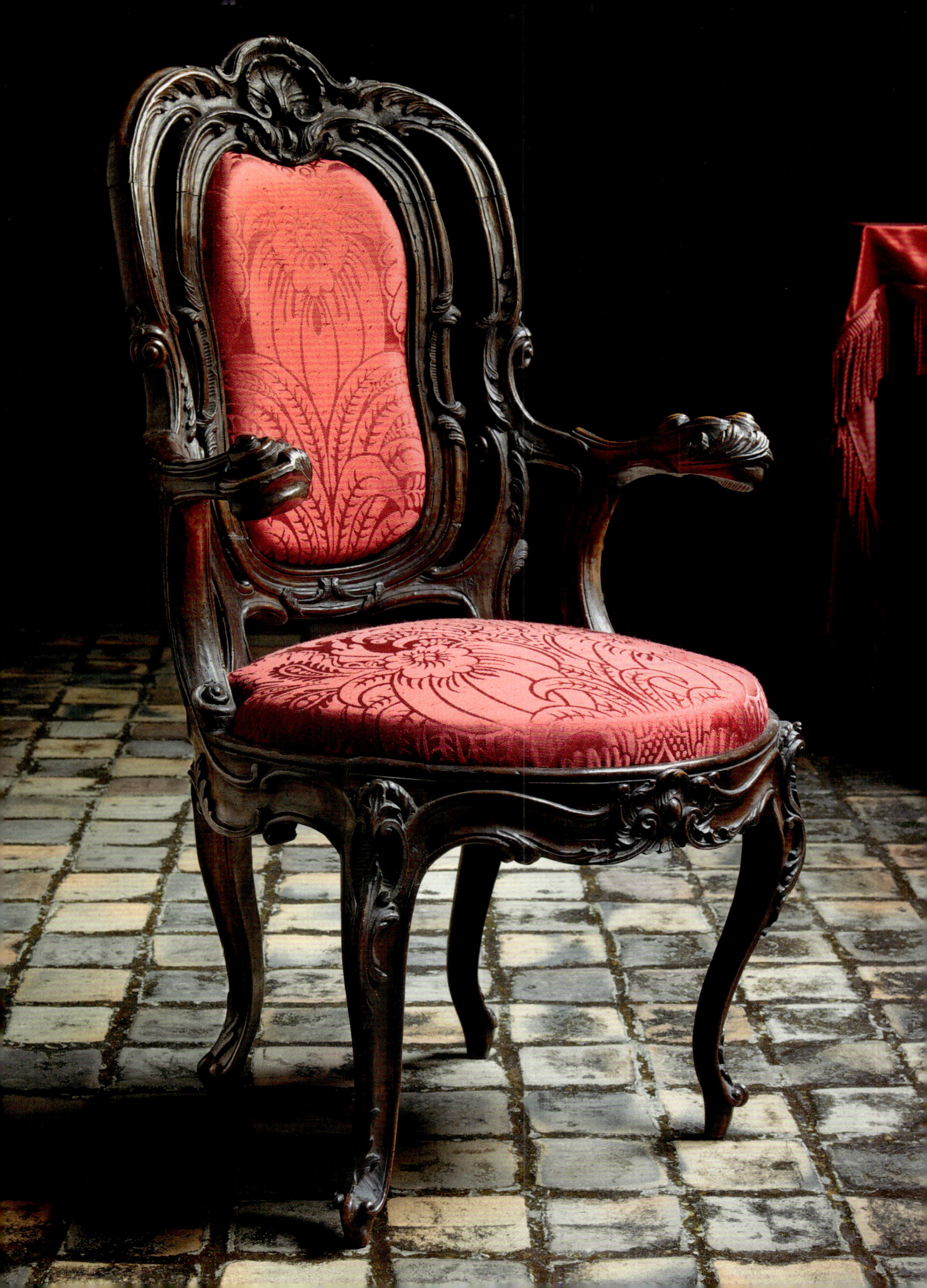

Fig. 7
Pair of wall lights, 1750–60, possibly by Jean-Claude Duplessis (French, 1699–1774), François-Thomas Germain (French, 1726–1791), or Jacques Caffieri (French, 1678–1755). Gilded bronze, each: 88.9 × 61 × 30.5 cm (35 × 24 × 12 in.)

action takes place principally at a *casino* (a small private house) on the island of Murano, rented by Bernis as a secret retreat for his mistress, where he entertained Casanova on multiple occasions. Bernis appears not to have neglected the interior decor: Casanova notes the presence of various candelabras and mirrors, and he also mentions the use of Sèvres porcelain dinnerware (H 4:38). The standard of elegance was sufficiently high that when Casanova selected his own *casino* in which to reciprocate the hospitality, he felt pressured to rent the most luxurious property available, formerly owned by the English ambassador. Its five rooms boasted mirrors, chandeliers, a marble fireplace, walls tiled in Chinese porcelain, and wainscoting embossed with ormolu and painted with arabesques (H 4:46–47). Casanova also arranged for Meissen porcelain to rival the Sèvres used at Bernis's *casino*.

Casanova would continue to have opportunities to appreciate Bernis's taste for the decorative arts after they had concluded their amorous intrigues with C.C. and M.M. In 1755 Bernis left Venice and returned to the French capital, summoned by the king to serve as minister of foreign affairs. Casanova followed less than two years later, arriving at the start of 1757 after his famous escape from Venetian prison. He made it an immediate priority to meet with Bernis, who warmly welcomed him at his apartments at the Palais-Bourbon—one of several residences he kept, including one at Versailles.[12] This meeting happened against a resplendent backdrop of painting, sculpture, and decorative arts (fig. 7). In a letter to his protector, the king's mistress Madame de Pompadour, Bernis mentions having spent two hundred thousand francs on the furnishings of his quarters at the Palais-Bourbon.[13] One guest the decor impressed was the duc de Croÿ, who after a visit in 1758 wrote that Bernis "furnished his house to a level of magnificence rarely seen, especially during so ruinous an age of war."[14] No inventories of the apartments survive, but we can assume they bore the influence of Pompadour. She was responsible for Bernis's rise, earning his supreme devotion, and she was also the leading tastemaker at court. There was no domain over which she exercised a more decisive influence than the visual arts.

Among the evidence that Bernis modeled his decor on Pompadour's is a passage in a letter by Voltaire from 1748. Bernis was then living in the Tuileries Palace, where his apartments were already beginning to resemble those of his later years in their sumptuousness—at least

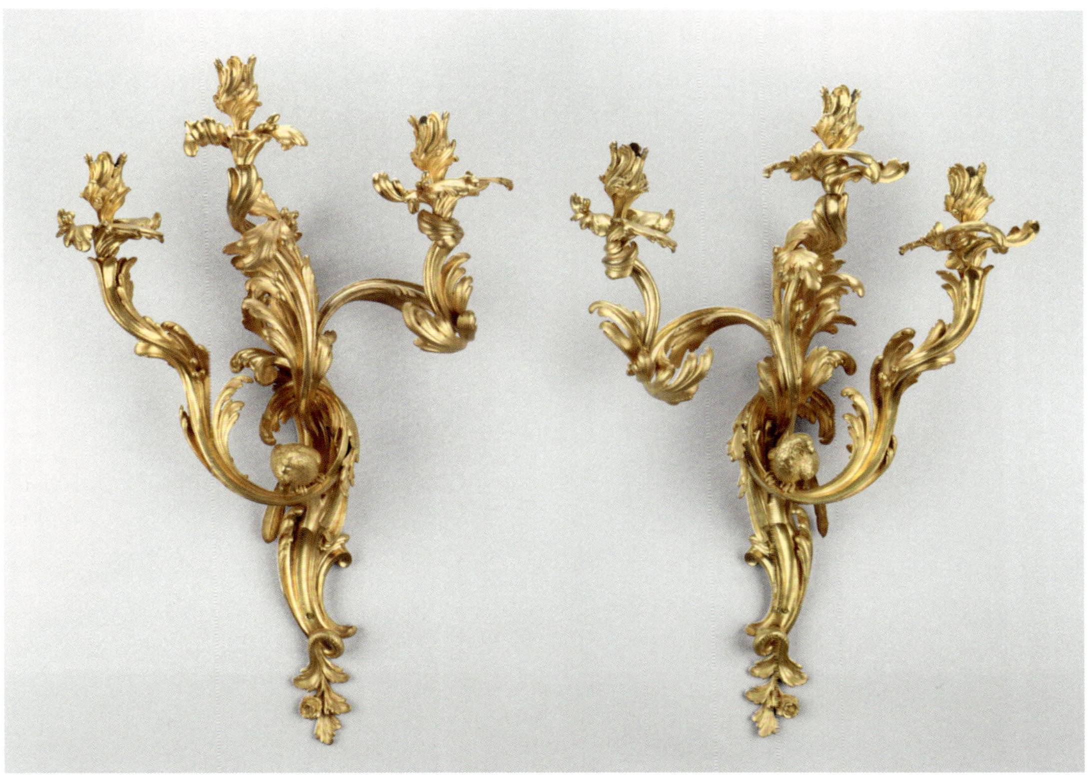

according to Voltaire: "An intoxicating atmosphere presided, among the porcelain magots [figurines] in blue of China and the pearly white statues by Pigalle and Falconet."[15] The reference to ceramics immediately calls to mind Pompadour, a great champion of the porcelain industry in France.[16] The porcelains Voltaire describes may have been from the royal manufactory at Vincennes, which began producing wares in the Saxon, or Meissen, style about 1740—a style that drew on Chinese examples.[17] As for the sculptors Voltaire names, Jean-Baptiste Pigalle and Étienne-Maurice Falconet, they were two of Pompadour's favorites.[18] Discussions with her may have inspired Bernis to acquire examples of their art. We can confirm that when she and Bernis were together, their conversations occasionally turned to matters of decoration: Bernis reports that while he was visiting her apartments one day, she gave him a roll of expensive fabric for decorating his walls.[19]

Although Casanova may not have picked up that Bernis was hosting him in a room that reflected the tastes of Pompadour, he surely recognized that the material surroundings were charged with an elegance appropriate to the man in front of him. This is precisely the reaction Bernis sought. However sincerely he may have loved his works of art for the inventiveness of the designs or the brilliance of the workmanship, he was drawn to collecting mainly for a reason similar to Pompadour's: the recognition that art could be an effective agent of personal and public relations. As minister of foreign affairs, he needed to project an image of cultivation and knowledge, while also signaling the affluence and power his royal office conferred. The right decor, which encompassed paintings and sculptures, helped broadcast these traits. It was not only diplomats who were expected to discern the message; Casanova, as a kind of courtier, was also in the intended audience. The setting conveyed to Casanova that his old friend was in a position to be of use to him. Bernis, for his part, was eager to bring courtiers like Casanova into his fold, as reciprocal favors with them were how he accomplished his diplomatic work.

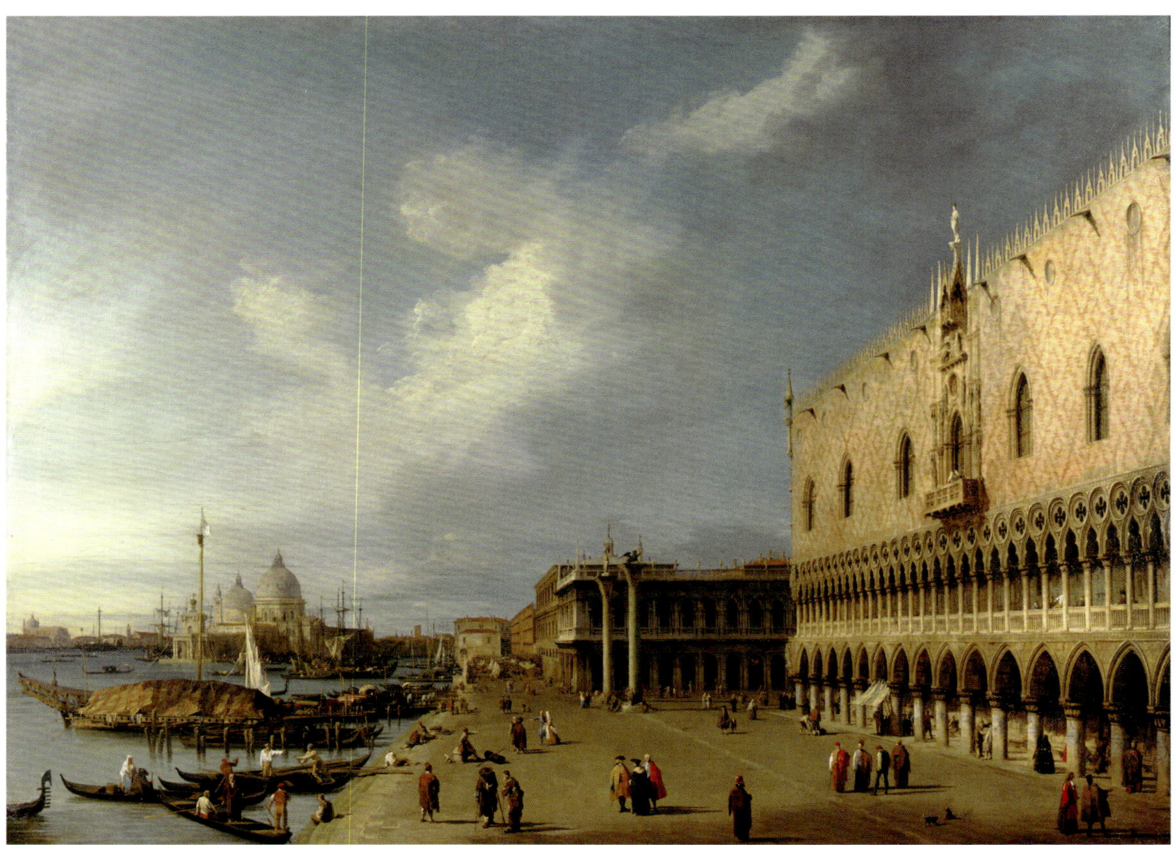

Fig. 8
Giovanni Antonio Canal, called Canaletto (Italian, 1697–1768), *View of the Molo*, about 1730–35. Oil on canvas, 113 × 160.7 cm (44 ½ × 63 ¼ in.)

Across eighteenth-century Europe, men and women at court—from kings and queens to ministers like Bernis—were employing art to mediate the relationships that were at the heart of court business. Roving courtiers such as Casanova participated in this dynamic. Among the reasons they were invited to functions at court was to appreciate the world of luxury on display, which helped them understand their relative place in the social hierarchy, as well as encouraged their loyal service through the promise of rich rewards. Casanova was not expected to walk into a gallery and name the artists represented, or sit down at a banquet and distinguish between the types of porcelain and silverware. Instead, the cumulative effect of the art that surrounded him provided a backdrop to the complex game of social one-upmanship that was the courtier's calling.[20] Casanova's relative silence about art in *History of My Life* does not mean he was immune to its powers—at least not to its capacity to fill a person with wonder at the considerable resources required to collect great art or decorate the perfect room. Yes, this would still mean his interest in art did not run very deep. But it also underscores the extent to which so much of the art produced during the eighteenth century was about making just this kind of impression.

Thanks to a favor worked by Bernis—a direct outcome of their first meeting at the Palais-Bourbon—Casanova had the opportunity to play decorator himself and become the one doing the impressing. Bernis provided him with an introduction to the comptroller general of France, Jean de Boulogne, comte de Nogent-sur-Seine, as well as to the future duc de Choiseul, Étienne-François. Casanova was advised that when he met with these men, he should play the part of financier and suggest a scheme that could generate revenue for the state. The idea he put forth was a national lottery. He succeeded in talking the men into granting him control of six ticket offices, including the most lucrative one, on rue Saint-Denis (H 5:34–35). He was soon flush with cash. His experiences as a courtier helped him know how to spend it most advantageously to raise his social standing—for instance, by keeping his own carriage: "It gave me a reputation and unlimited credit. Paris was, and still is, a city where people judge everything by appearances" (H 5:36–37). A more substantial step up the social ladder was leasing a suburban retreat, named Cracovie-en-bel-air, in 1759 (H 5:179–80).[21] Located in an area of Paris known as the Petite Pologne, it was more manor house than country cottage, with two gardens (one a terrace accessible from the second floor), three suites of apartments, stables for twenty horses, baths, a good cellar, and a great kitchen with all the necessary equipment. If there ever was a moment in his life when he might try to collect art, this was surely it: he would never come closer to owning a home, and he would never be richer. A disincentive for collecting may have been that the house came finely furnished, suitable for Casanova to host dinner parties for distinguished guests, including his great patroness at the time, Jeanne d'Urfé, who reportedly was enchanted by the place (H 5:180). None of the decorations is described, nor is there any mention of acquisitions.

If Casanova made any improvements to the decor, they almost certainly would have involved silk fabrics painted with decorations inspired by Chinese art (see fig. 91). This decorative style, known as chinoiserie, had become all the rage in Paris during the 1750s, and Casanova was not immune to its popularity. He was introduced to a man who proposed that he became a partner in a scheme to produce silk fabrics "de Pekin," or *à la chinoise*. Casanova's description of the samples he was offered demonstrates that he was perfectly capable of responding to art: "What won me over was the design and the beauty of the colors, of which he had the secret.... The beauty of the foliage in silver and gold surpassed what was admired in silks from China which were sold at very high prices in Paris and everywhere." Casanova asked the man to let him observe the work for a week: "He did it very rapidly, and he left me all that he had produced, saying that so far as the lastingness of the colors was concerned I could put the pieces he had painted to any test. I carried the samples in my pockets for five or six days, and I saw that all my good friends were delighted with their beauty and my project" (H 5:231). The enterprise would fail within months, with a dispirited Casanova bemoaning that he would have to give up on something so beautiful (H 5:232). Surely, as proprietor of the workshop, he would have reserved at least some fabric for his home in the Petite Pologne—perhaps as a wall covering or for a folding screen.

During the year or so Casanova was residing at Cracovie-en-bel-air, he was also navigating his difficult relationship with the captivating Manon Balletti, the one woman he seems to have seriously regretted not taking as his wife.[22] There has been frequent speculation that Jean-Marc Nattier's sensitive portrait of Manon was commissioned by Casa-

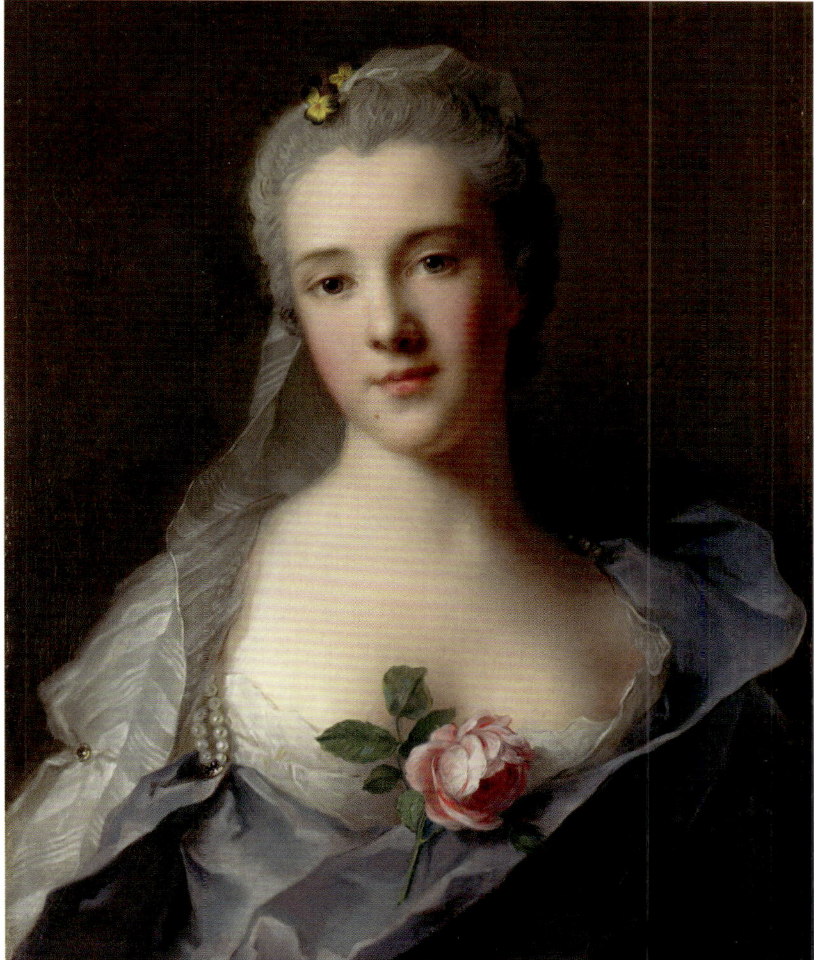

Fig. 9
Jean-Marc Nattier (French, 1685–1766), *Manon Balletti*, 1757. Oil on canvas, 54 × 47.5 cm (21 1/4 × 18 3/4 in.)

nova (fig. 9).[23] If so, he ordered the portrait in 1757, as it was exhibited at that year's annual exhibition of paintings and sculptures at the Louvre, known as the Salon. In considering the possibility he was the patron, it bears noting that he was a personal friend of Nattier through Manon's mother, Silvia, herself a member of the circle of artists and performers with whom Casanova enjoyed socializing in Paris (see fig. 52). In a later section of *History of My Life*, Casanova recalls having asked Nattier about the source of his "magic" as a portraitist (H 6:214). He introduces the question by describing a portrait by Nattier that he had found to be particularly remarkable, but it is not the painting of Manon. Surely, if he had commissioned Manon's portrait, he would have taken this opportunity to alert readers. The portrait was most likely made for Manon's par-

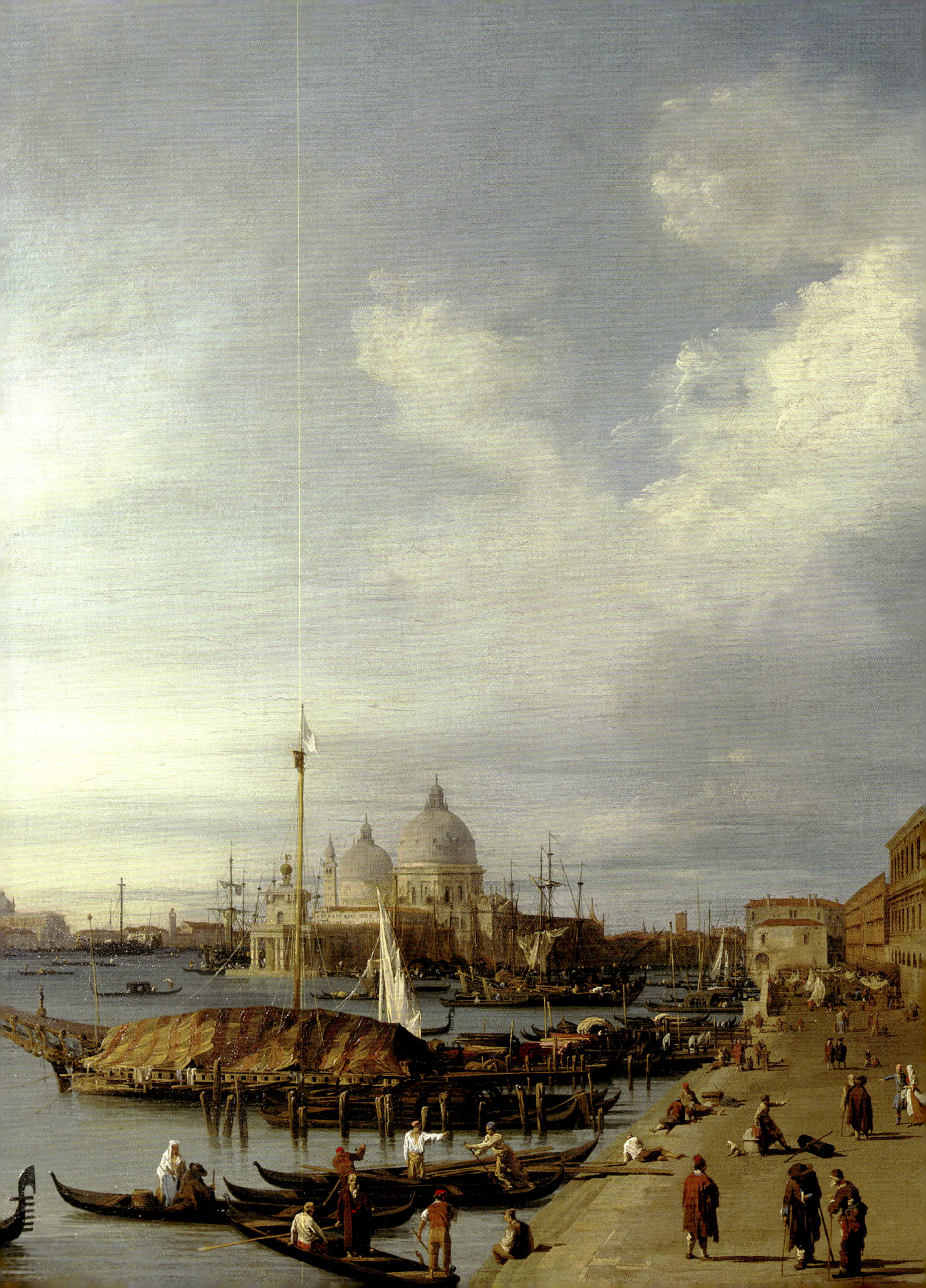

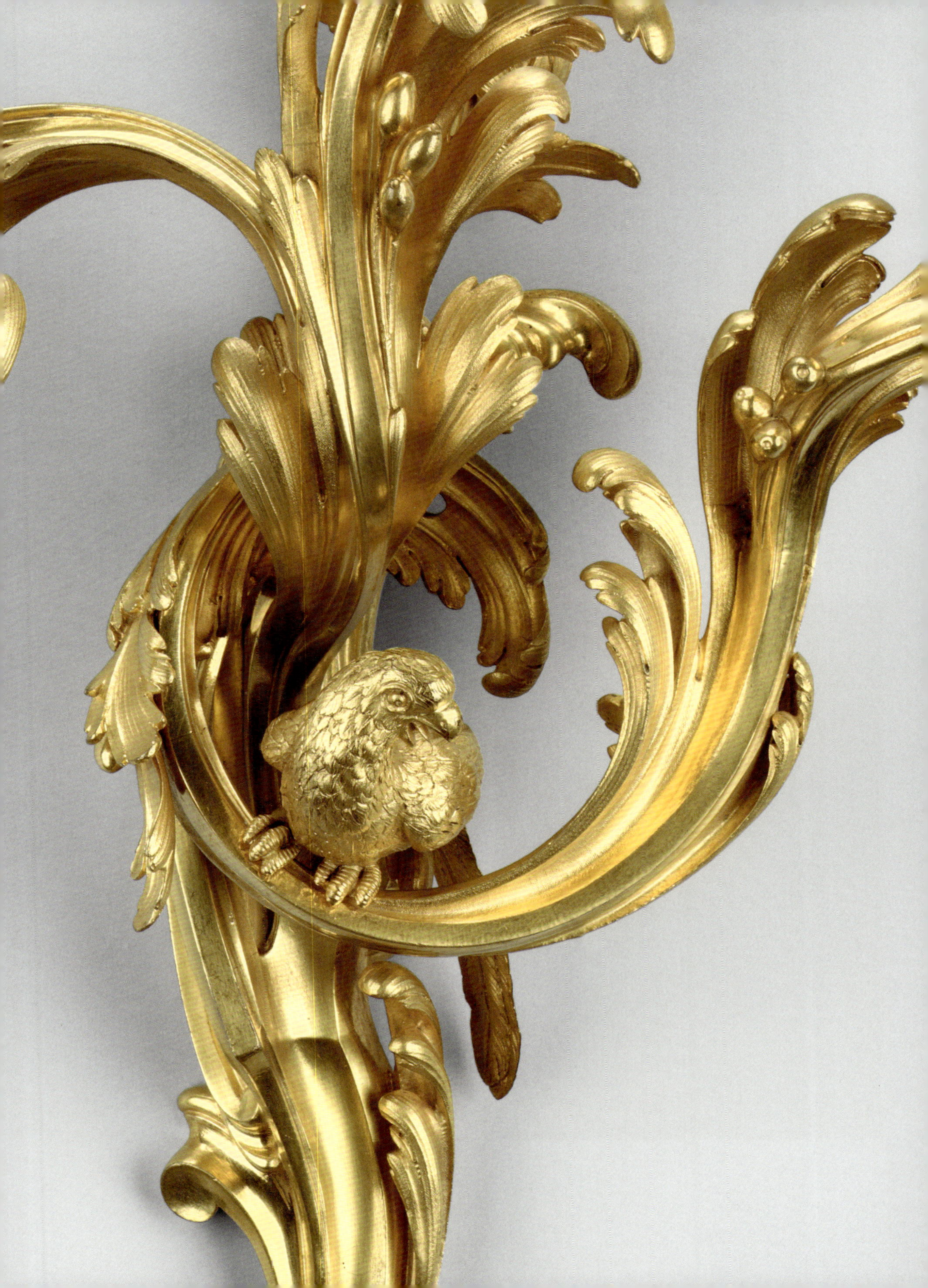

antiquities at the villa that most astonished him (H 7:181–83). Later, he was delighted when his brother gave him an antiquity of his own, an onyx cameo with a depiction of Venus at her bath, reportedly carved by Sostrastus. Casanova writes that he sold the cameo two years later in London and that it may have entered the collection of the British Museum (H 7:256–57).

When Casanova was in Madrid six years later, he became reacquainted with Mengs, now court painter to King Charles III of Spain. As before, Mengs warmly welcomed his visitor, inviting him to dinners and allowing him to watch as he painted at his studio. Presumably, it was during one of these trips to the studio that Casanova leveled a critique against a portrait Mengs was finishing. He recognized that Mengs had made an anatomical mistake, painting the ring finger of a figure's hand shorter than the index finger (H 11:51). The story makes clear that he was prepared to look closely at art, and that he understood one of the most time-honored conventions of judging art, the rule of truth to nature.

Casanova's relationship with Mengs eventually soured when the painter refused to defend him against charges of heretical behavior leveled by a local priest. But he had spent sufficient time with Mengs by then to form at least some idea of how a major European painter approached his work. This insider's perspective was likely deepened by his frequent interactions with other painters. Aside from his brothers and Nattier, Casanova claims to have known Francesco Guardi and Antonio Joli.[30] Whoever painted the nude miniature of O'Murphy—possibly Gustaf Lundberg or Johann Anton de Peters—can be added to this list, which grows even longer with the addition of artists who rendered Casanova's portrait.[31]

There are four certain portraits.[32] The most impressive is a red chalk drawing by his brother Francesco (fig. 14). The other three are a miniature, now lost, of a thirty-year-old

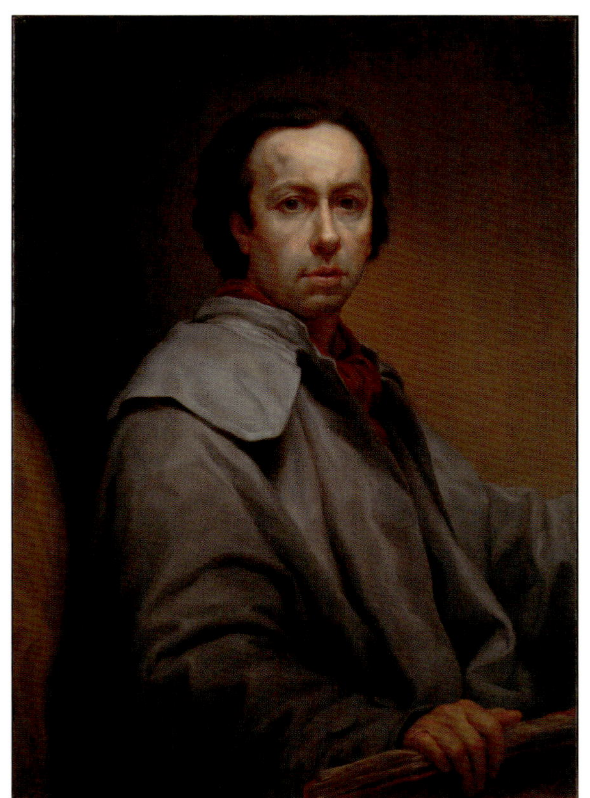

Fig. 13
Anton Raphael Mengs (German, 1728–1779), *Self-Portrait*, 1776. Oil on canvas, 90 × 65.5 cm (35 ½ × 25 ⅞ in.)

Fig. 14
Francesco Casanova (Italian, 1727–1803), *Giacomo Casanova*, about 1751. Red chalk on paper, 20 × 15 cm (7 ⅞ × 5 ⅞ in.)

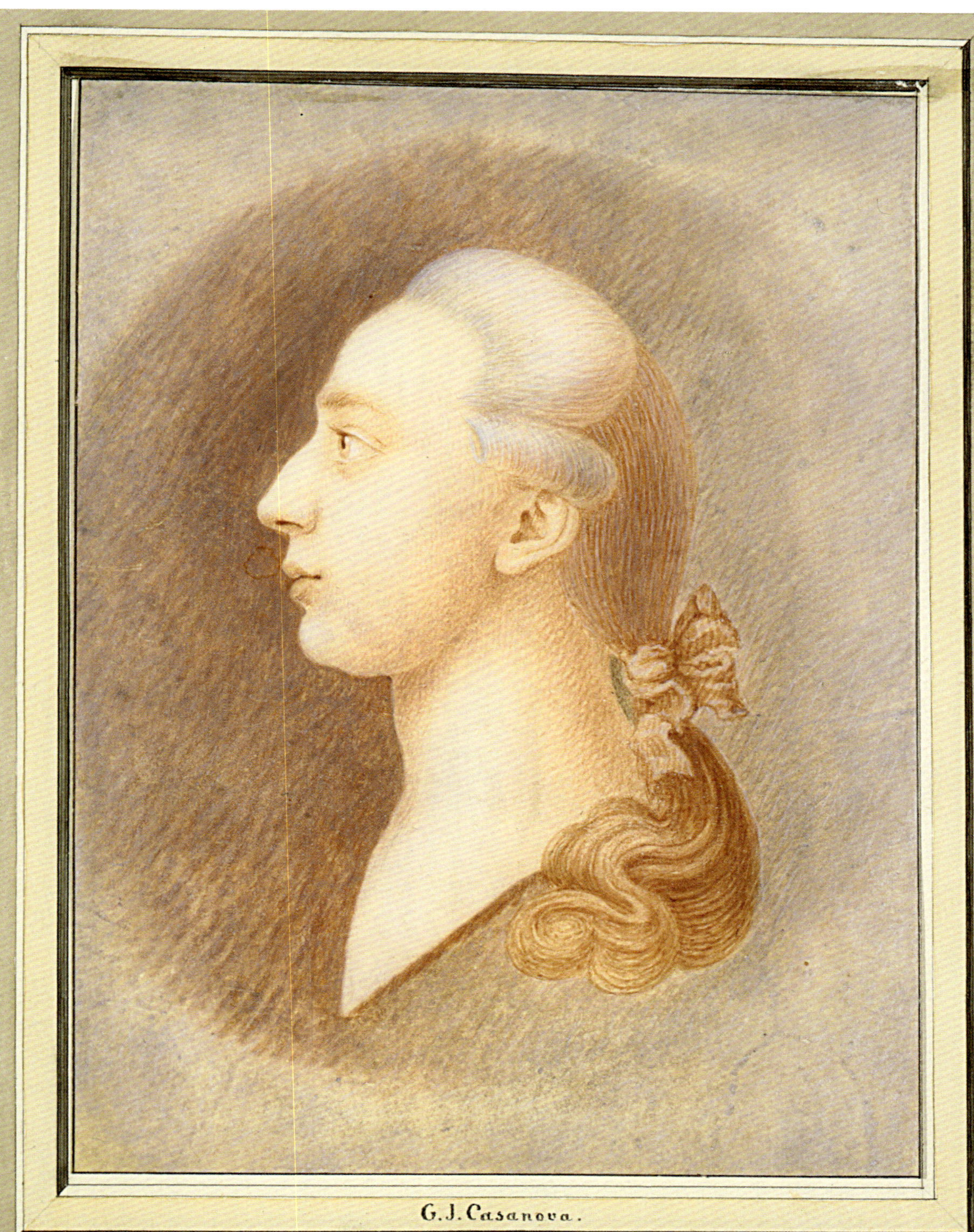
G. J. Casanova.
F. Casanova delineavit.

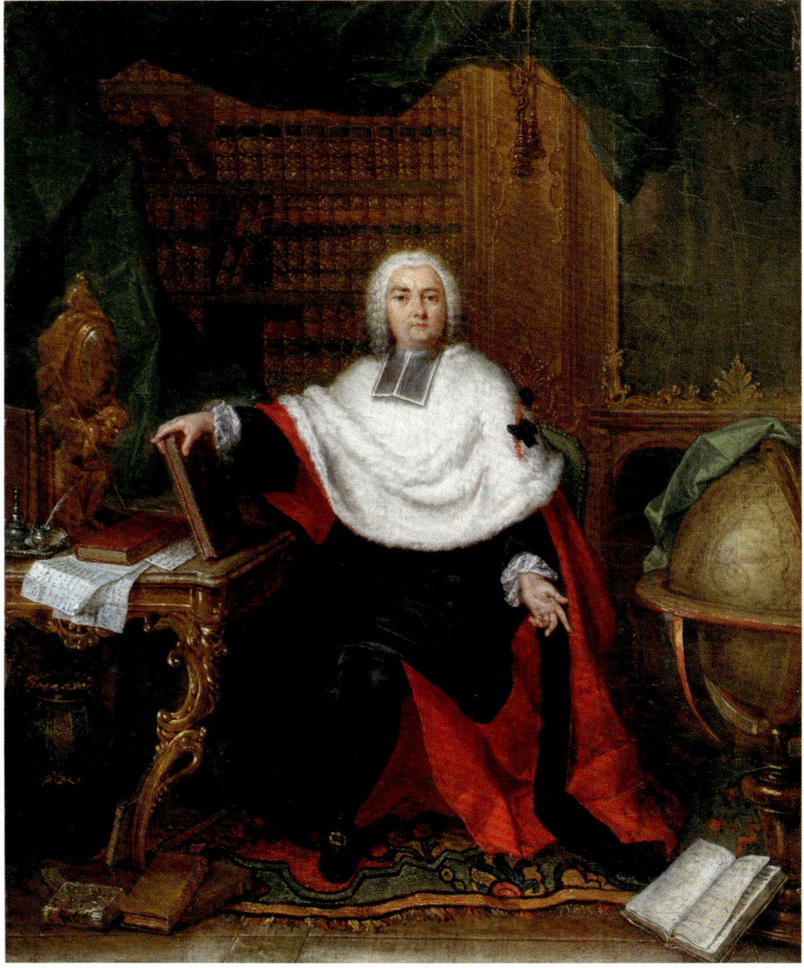

Fig. 15
Pietro Longhi (Italian, 1701–1785), *Abate François-Joachim de Pierre de Bernis, French Ambassador to Venice*, 1753–55. Oil on canvas, 46.6 × 38.5 cm (18 3/8 × 15 1/8 in.)

Casanova in profile, by an unknown artist; a miniature of a seventy-one-year-old Casanova in profile with an inscription identifying Francesco as the portraitist; and an engraving of a sixty-two-year-old Casanova in profile by Jan Berka, a printmaker from Prague (see fig. 31). There are a handful of other portraits that may or may not represent Casanova. The one with the strongest claims is a large oil on canvas that is currently attributed to Francesco Narice. It shows a handsome and well-dressed young man seated with his left hand resting on an open book, as a winged putto hovers nearby (fig. 3). If it does represent Casanova, it was almost certainly done at his behest—not necessarily the case with the two portraits by his brother, which may have originated as casual studies for Francesco's own purposes.

By commissioning portraits, Casanova was participating in deliberate image manipulation. According to one contemporary, Casanova was not blessed with beauty, which is sure to have been unfortunate for a man who fancied himself the answer to every woman's dreams.[33] Casanova seems to have recognized the power of portraiture to amend the truth in ways favorable to the sitter. His portraits reinforce the self-image he projects in *History of My Life*: handsome, intelligent, and suave. His understanding that portraiture could be used to influence the thinking of others was virtually inevitable in his role as a courtier. Portraits were part of the carefully orchestrated experience of going to court, meeting the powerful, and seeking their favor.

When Casanova visited Bernis at his apartments at the Palais-Bourbon in 1757, he was surely paraded past a portrait of his host—possibly the painting by Pietro Longhi from Bernis's time as ambassador to Venice (fig. 15).[34] The work is likely to have returned with Bernis to Paris and, in spite of its diminutive size, probably occupied a privileged position in one of his dwellings, where it would have advertised to visitors that the man they were about to meet wielded the greater power. Dressed in full ambassadorial garb in a richly appointed interior, and surrounded by books and other objects of learning, Bernis proclaims his authority and worldliness. Casanova would have first processed the portrait in these terms before bothering to register the artistry it involved—just as he would have swept his eyes over the surrounding decorative arts and made a mental note of the cumulative luxury but paid little mind to any single object. If we may regret that social politics dominated his reaction, we should not be distracted from the value of viewing the display from the vantage of a courtier like Casanova: the arts of eighteenth-century Europe gain increased accessibility, appearing to us as they appeared to so many of those whom they were originally meant to impress.

Venice

Venice

FREDERICK ILCHMAN

Giacomo Casanova's story begins in Venice. He was born and grew up there, and returned repeatedly during his travels. He spent more than a quarter of his life in the city, far longer than in any other place. Casanova's Venetian origin helped determine his character, predilections, and professional and social opportunities. Although he moved effortlessly in the highest circles across Europe, spoke with kings and philosophers, wrote fluently in French, and was one of the most cosmopolitan figures of his time, he nevertheless remained thoroughly Venetian. Anecdotes from Casanova's years in Venice and consideration of characteristic Venetian spaces, institutions, and works of art can help explain what made him, for better or worse, the man he was.[1]

Venice, in turn, begins with water. Built only marginally above sea level, Venice is protected from the rough waves of the Adriatic by the long sandbar called the Lido. Unthreatened by coastal surf, smaller craft easily navigate the waterways, while their rowers stand upright. Venice claims the most celebrated city canal in the world, the Grand Canal, as well as its own boat, the iconic gondola. Canaletto's jewel-like *Entrance to the Grand Canal* sets the stage for Venice—and for Casanova (fig. 16). At the painting's left, the imposing dome of Santa Maria della Salute (Saint Mary of Health), constructed to commemorate the city's survival of the plague of 1630, marks the start of one of the most spectacular streets in the world, which divides the three northern *sestieri* (or districts) of Venice from the three southern. On the right bank, tall palaces crowd together, demonstrating that land is precious and that the front door

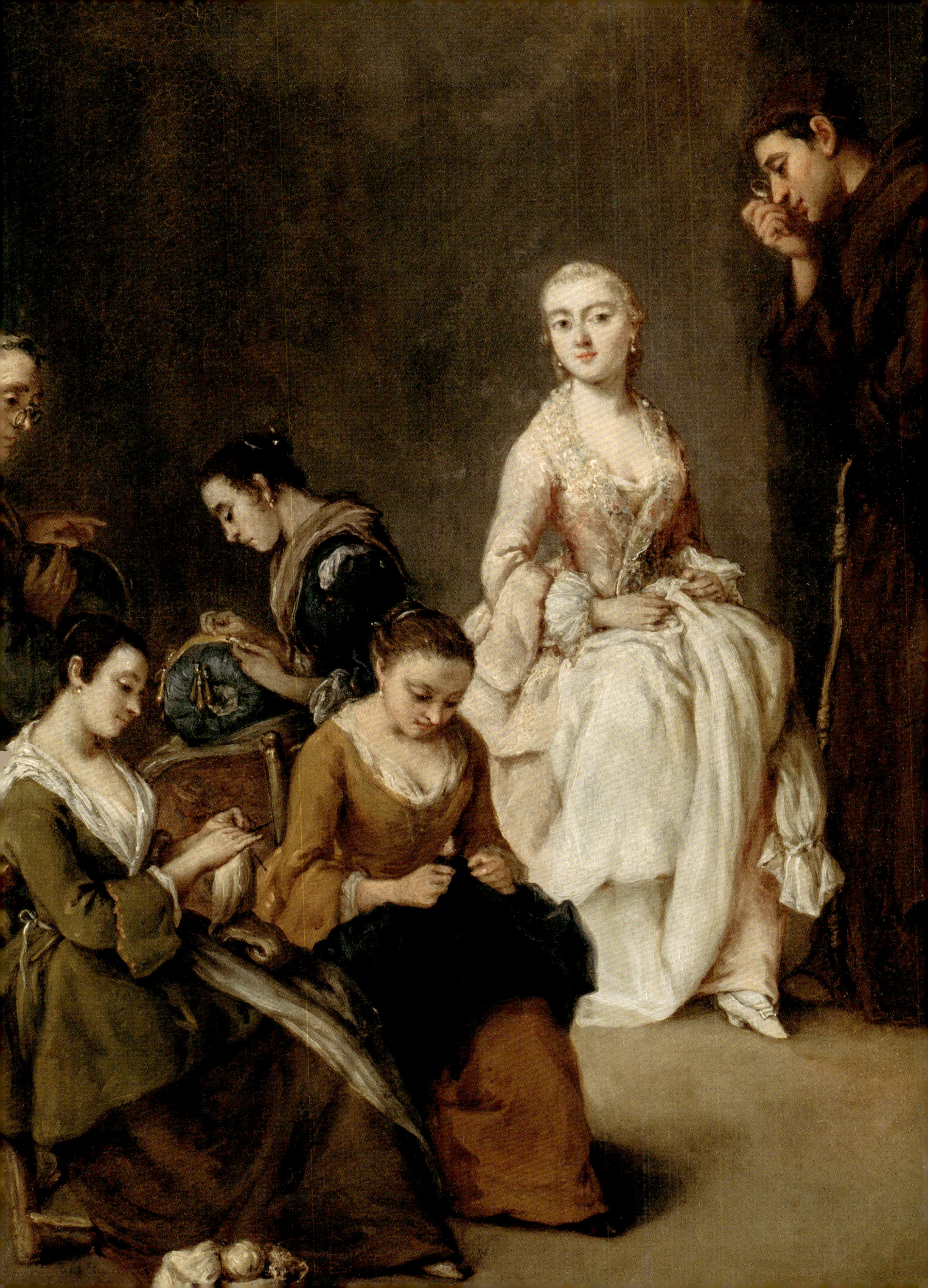

to any substantial building is on the water. Only a few minutes by oar around the bend of the canal to the right is the parish of San Samuele, where Casanova was born, on April 2, 1725, in a modest home on a back street, to an actress named Zanetta Farussi.[2] Although at the time she was married to Gaetano Casanova, a fellow actor, the identity of her son's father remains in dispute. A member of the patrician Grimani family is the most probable candidate.

Just a few years after Casanova's birth, Canaletto created this painting. Rowed boats slowly skim the water's surface, rendered with delicate reflections and varied ripples. The diversity of watercraft and the postures of the boatmen underscore the relation of each boat and gesture to a commercial exchange. At center, two gondoliers in red breeches power an elegant gondola, with a *felze* (cabin with curtains) protecting passengers from weather or prying eyes. Gondolas are invariably painted black, to satisfy sumptuary laws promulgated as early as 1562.[3] The pendant painting, *The Grand Canal Near the Rialto Bridge*, emphasizes the merchants of Venice in the return of large empty barrels in the *topo* (barge) in the left foreground, with a wooden shed for the sale of lottery tickets just beyond, while the foreground gondola features rowers in festive striped livery, dressed for a special event, such as a regatta, or a special passenger (fig. 17). Being on the water offered a welcome contrast with the narrow streets and cramped houses.

Canaletto's *vedute* (view paintings) convey the centrality of boats to daily life in Venice, in Casanova's day and in ours. Venetians still employ the saying "Barca xe casa," or "Your boat is your home," and Casanova's first home was a world of watercraft. Many of Casanova's most striking anecdotes of Venice involve boats. Indeed, his earliest memory, from August 1733, involves a trip to Murano by gondola to stanch a serious nosebleed. Casanova's memoirs recount how he, at the age of eight, was taken by his grandmother to this densely populated island. There he was presented to an old woman, a kind of witch doctor, whose elaborate spells produced the desired relief (H 1:44–46).[4]

Casanova's first absence from the Venetian lagoon, on his ninth birthday, also occasioned his earliest intellectual feat. The aristocratic Grimani family, proprietors of a theater and protectors of Casanova's family, in conjunction with the poet Giorgio Baffo, had determined that the young boy ought to be educated in the nearby university city of Padua.

Trips across the lagoon and into the canals and rivers on the Venetian mainland were accomplished in a *burchiello*, a houseboat with a large covered cabin, which can be seen in the middle ground of Canaletto's *Porta Portello, Padua* (see fig. 130; see also fig. 46). This *burchiello*, whose journey from Venice to Padua is nearly completed (the towers of the destination are visible in the distance), has paused by a flight of steps as a boatman negotiates with a passenger on shore. The overnight trip took Casanova and his mother, along with Alvise Grimani and Baffo, eight hours. At daybreak, the boy was astonished to see trees passing by the windows, since he could not detect the boat's motion. He quickly inquired, "How is it that the trees are walking?" While Grimani laughed, his mother explained that the boat was moving, and not the trees. The young Casanova then made a precocious mental leap, declaring, "Then it is possible, Mother, that the sun does not move either, and that it is we who turn from West to East." Baffo congratulated Casanova on his deduction, praise that he recalled as the "first real pleasure" in his life and that inspired him to begin systematically cultivating his mind (H 1:50–51).

Venetian gondolas also afforded opportunities for mischief. In 1745, as an unmoored twenty-year-old, having abandoned his career as a priest (and barely scraping by as a violinist in a theater orchestra), Casanova joined a roguish gang with a penchant for late-night practical jokes: "We amused ourselves by untying the gondolas moored before private houses, which then drifted with the current... and making merry over the curses the gondoliers would call down on us the next morning" (H 2:185). Such hijinks seem foreign to the orderly world of Canaletto's painted Venice.

Yet a gondola soon also afforded the occasion of the young Casanova's single greatest stroke of luck. An hour before dawn, as he was leaving a palazzo where he had been playing violin at a wedding, he found and returned a letter dropped by a red-robed senator, who offered him a ride home. In the gondola, the senator suffered a stroke. Casanova insisted on finding medical help and accompanied the stricken man to his palazzo in Campo Santa Marina. At a critical moment in the man's treatment, he overruled the physician's orders and removed a mercury compress that was harming the patient. Such quick action saved the life of the senator, Matteo Bragadin, who in gratitude invited Casanova to live at the palazzo and provided him with a servant, a gondola, and an allowance. In

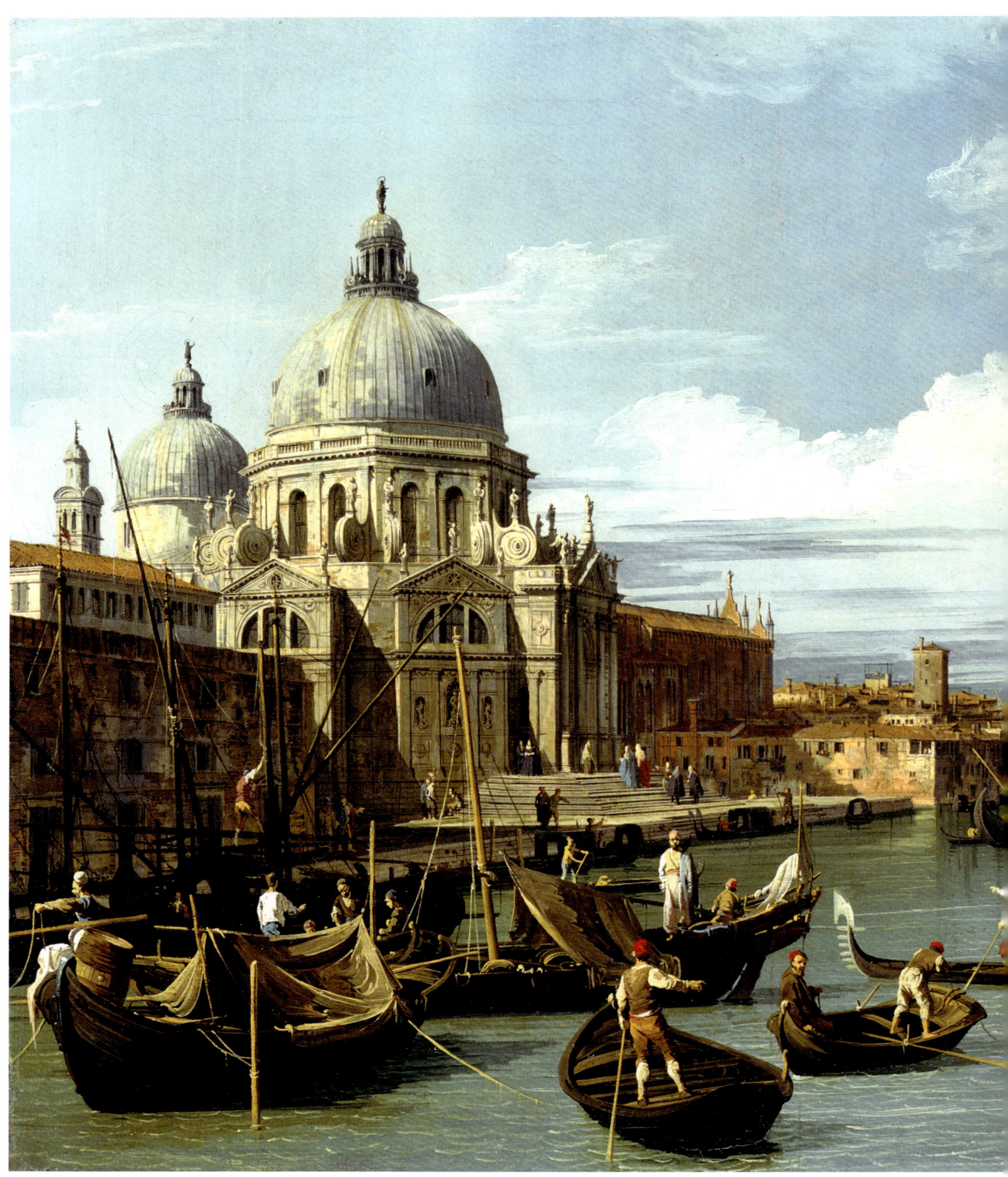

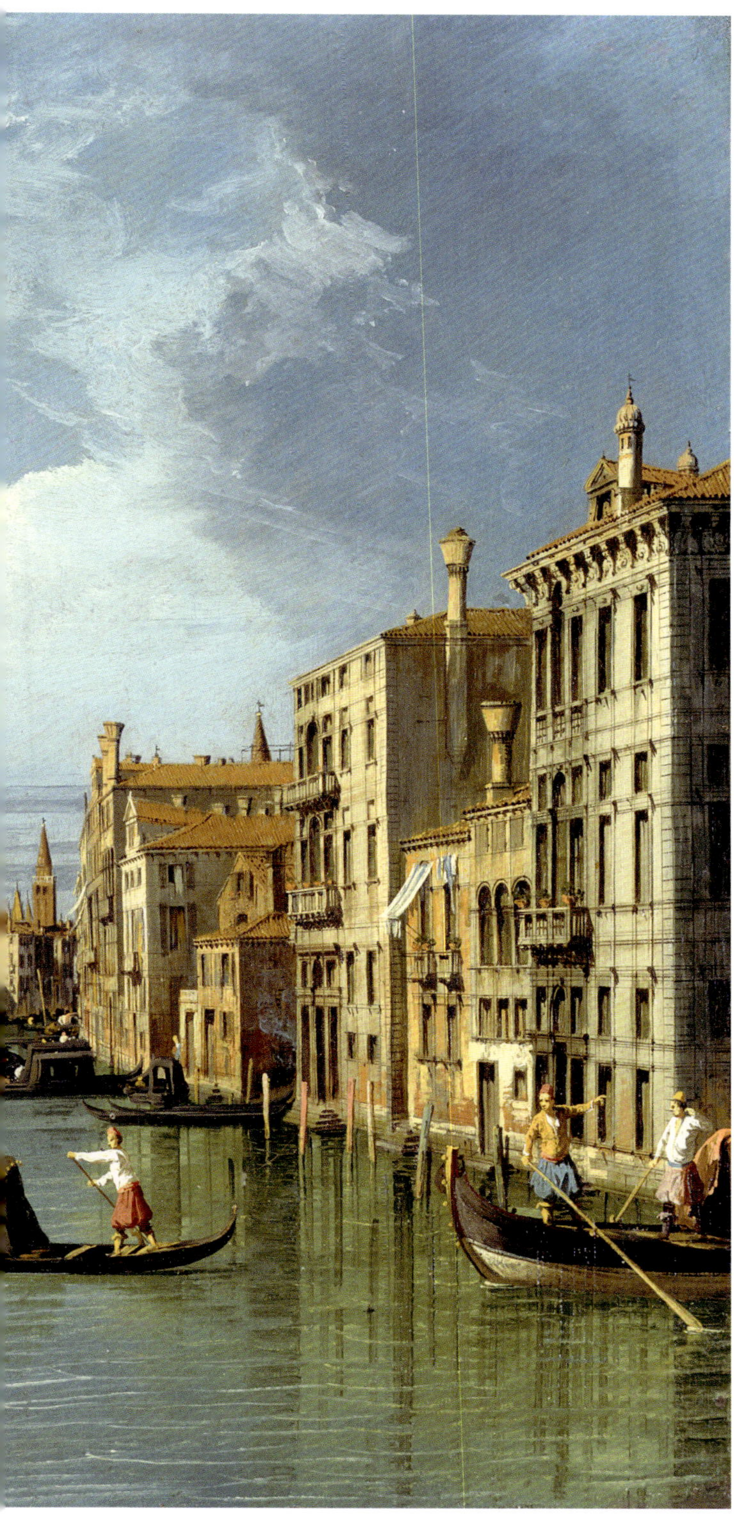

Fig. 16

Giovanni Antonio Canal, called Canaletto (Italian, 1697–1768), *Entrance to the Grand Canal*, about 1730. Oil on canvas, 49.6 × 73.6 cm (19 ½ × 29 in.)

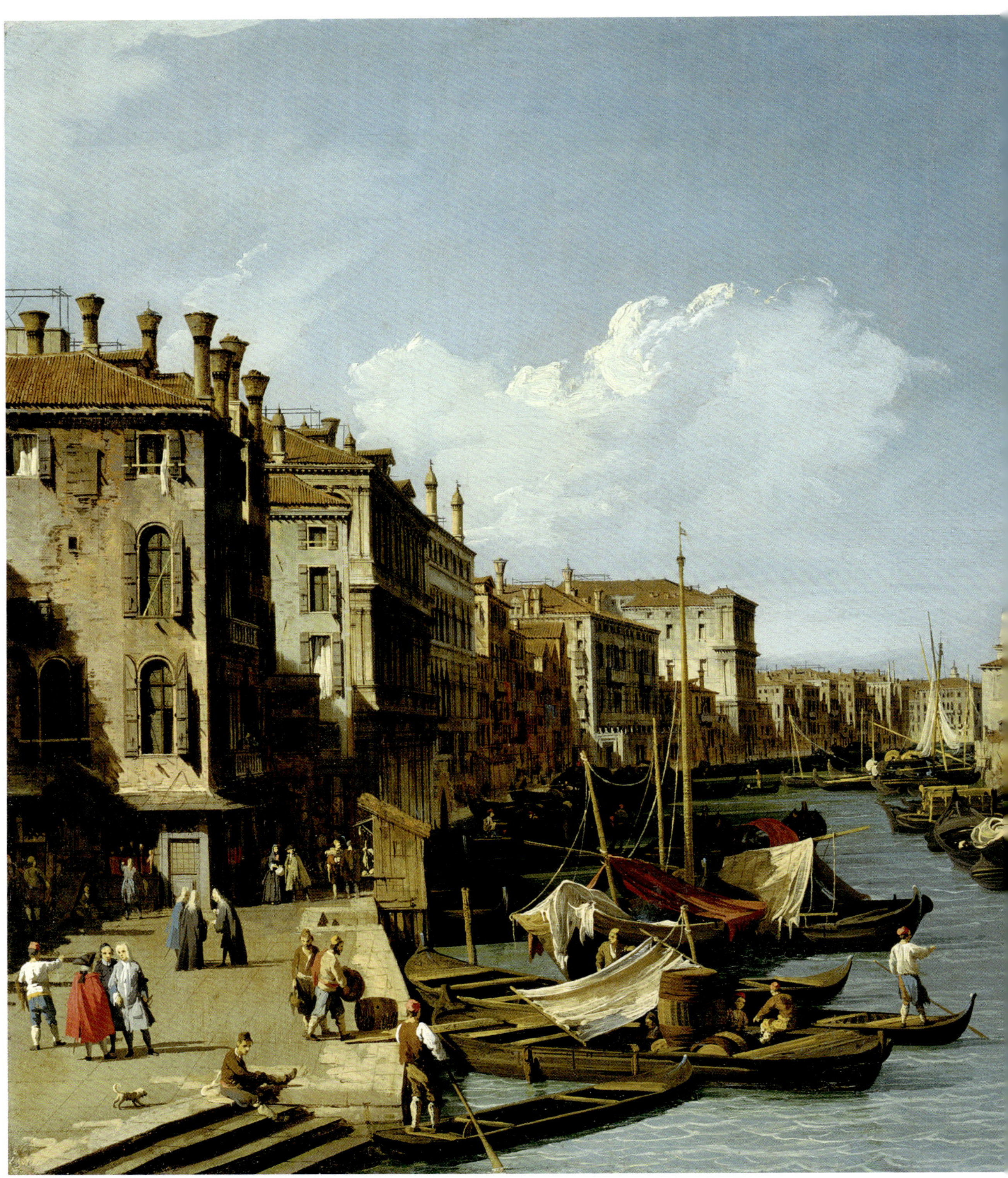

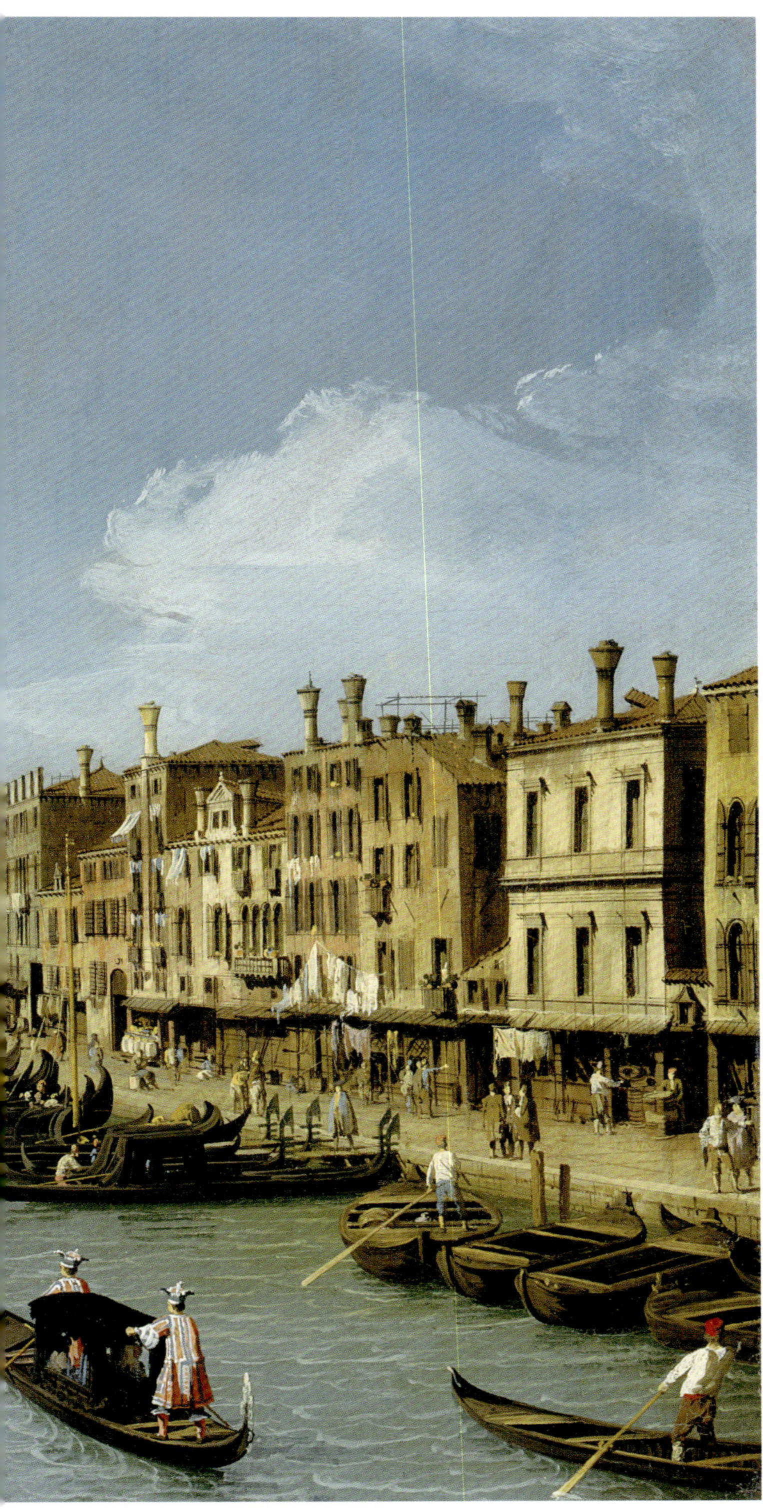

Fig. 17

Giovanni Antonio Canal, called Canaletto (Italian, 1697–1768), *The Grand Canal Near the Rialto Bridge*, about 1730. Oil on canvas, 49.7 × 73 cm (19 5/8 × 28 3/4 in.)

Fig. 18

Giovanni Antonio Canal, called Canaletto (Italian, 1697–1768), *The Grand Canal from Campo San Vio*, 1730–35. Oil on canvas, 114 × 161.3 cm (44 7/8 × 63 1/2 in.)

his own gondola, Casanova could now move about the city as he pleased and enter buildings through the front door.[5] He had been raised "at one bound from the base role of a fiddler to that of a nobleman" (H 2:191–200). A gondola thus proved to be more than a mode of transport; it was a means of social transformation.

A grander Venice now unfolded for Casanova. A pair of sizable canvases by Canaletto portray this more monumental city, controlled by its ruling class and envied across Europe for its political stability that earned it the name of *La Serenissma* (the most serene). A sense of quotidian calm, from the chimney sweep at upper right to the gondoliers ferrying passengers in the middle distance, pervades *The Grand Canal from Campo di San Vio* (fig. 18).[6] The view looks back toward the entrance of the canal, with the Riva degli Schiavoni in the distance; the great dome of the Salute, which dominated the left side of the *Entrance to the Grand Canal*, now is on the right, partially hidden behind a row of palazzi with their facades in shadow. At left, the sixteenth-century Palazzo Corner, so large that it was known as Ca' Granda (the Great House), looms over the tiny gondolas before it, while the expansive blue sky dwarfs everything. By the time of this painting, Canaletto had achieved a new sophistication in composing his views; the verticals of masts and mooring poles echo the lines of the architecture to draw the viewer's eyes up. Palazzo Corner, designed by the architect Sansovino, shares the Venetian characteristic of deploying architectural ornament and costly materials on the main facade, while comparatively neglecting the sides of buildings. Such an attitude applied to personal presentation, too. For Casanova and his peers, creating the crucial first impression required display of sumptuous interiors and fine clothing.

In the pendant painting, *View of the Molo*, the vista is more magnificent still (see fig. 8).[7] A strong perspective draws our eyes down the length of the Molo, or quayside, the ceremonial entrance by water to the government district of the San Marco *sestiere*. With the church of the Salute and the mouth of the Grand Canal in the left distance, the composition centers on the arcaded, two-story structure of Sansovino's Biblioteca Marciana (Library of Saint Mark, begun 1537), behind the two columns. A library on the main square indicates the prestige the Venetian state conferred upon learning. Dominating the right side of the painting is the enormous Palazzo Ducale (begun about 1340), the seat of

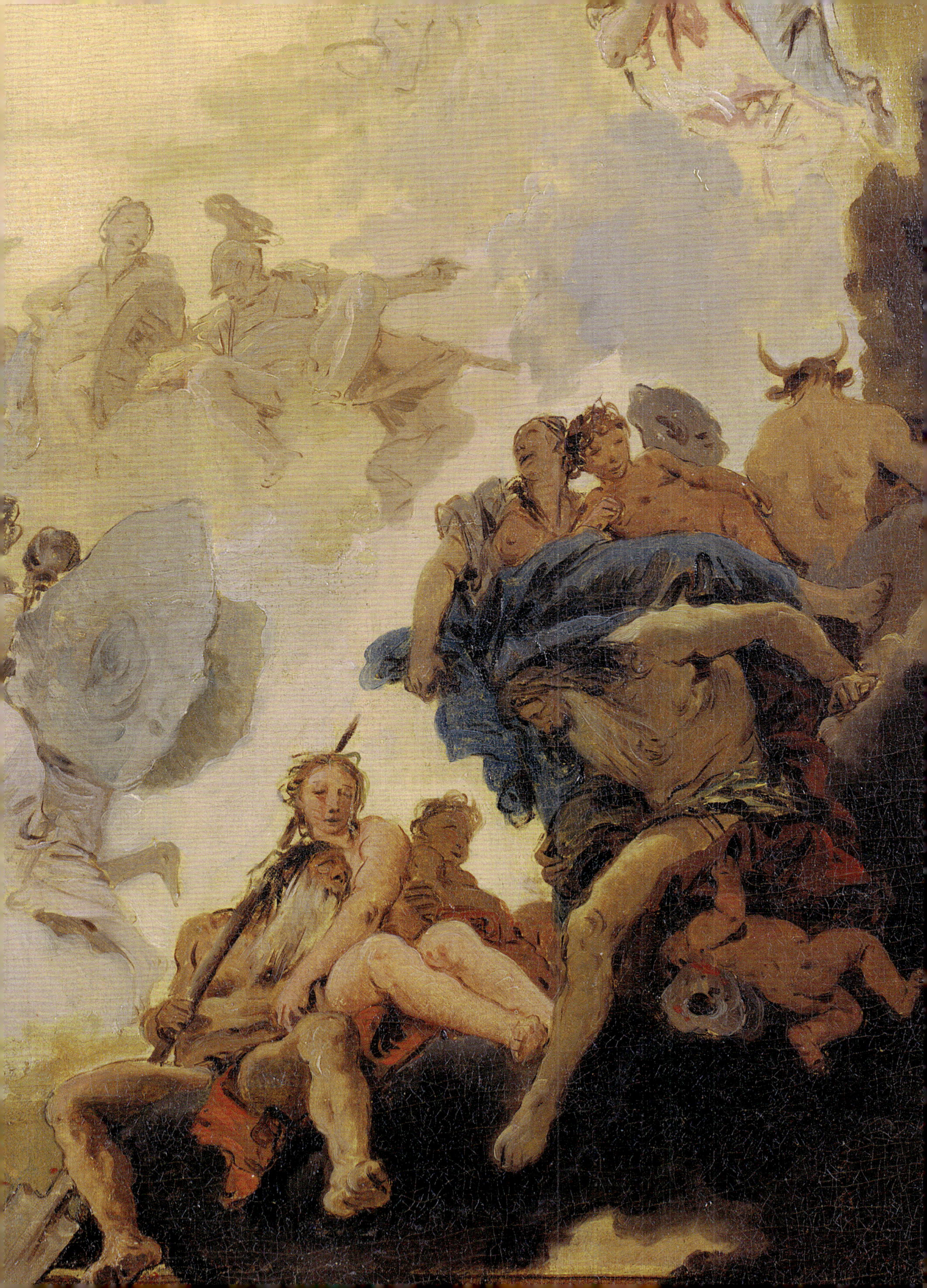

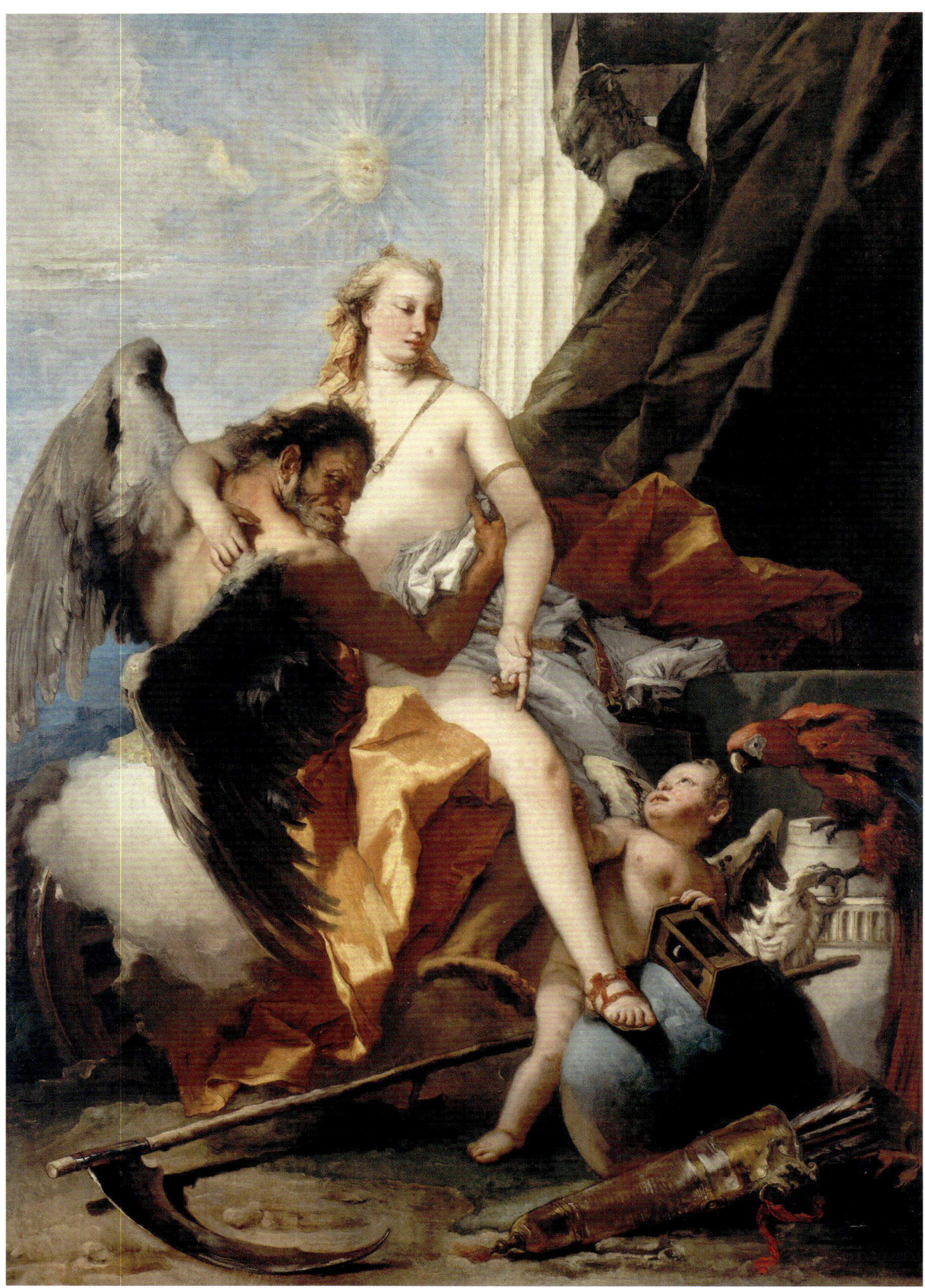

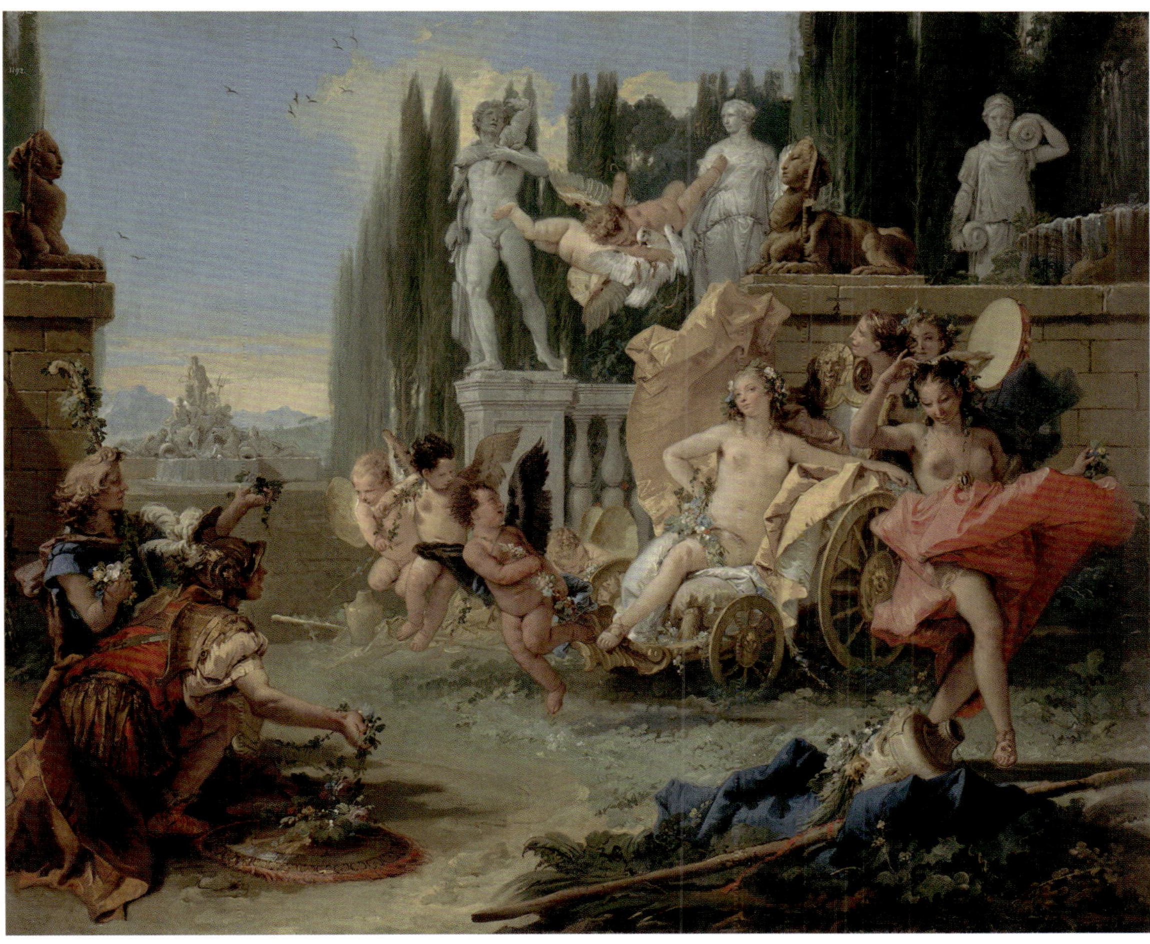

Off the *portego* were more intimate spaces, the often windowless sitting rooms and bedrooms, to which an honored guest might be invited. Although Tiepolo's *Empire of Flora* would have been ideally suited for such a room in a Venetian palazzo, it was in fact intended to be exported (fig. 21). In 1743 Count Francesco Algarotti, an acquaintance of Casanova's and yet another Venetian successful abroad, commissioned the painting as a diplomatic gift for Count von Brühl in Dresden. With its highly finished details of billowing fabric, supple flesh, and delicate flowers, not to mention a flattering reference to the recipient's own gardens, this virtuoso painting could not fail to impress.[16] Here the classical goddess of flowers, seated in a chariot pulled by cherubs, reigns over a lush Italianate garden populated by stone statuary and human admirers.

Fig. 20

Giovanni Battista Tiepolo (Italian, 1696–1770), *Time Unveiling Truth*, about 1758. Oil on canvas, 231.1 × 167 cm (91 × 65 ¾ in.)

Fig. 21

Giovanni Battista Tiepolo (Italian, 1696–1770), *The Empire of Flora*, about 1743. Oil on canvas, 71.8 × 88.9 cm (28 ¼ × 35 in.)

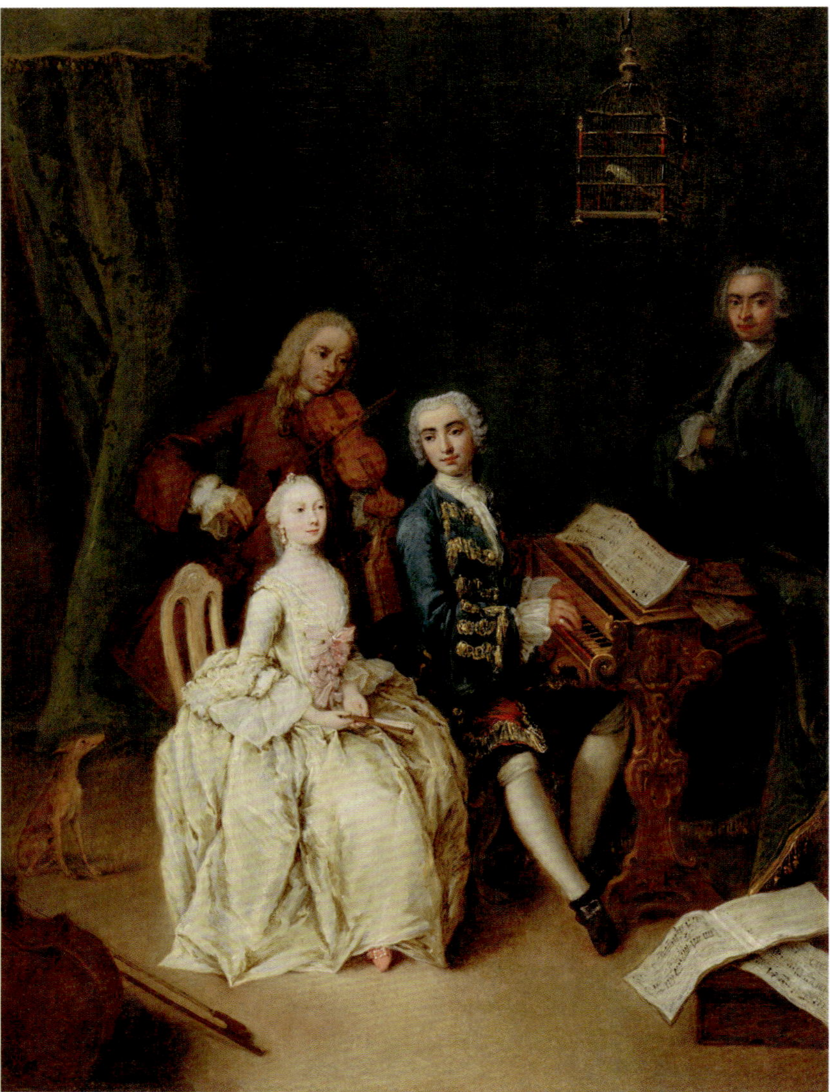

Fig. 22

Pietro Longhi (Italian, 1702–1785), *The Music Lesson (The Bird Cage)*, about 1740–45. Oil on canvas, 56.5 × 43.8 cm (22 1/4 × 17 1/4 in.)

Fig. 23

Pietro Longhi (Italian, 1702–1785), *The Concert (The Mandolin Recital)*, about 1760. Oil on canvas, 58.4 × 47.6 cm (23 × 18 3/4 in.)

Another important element in Venetian decor was costly fabrics used to adorn furniture and walls. Fabric-covered walls helped make smaller rooms in palazzos, which typically had very high ceilings, seem more inviting in all seasons and feel warmer in winter. The green silk damask on the walls in two scenes of Venetian aristocratic life by Pietro Longhi, *The Music Lesson* and *The Concert (The Mandolin Recital)* would have also served as soundproofing, isolating the music from other activities in the building (figs. 22, 23). Longhi's paintings appear to be accurate depictions of Venetian life with their attention to textures and sense of paused narrative. They are sometimes populated by well-known figures: the man at the keyboard in *The Music Lesson* may be the famous castrato singer Farinelli (see fig. 34), whom Casanova knew in Bologna in 1772 (H 12:139–40).[17] A Venetian viewer of the eighteenth century, however, would see below the surface and register the hints of more complex social relations. For example, the caged bird in *The Music Lesson* very probably refers to the virginity of the girl at center. Casanova could have imagined himself taking control of the action in such scenes, charming and impressing the characters within.

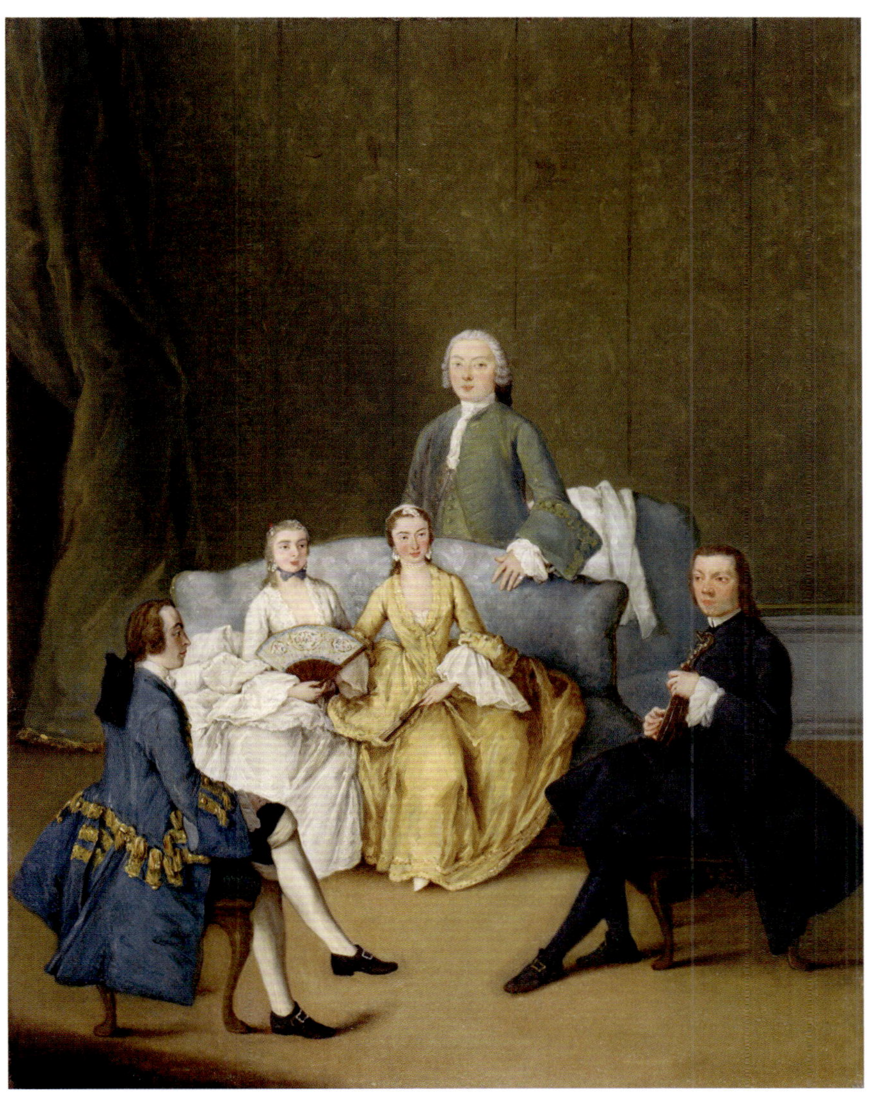

Fig. 24
Pietro Longhi (Italian, 1702–1785), *The Temptation*, about 1745. Oil on canvas, 49.5 × 61 cm (19 ½ × 24 in.)

Other paintings by Longhi present a more dissolute side of Venetian life. These images parallel Casanova's moral degeneration following his sudden elevation to wealth, when he "began to behave in complete disregard of anything which could set bounds" to his desires (H 2:201). Longhi's *Temptation* shows a utilitarian room in a palazzo, with an elegantly dressed noblewoman surrounded by maidservants engaging in needlework (fig. 24).[18] A Franciscan friar, presumably visiting to lead prayers or hear confessions, pretends to admire the stitching through a monocle, though the true focus of his attention is his hostess's décolletage. A simple birdcage again represents the virtue of the women—the friar's was clearly dissipated long ago. Like the plays of Longhi's contemporary, Carlo Goldoni, who admired the painter greatly, and to whom he is often compared, the ostensibly simple narrative of a genre scene could abound with intrigue and multiple meanings.[19] Goldoni's world overlapped with Casanova's, as the playwright had written major roles for Casanova's mother, Zanetta.[20] Like Casanova, Venetian artists left the confines of the lagoon in search of adventure and renown. Goldoni left for Paris in 1762, and Tiepolo departed for Madrid the same year. Tiepolo and Canaletto found foreign patronage and spent years working far from home.

Clerics and laypeople mingled in other kinds of spaces in Casanova's Venice. One distinctive institution was the *parlatorio*, or visiting room at a nunnery. Such a liminal place between private and public was also the starting point for some of Casanova's most famous romantic exploits. His memoirs describe a visit to Murano, whose island setting added intrigue to affairs with nominally cloistered nuns. In 1753, Casanova traveled with a Countess S. to a Murano convent, probably Santa Maria degli Angeli, the far-left bell tower in the murky distance of Canaletto's view of islands in the lagoon north of Venice proper (fig. 25).[21] There he spotted for the first time the lovely nun he identifies in his memoirs by the initials M.M.[22] Casanova was astonished that the grating separating nuns from visitors in the small visiting room could be opened temporarily by the push of a button, allowing the two women a furtive embrace. Always thinking ahead, Casanova noted, "Any man of my stature could have passed through it" (H 4:16). After his affair with M.M was under way, Casanova visited to ask his inamorata for forgiveness for a misunderstanding, and "she put her beautiful hand

The Theater of Identity

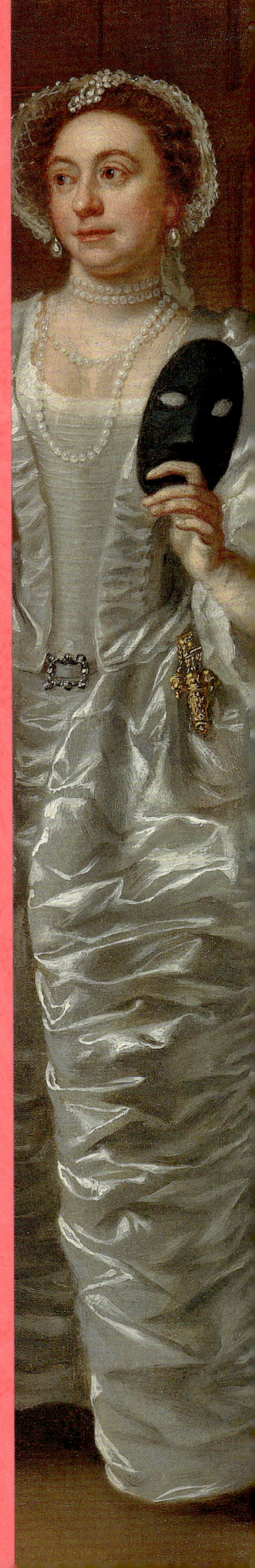

The Theater of Identity

JAMES H. JOHNSON

In *Dangerous Liaisons*, Choderlos de Laclos's stylishly sinister chronicle of seduction, Madame de Merteuil declares that to succeed in the "grand theater" of society one must "join the intelligence of an author with the talent of an actor."[1] To call all the world a stage was not new, but the trope found fresh vividness in the eighteenth century, when cafés, salons, promenades, and theaters turned daily life into a public spectacle. Fashionable strollers judged one another's taste by the cut of their clothes and the quality of their fabrics. Conversation in cafés and salons, however refined, had its winners and losers, their triumphs and humiliations on display for all to see. Spectators watched plays and operas with one eye on the stage and the other on the house, to check or confirm responses according to the reactions of the powerful. "One never judges things by what they are," wrote the guardian of courtly etiquette Saint-Simon, "but by the people they concern."[2] To win the esteem of those above you on the social ladder meant mastering the fluent speech and fine manners of society, a performance judged excellent only if it looked natural. For the century's cultivated classes, such politeness—a self-censoring discretion that hid all harshness for the sake of community—was a triumph of civilization. Humanity's brutish instincts could now be tamed. But for others, the very word stood for flattery and shallow pretense. Polish, the root of *politesse*, referred only to the surface, the blinding gleam of appearances. "The man of the world is wholly his mask," wrote the philosopher Jean-Jacques Rousseau. "What he is, is nothing. What he appears to be, is everything."[3] Whether one believed

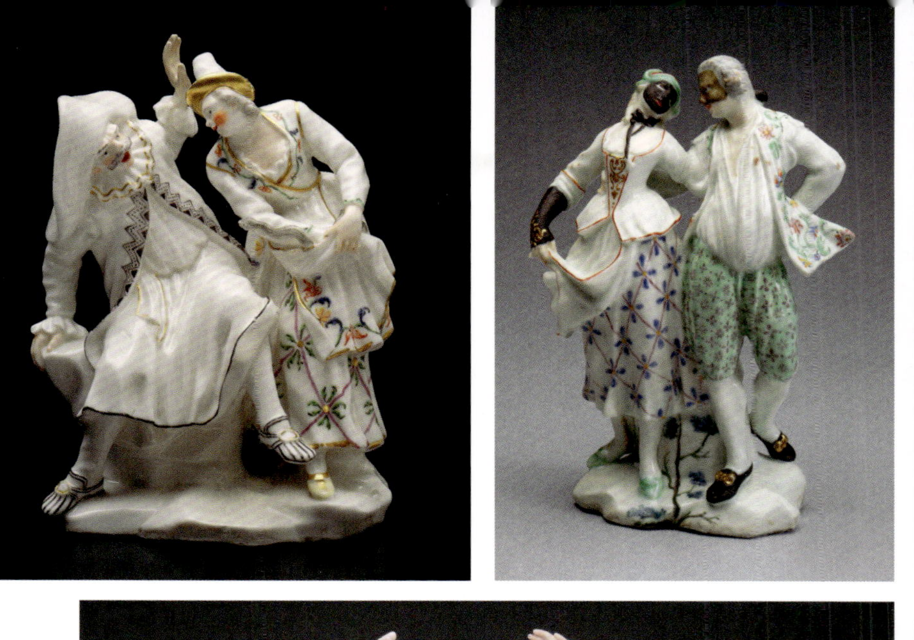
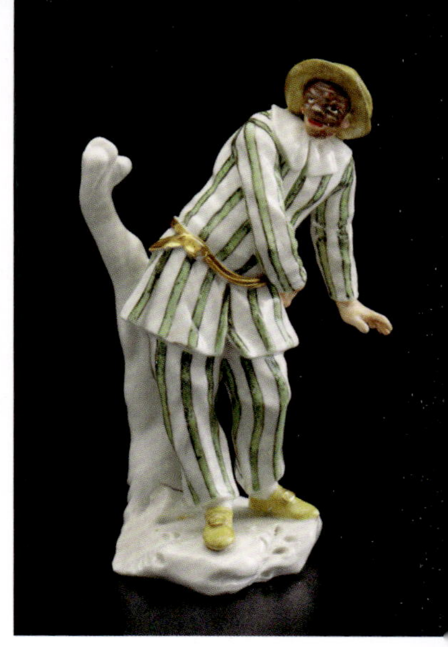
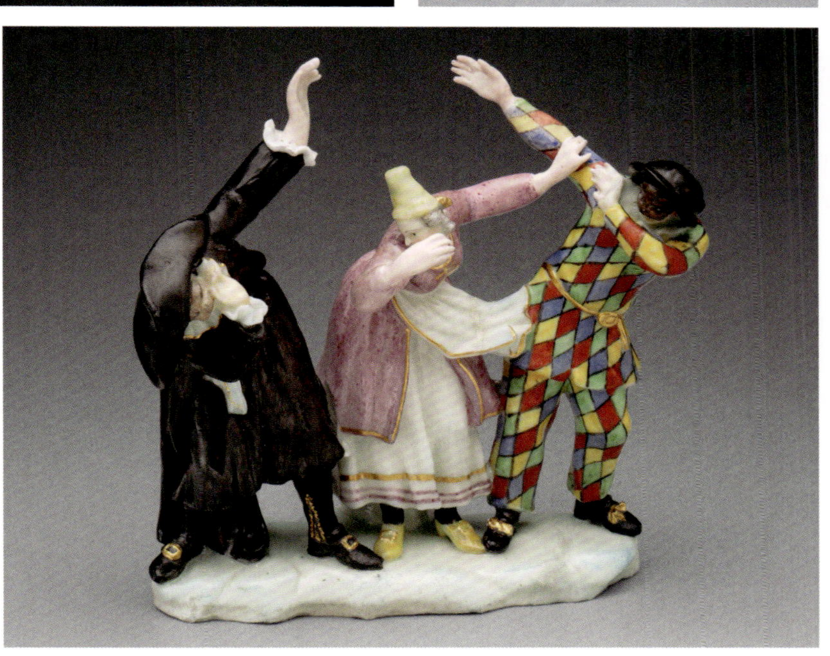
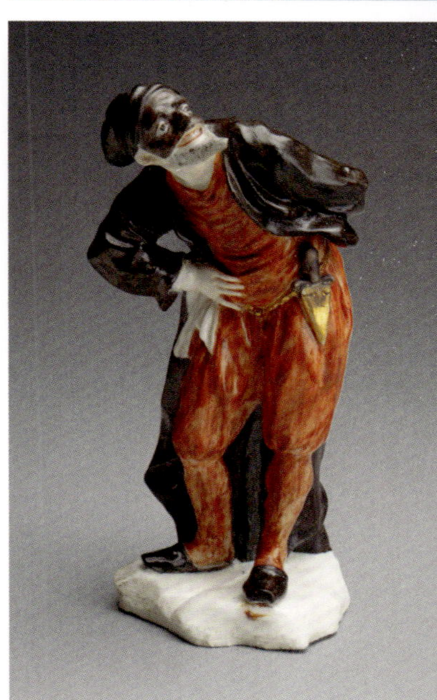

ous settings that made Venice famous for its music—the Ospedale della Pietà, for instance, where Antonio Vivaldi led a chorus and orchestra of superbly trained young women, or the grandeur of Saint Mark's basilica—theater orchestras offered little prestige and few opportunities. But when a senator named Bragadin offered to share his gondola after a ball where Casanova had played, Fortune smiled. The man suffered an apoplectic stroke mid-journey, Casanova claimed to know medicine and stayed by his side, and Bragadin, convinced that the young musician had saved his life, rewarded him with money, protection, and an entrée into society.

Fig. 33
Gabriel de Saint-Aubin (French, 1724–1780), *Quinault and Lully's Opera "Armide" Performed at the Palais-Royal Opera House*, 1761. Pen and brown ink, watercolor and gouache over graphite pencil on paper, 31.1 × 50.2 cm (12 ¼ × 19 ¾ in.)

Most of Casanova's later stays in foreign cities included a visit to the theater and introductions to its circle. The reigning operatic language of the day was Italian, and adaptations of commedia dell'arte had spread across Europe. As a result, Italian composers, librettists, playwrights, and performers circulated freely throughout the Continent, animating the cultural life of every major city. In Vienna, Casanova attended performances with the venerated poet Pietro Metastasio, librettist of more than twenty operas and lyricist for dozens of occasional pieces, oratorios, and cantatas. In Berlin, he sat by the sickbed of Ranieri Calzabigi, a Tuscan poet whose librettos were revolutionary for their sober plots and intense emotions. In Prague, he dined with the composer Pietro Locatelli, director of the city's Italian Opera, who laid a table every night for actors, singers, and dancers. And in Paris, he saw a French version of Venetian carnival in *Les fêtes vénitiennes*, an opera-ballet by André Campra. A luminous gouache of the theater's interior by Gabriel de Saint-Aubin gives an idea of the splendor and barely contained tumult that greeted him (fig. 33).[10] At the Paris Opera, floor lamps lit the stage scenery, and wax candles on suspended chandeliers provided enough light for spectators to identify one another from across the hall. In the crowded parterre, men stood, strolled, sang, and sometimes fought during performances. Two armed guards, visible on either side of the stage, were among forty royal musketeers assigned to keep order. Watching from their spot in the parterre, Casanova and his French host kept up a running commentary on what they saw, marveling at Louis Dupré's stately dancing, speculating about whether the ballerinas were wearing drawers, and roundly condemning the set, which placed the basilica at the wrong end of Piazza San Marco.

Casanova's thoughts were often drawn to performers' erotic lives. The sweet, unearthly voices of castrati in Rome, where a prohibition on women's voices in church encouraged the necessary procedure, unnerved him. "When [the singer] swept his gaze over the boxes his black eyes revolved so tenderly and modestly that they ravished the soul.... The Holy City... thus drives the whole human race to become pederasts" (H 7:251). He met the castrato Farinelli after the singer had left the Spanish court and was living in Bologna. Farinelli's appointment as "royal servant" to Spain's Philip V, for whom he gave nightly concerts to help ease the king's crippling depression, had capped a career that had made

Venetian gondola propelled by two oarsmen goes smoothly and does not cause a nausea which turns one inside out."[12]

Motion sickness was but one of the inconveniences that eighteenth-century travelers endured, and that Casanova fell victim to. The roads he traveled on varied from the exemplary highways of England and France (which Casanova praised as "the immortal work of Louis XV") to the often primitive infrastructure of southern Italy and Spain (H 3:120–21). On his way to Madrid in 1767, Casanova found the first twenty leagues out of Pamplona magnificently paved, the legacy of a French governor of Navarre. Thereafter the road vanished, leaving "uneven stony climbs and descents, where one nowhere saw the least sign to indicate that carriages passed there. Such was the whole of old Castile" (H 10:303–4). Even good roads held dangers, as when Casanova's carriage overturned at midnight on an otherwise smooth stretch near Benevento. Convinced his vanished postilions were in league with highwaymen, he armed himself with two pairs of pistols, a carbine, and a sword, ready to make a stand; in the end the peasants proved friendly, thanks to ready coin, and he made it safely into town at daybreak (H 7:236–38). The ever dyspeptic English traveler Tobias Smollett related a similar tale in 1765 of the loss of a wheel and broken axle-tree in desolate country between Montefiascone and Viterbo, luckily repaired by a handy postilion. "I mention this circumstance," Smollett explained, "by way of warning to other travellers, that they may provide themselves with a hammer and nails, a spare iron-pin or two, a large knife, and bladder of grease, to be used occasionally in case of such misfortune."[13]

The extremes of danger during travel were captured in four large canvases painted by Giacomo's younger brother Francesco about 1770 for the composer Jean-Benjamin de La Borde, *premier valet de chambre* to Louis XV, and sold in 1773 to the royal collection for twenty-four thousand francs.[14] Francesco, a landscape and battle painter trained under Antonio Guardi and Francesco Simonini, had come to Paris at his brother's urging in 1751, returning after further study in Dresden to fill the void left by the death in 1752 of the famed battle painter Charles Parrocel.[15] Perhaps stimulated by his own journeys, Francesco applied a sense of epic conflict to scenes of roadside catastrophe, whose heightened drama and proto-Romantic emphasis on man's helplessness against the elements reflect the rising allure of the sublime, an aesthetic often linked

Fig. 48

Francesco Casanova (Italian, 1727–1803), *Collapse of the Bridge*, about 1770. Oil on canvas, 226 × 282 cm (89 3/8 × 111 3/8 in.)

Fig. 49

Francesco Casanova (Italian, 1727–1803), *Travelers in a Storm*, about 1770. Oil on canvas, 229.5 × 286 cm (90 3/8 × 112 5/8 in.)

to the Grand Tour. As Horace Walpole put it while crossing the Alps in 1739, invoking an earlier painter of landscapes: "Precipices, mountains, torrents, wolves, rumblings, Salvator Rosa.... Where I shall finish my neighbor Heaven probably knows."[16] The fates of Francesco's voyagers are all too clear. In one canvas, the rupture of a log bridge plunges a carriage and its occupants into a rocky crevasse, to the horror of onlookers; in another, a bolt of lightning strikes a cart's passengers while others run for shelter (figs. 48, 49). A third depicts a moonlit ambush by bandits, and the fourth a hurricane in which a broken tree crushes a rider crossing a raging torrent. All were calculated to strike a delicious terror into past or future travelers, and in fact, after their purchase by the crown, the paintings were hung, with evident black humor, in the apartments of the minister of foreign affairs at Versailles. Giacomo had his own brush with Mother Nature near Pordenone, when a thunderous squall threw the fellow occupant of his two-wheeled chaise—a new bride he'd been pursuing—into his lap, a situation he immediately turned to advantage (H 1:152–53). Given Casanova's prowess as a raconteur, did Francesco's visions of mortality on the road include his brother's "little death" in Friuli?

Whatever challenges the journey posed, new ones began upon arrival. Eighteenth-century inns, especially in rural areas, often obliged patrons to share not just rooms but also beds. This could be an advantage, as in Senigallia, where the need to bunk double finally unmasked the castrato "Bellino" as Theresa; or an obstacle, as in Marino, where the "accursed blabbing" of the creaky beds thwarted Casanova's designs on the lawyer's wife (H 2:22–25, 1:255). Even single rooms were not always secure. In Cesena, Casanova learned that the Holy Inquisition prohibited bolts on doors throughout the Papal State to facilitate the supervision of travelers' morals. "Twenty years later in Spain," he added, "I found that all rooms in inns had a bolt on the outside, so that foreigners who slept in them could be to all intents and purposes imprisoned."[17] Meals, too, were typically communal, and "when the vetturino has contracted to feed his passengers, it is customary for him to eat with them" (H 1:249). Given these limitations, travelers staying longer often leased furnished apartments, as Casanova did in Parma, Paris, Vienna, Moscow, and Warsaw. Customization was sometimes necessary. In Saint Petersburg, where the heating was admirable, he was obliged to purchase a chest of drawers

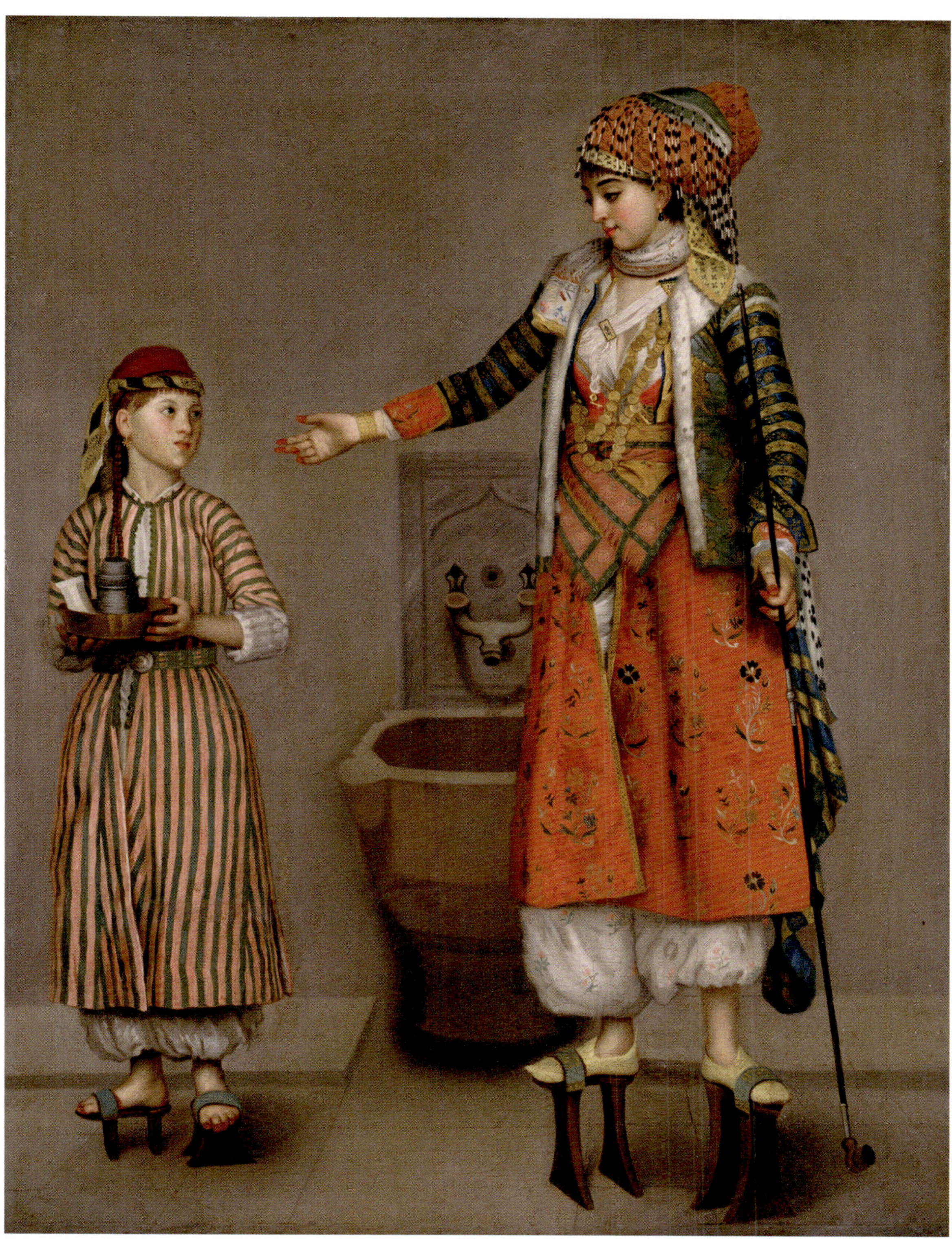

Islam; and the former minister of foreign affairs Ismail Effendi, who offered Casanova the one kind of love in which he professed no interest.[27] Strongly tempted by Yusuf's proposal, he firmly rejected Ismail's. Yet after an artful moonlit night's seduction involving a glimpse of bathing beauties, Giacomo yielded to local custom and to Ismail—"It would have been impolite in me to refuse"—with good humor and without regret (H 2:95–96). Still, ultimately Casanova followed his maxim of "sequere Deum" (follow your God) and did not turn Turk, perhaps recalling the *bailo*'s warning that in Constantinople "boredom is more a threat to foreigners than the plague."[28] Instead, like all tourists, he shopped for souvenirs—"rolls of Damascus cloth glazed with gold or silver, purses, portfolios, belts, scarves, handkerchiefs, and pipes"—that he promptly sold once back in Corfu, retaining only Ismail's gift of rare Scopolo wine (H 2:99–101). In the end, Constantinople was no more than a way station on a journey that, without further exception, unfolded in Christian Europe.

If Constantinople proved to be a bridge too far, what kept Casanova on the road? What compensated for travel's inevitable discomforts, and what, ultimately, did travel provide? Had Casanova been an idealist, he might have embraced traditional encomia to travel as a semi-spiritual quest for self-improvement and moral uplift. Proper travel, as the Marburg professor Hermann Kirchner had cautioned earlier generations, was not merely "a certayne gadding about, a vaine beholding of sundry places, a transmigration from one country to another," but a search to enlarge one's understanding, further one's studies, and lose one's prejudices.[29] The true traveler, Kirchner asserted, "moveth more in minde then body." Can this be said of Casanova? The evidence suggests not—rather, that Casanova traveled because his nature compelled it, and not for any greater good. Indeed, his ceaseless motion seems to have concealed a spiritual stasis; unlike Johann Wolfgang von Goethe or Vittorio Alfieri, Casanova traveled not to find himself but to find new fields in which to cultivate the familiar pleasures of conversation, gambling, the table, and the bedroom.[30] For all his peregrinations, Casanova rarely engaged in sightseeing or expounded on what he encountered (except for women) along the way. Nor, having lived most of his life outside Venice, did he feel anything but Venetian, feuding with the cook at Duchcov over polenta or macaroni, "as to which he was very exacting."[31]

Cosmopolitan as he seems, recounting (in French) his success in salons across Europe, Casanova always missed his fatherland—even if, whenever he returned to it, misdeeds or restlessness forced him out again.

For Casanova, travel was its own reward, a journey in search of pleasure that bred pleasures of its own. As age crept up on him in Genoa, he reflected on how the "very free conversation and companionship of travel" had a way of sparking affairs, recalling "the pleasant idleness which, to replace doing nothing, forces the body and the soul to do everything. One grows tired of talking, of insisting, of reasoning, and even of laughing; one lets oneself go, and one acts because one does not want to know what one is doing. One thinks about it afterward, and one is very glad that it all happened" (H 9:21). Far from nearing some desired destination, Casanova spiraled farther and farther away from it, confessing at journey's end that he had "never aimed at a set goal," and that "the only system I followed, if system it may be called, was to let myself go wherever the wind which was blowing drove me" (H 1:26). To an extent rarely equaled, travel was Casanova's metaphor for life. As a budding ecclesiastic he was "on the road to the highest dignities of the Church," "on the road to the Papacy," and "on the high road to fortune"; in Venice, his soldier's garb convinced friends he was "on the road to political office," until a detour to Naples put him "on a different road," before Cardinal de Bernis, in Paris, again "put me on the road to fortune."[32] For Casanova, seeker of pleasure, to stay put was to stagnate. "I loathed the idea of settling down anywhere," he confessed in 1761, admitting that prudence was "absolutely foreign to my nature" (H 7:239).

Perhaps what Casanova relished most was the perspective of the outsider, the insight that "there is not a place on earth where the observer does not note aberrations if he is a foreigner, for if he is a native of the country he cannot discern them" (H 3:144). Or perhaps what drove him ever onward was a passion for liberty, an escape from the constraints of inquisitors, family, or possessions.[33] And perhaps, despite abandoning the priesthood, he was not so unlike the Jesuits of two hundred years earlier, who "consider that they are in their most peaceful and pleasant house when they are constantly on the move, when they travel throughout the earth, when they have no place to call their own."[34] If so, Casanova too inhabited the "house of journey," his religion the freedom to be oneself that only the open road can give.

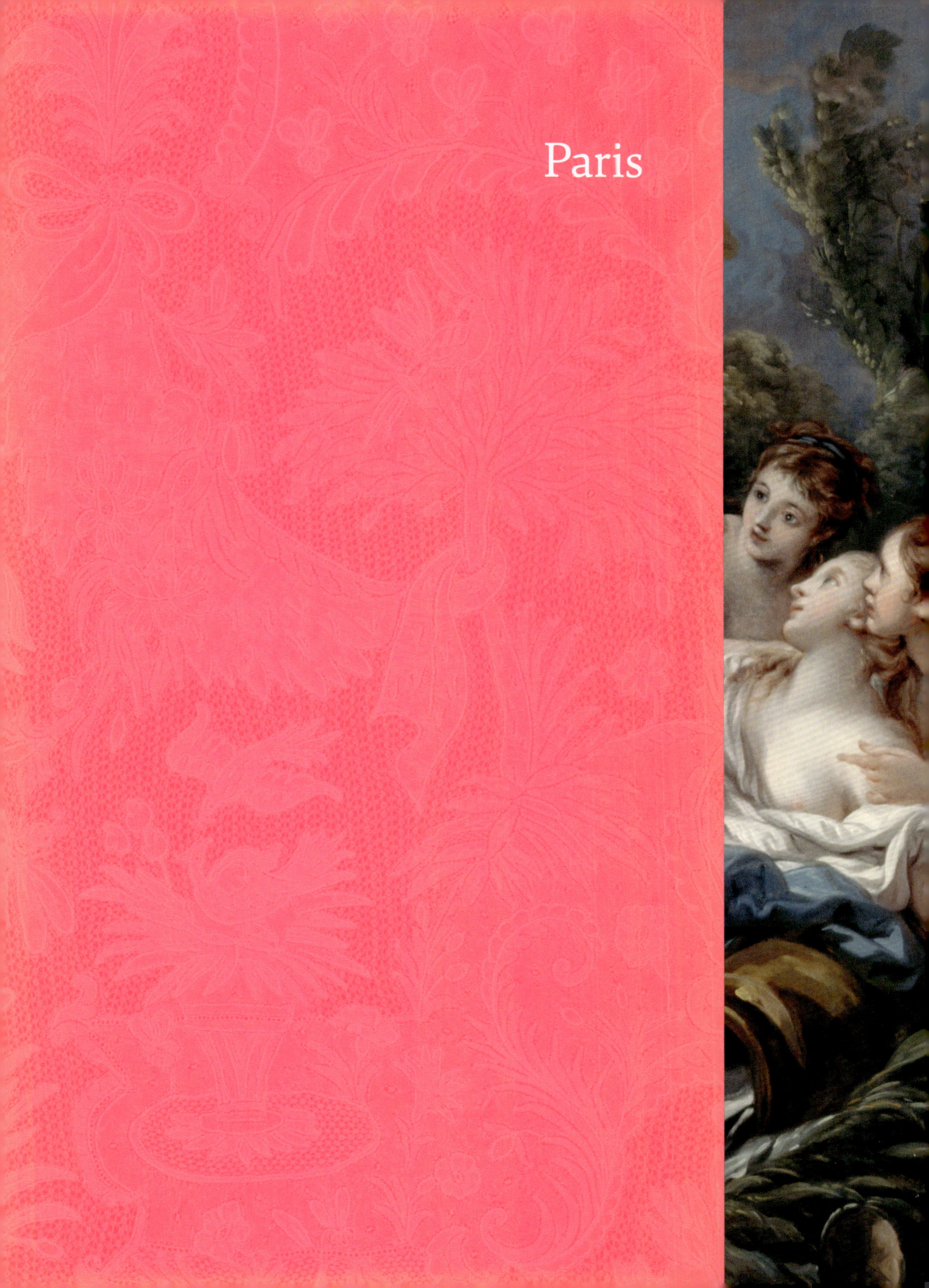

Paris

Paris

ESTHER BELL

From a one-eyed brothel keeper to King Louis XV, the colorful characters of eighteenth-century Paris provided Casanova with many of the highlights in his *History of My Life*. Arriving in the cultural capital of Europe for the first time in August 1750 at the age of thirty-one, Casanova—ambitious and ever virile—entered the social apex of his life and career. During his first stay, which would last two years, his only goal was "to enjoy life." He studied French pronunciation with the playwright Prosper Jolyot de Crébillon, visited the salon of Madame de Graffigny, and argued philosophy with Jean Le Rond d'Alembert. During his second tenure in the city, from 1757 to 1759, he was even more determined to "make acquaintance with the great and the powerful, exercise strict self-control, and play the chameleon to all those whom [he] should see it was an interest to please" (H 5:19). We can trace his movements through the vibrant streets, coffeehouses, and public gardens, but it is his machinations behind the scenes of the city's premiere cultural and court institutions that reveal his greater ambitions.

In midcentury Europe, Paris's permanent population was second only to London's, and the French capital greeted many European visitors such as Casanova.[1] High culture was more readily available to those with family or professional ties to the city, but certain avenues of access were open to everyone, including printed materials, theaters, music, and the public art exhibition known as the Salon, held regularly from 1737 onward in the Louvre. Casanova reveals much about Enlight-

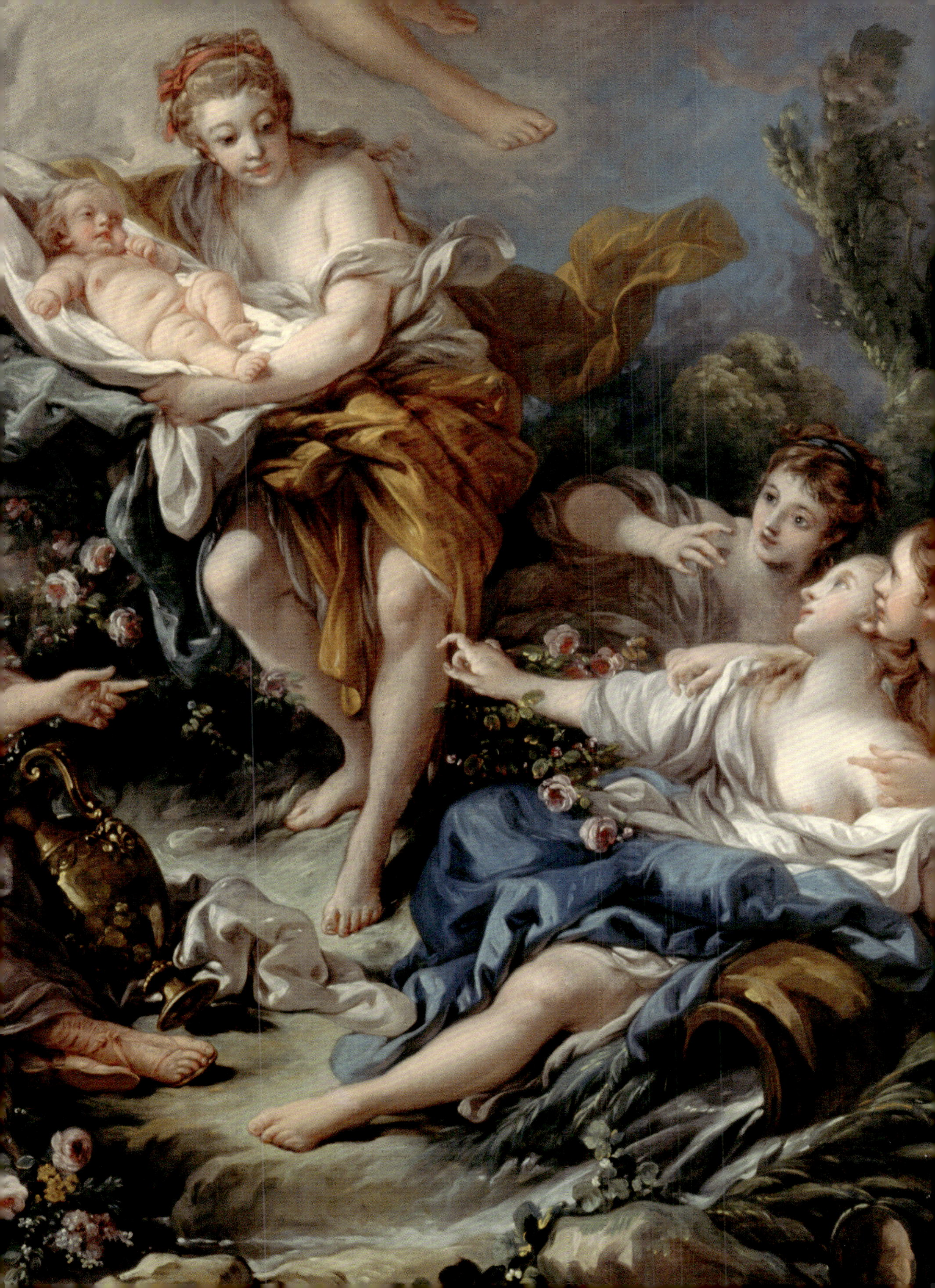

Fig. 52
Jean-Marc Nattier (French, 1685–1766), *Zanetta Balletti, called Mademoiselle Silvia*, 1750–58. Oil on canvas, 48 × 42.5 cm (18 7/8 × 16 3/4 in.)

enment leisure through his accounts of experiences and relationships at the Théâtre Italien, Opéra de Paris, and Comédie-Française. He also insinuated himself, largely through his brother Francesco, into the orbit of the Royal Academy of Painting and Sculpture—then dominated by artists of the Generation of 1700, such as François Boucher, Carle van Loo, and Charles-Joseph Natoire.[2] Casanova's strategic social alliances granted him access to some of the most privileged spaces in Paris and its environs, many of which were sumptuously decorated in the height of Rococo excess. In Paris, Casanova became an ultimate insider—climbing back staircases at the Palais-Royal, sneaking into private apartments at Versailles, and catapulting himself into the inner circles of Ancien Régime society.

Approaching the gates of Paris for the first time, in an uncomfortable oval coach, Casanova and his friend, the actor Antonio Balletti, were intercepted on the road by two figures who would become centrally important in our protagonist's life. It was then that he first met his adopted materfamilias, Silvia (née Zanetta) Balletti, accompanied by her nine-year-old daughter and his future love, Manon Balletti. Antonio's parents, celebrated actors at the Théâtre-Italien (otherwise known as the Comédie-Italienne), would provide Casanova with a roof over his head and the social introductions that would enable him to take root and flourish in his new city. Jean-Marc Nattier's oil study of Silvia portrays the actress with a warmth and sympathy that corroborate Casanova's description of her as "elegant... full of wit... completely unpretentious" (fig. 52).[3] The arrival of Casanova and Antonio was celebrated by a grand dinner, with other relatives in attendance, including the aging actor and theorist Luigi Riccoboni (stage name Lélio)—one of the central figures of eighteenth-century Parisian theater.[4] Riccoboni had been responsible for bringing the Italian troupe of comedic performers back to Paris in 1716 at the order of the regent, after it had been exiled by royal decree in 1697.[5] During Casanova's first stay in Paris, he kept close company with these Italian actors, who wanted to show him "how lavishly they lived" (H 3:146). Carlo Veronese, who played Pantaloon and was the wealthiest member of the troupe, introduced Casanova to his beautiful daughter Corallina, with whom the newcomer would become deeply infatuated. He frequented their theater at the Hôtel de Bourgogne, on the rue Mauconseil (now the rue Étienne Marcel) in the Les Halles neighborhood,

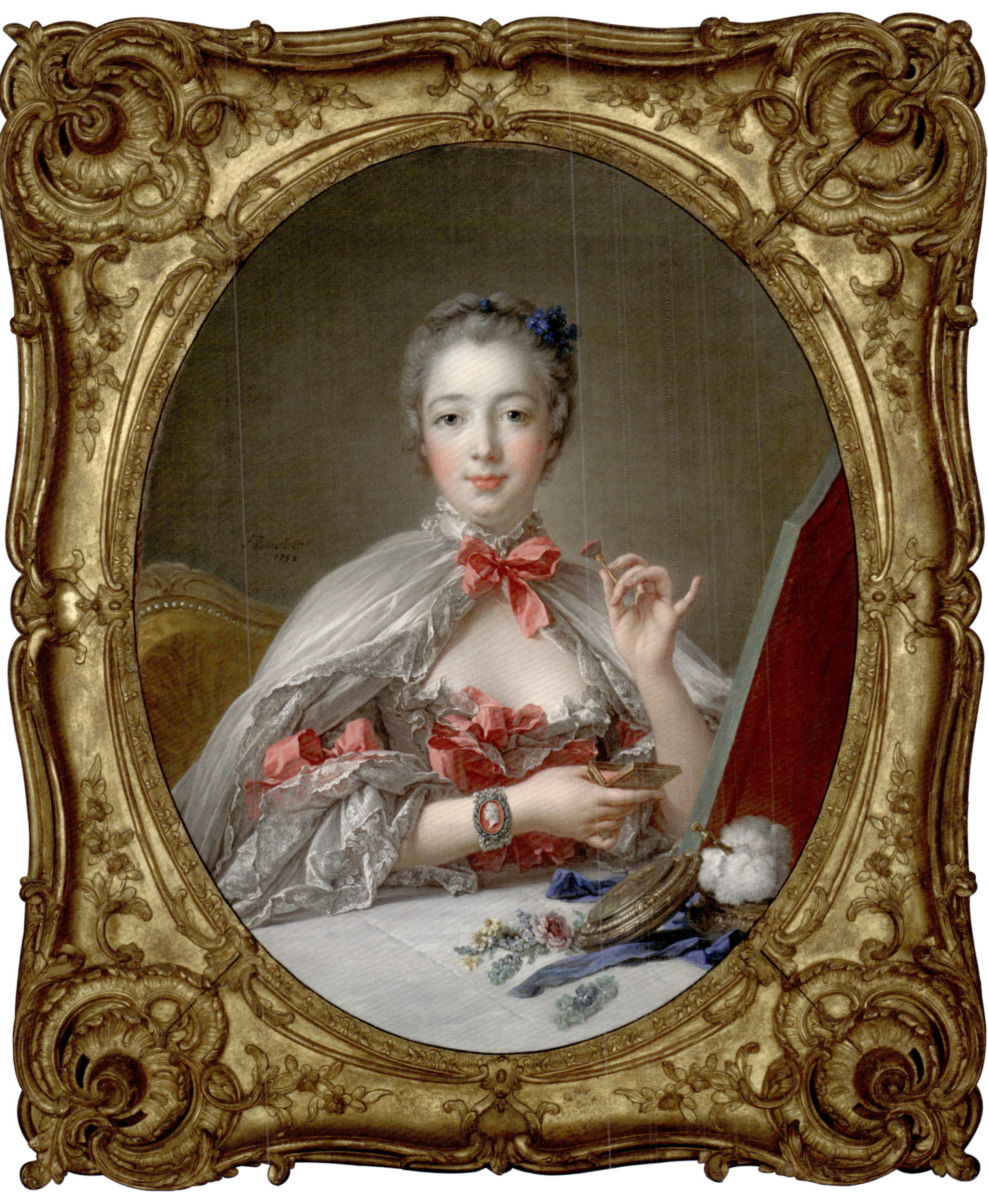

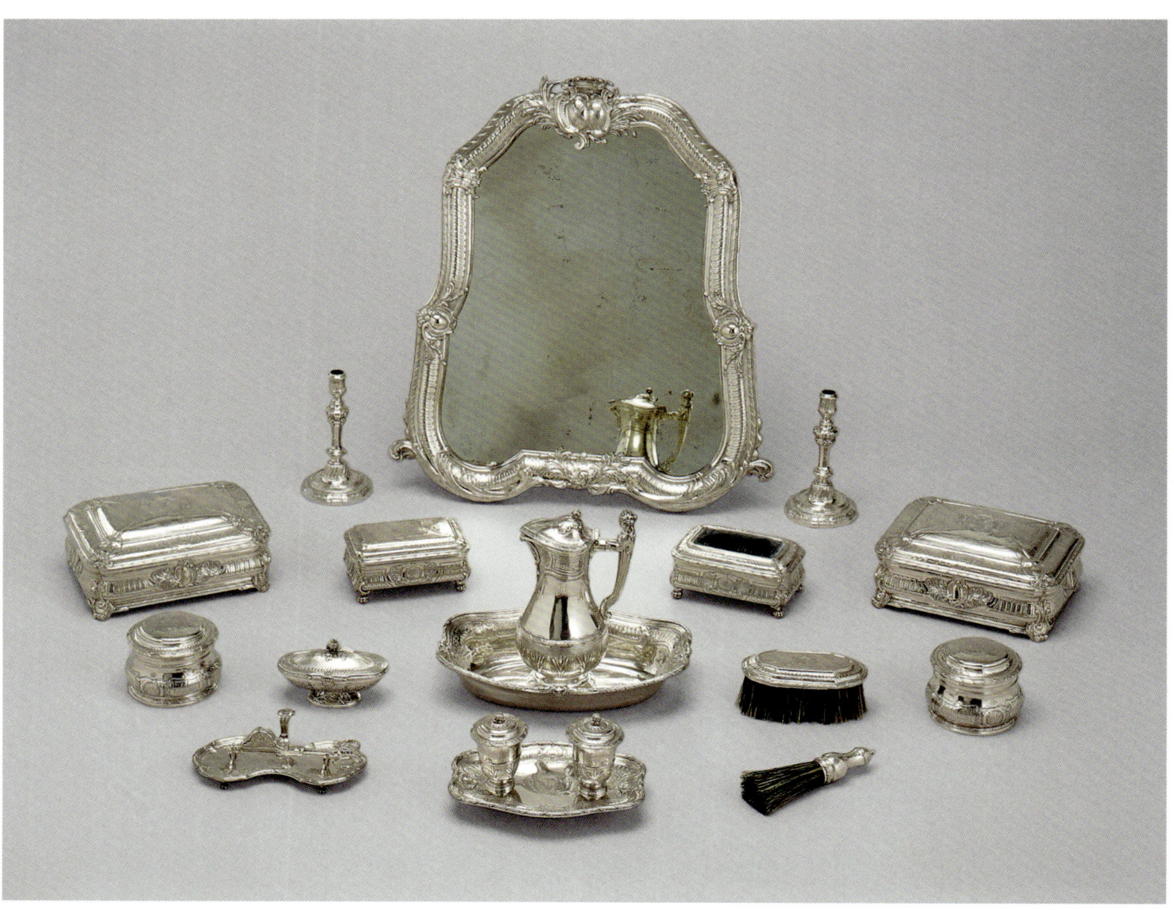

a half-length portrait by François Boucher, one of the marquise's preferred painters, she is presented in the act of applying rouge (fig. 55). Seated upon a yellow brocaded chair, she is surrounded by the trappings of her toilette: artificial flowers and ribbons to adorn her hair, a voluminous white powder puff positioned for use, and a mirror strategically angled in her direction (fig. 56).[15] Most conspicuous of all is the bejeweled cameo of Louis XV on her wrist, placed on the center line of the composition to underscore their relationship. Painting one's face with cosmetics was not simply a beauty ritual, but a practice with social implications. Face paint (or *maquillage*), and thereby cosmetic artifice, was a sign of courtly nobility. In Boucher's portrait, the viewer is confronted with the ways that Pompadour "made up" her identity and in the process asserted her agency.[16] When Casanova wrote about the circumstances in which Pompadour "contrived" to make the king's

Amorous Pursuits

Amorous Pursuits

SUSAN M. WAGER

Modern ideas about love, sex, and family originated in the social transformations that swept eighteenth-century Europe. Casanova's *History of My Life* incarnates these changes as he recounts a six-decade, transcontinental succession of sexual conquests, assignations, and affairs with well over a hundred partners: married women, men, prostitutes, nuns, and even his own family members. Europe and especially France in the age of Casanova witnessed a rise in sexual promiscuity alongside a growing investment in the primacy of romantic, passionate love. These alterations in intimate behavior reflected the growing cultural and philosophical value placed on selfhood, personal liberty, privacy, and the individual's right to pursue happiness.[1]

In his preface, Casanova insists that the memoir is intended primarily for its author: he aims to relive his amorous past through the act of writing, finding "no pleasanter pastime than to converse with myself about my own affairs."[2] The conceit of personal conversation, in lieu of narrative structure, underscores Casanova's predilection for unpredictability and renewal.[3] He characterizes himself as "extremely susceptible to the seduction of any pleasurable sensation... eager to pass from one enjoyment to another and ingenious in inventing them," from which came his "inclination to make new acquaintances" and "readiness to break them off" (H 1:30–31). A visual counterpart to the intimacy and unpredictability of Casanova's *History* could be found in Jean-Honoré Fragonard's painting *The New Model* (fig. 68).[4] In a studio, a painter with palette in hand turns from his easel to confront the half-naked model

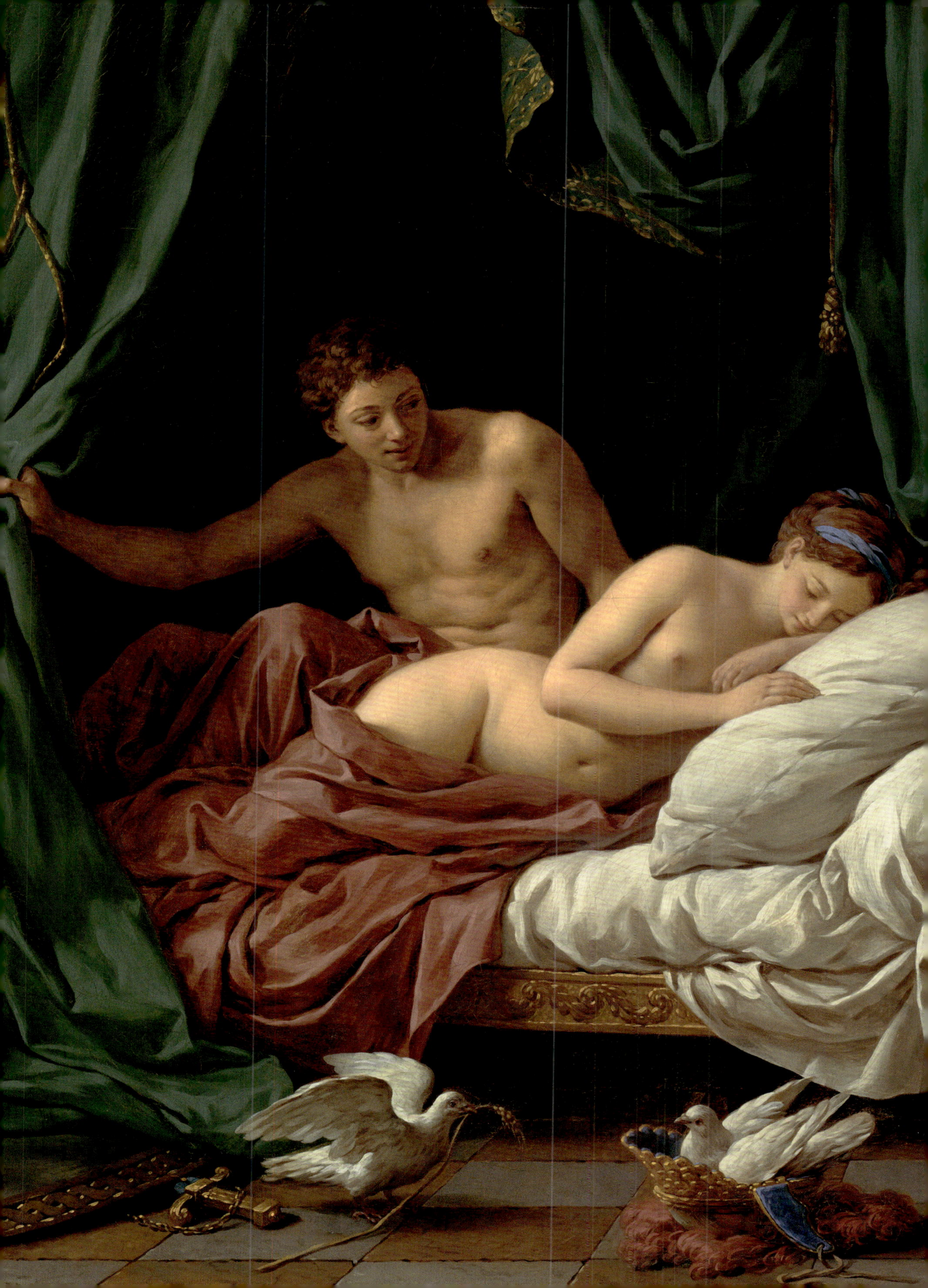

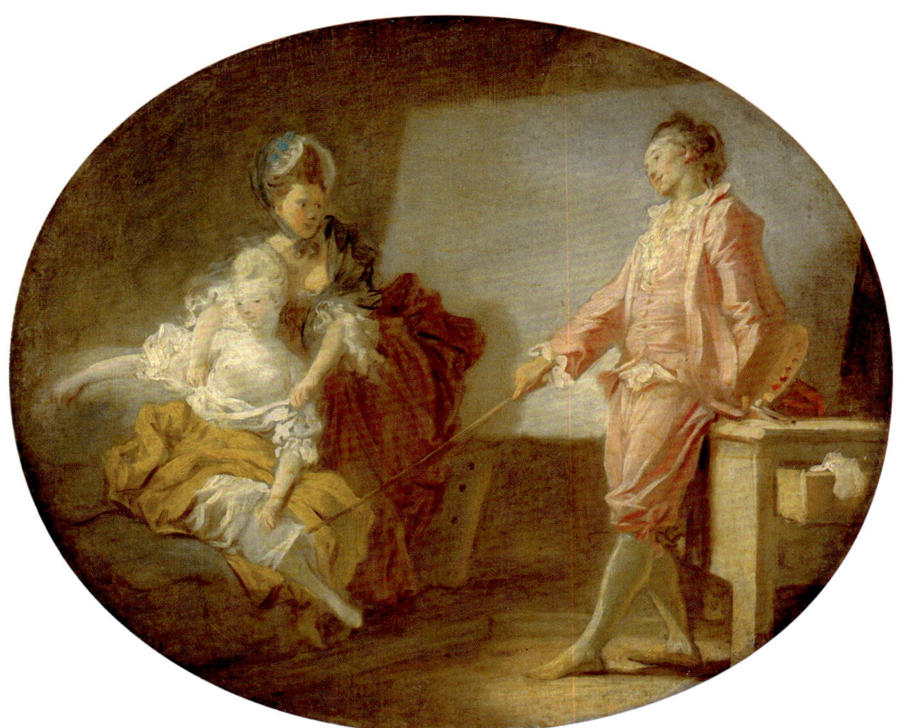

Fig. 68

Jean-Honoré Fragonard (French, 1732–1806), *The New Model*, about 1770–73. Oil on canvas, 52 × 64 cm (20 ½ × 25 ¼ in.)

Fig. 69

Jean-Honoré Fragonard (French, 1732–1806), *Aurora Triumphing over Night*, about 1755–56. Oil on canvas, 95.3 × 131.4 cm (37 ½ × 51 ¾ in.)

seated before him. With his mahlstick (used for steadying the brush), the painter pruriently lifts the model's skirts. The scene captures the erotic excitement of a first encounter—the new model and blank canvas represent fresh beginnings, while the loose handling of the model's drapery and patch of white behind her right arm convey the unfinished and inchoate. The small size and oval shape of the picture evoke the act of private reminiscence, of the mind turning elliptically as it explores a cache of memories.

But *The New Model* is not self-referential. Its actual scale and shape contrast markedly with the massive and rectangular blank canvas depicted within the picture. For the nude model to be represented on such a large and public scale, she would likely be inserted into a history painting—a mythological or religious narrative intended to elevate and instruct the mind through its universality and timelessness.[5] Fragonard's *Aurora Triumphing over Night*, for example, shows the bare-breasted goddess of dawn sprinkling rose petals above her equally exposed nocturnal counterpart (fig. 69).[6] Their nude bodies would not offend in a public setting because they have been safely removed from the earthly to the celestial world, and from the immediacy of the present to the cyclical time of day's passage from light to dark. In *The New Model* the imposing presence of the blank canvas and its association with history painting introduce a sense of the timeless into an erotic image of new beginnings and sensual immediacy. By collapsing these contrasting modes of representation, *The New Model* points to the eighteenth-century reshuffling of relationships between different kinds of love: fleeting and permanent, private and public, carnal and ideal.

One turning point in early modern conceptions of love might be located around 1715, when power at the French court passed from Louis XIV to the notoriously wanton regent, Philippe d'Orléans.[7] The heroic, chivalrous, and generous love identified with the seventeenth century was soon displaced by a culture of debauchery and self-interested lust. In his 1781 *Tableau de Paris*, the dramatist Louis-Sébastien Mercier wrote, "Licentiousness has replaced the love that still reigned in Paris not more than a century ago. In the time of Louis XIV, one's tastes were governed by decency and sensitivity."[8] This is, of course, an oversimplification; but nonetheless, the first decades of the eighteenth century saw several reorientations in the visual arts that reflect broader changes in ideas about love: the focus on amorous rather than heroic conquests in paintings of

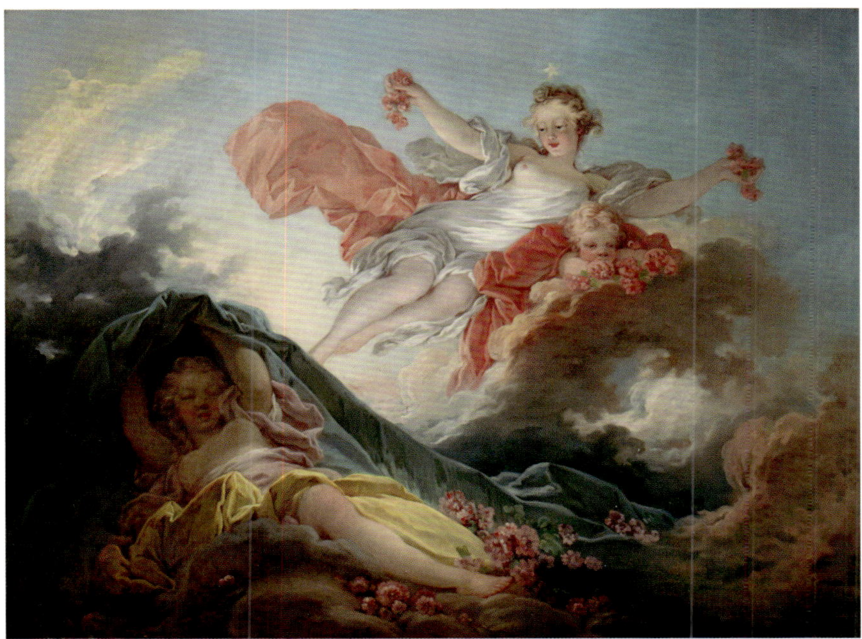

subjects from classical mythology; the introduction of privacy and intimacy in architectural design; and the injection of sexual innuendo into gallant pastoral paintings.[9]

Though painted in 1770, Louis-Jean-François Lagrenée's *Mars and Venus* reflects the amorous shift in mythological painting that began around the turn of the century (fig. 70).[10] The composition depicts a tender postcoital moment shared by the god of war and the goddess of love. Mars pulls back a sumptuous green curtain to admire Venus, who slumbers on the rose and white linens of their bed. The smoothness of Venus's marmoreal flesh contrasts with the deeply rumpled linens that hint at the ardor of the previous night's encounter. On the tiled floor in the foreground, doves build a nest in Mars's helmet, thrown off in the heat of the moment. The doves' occupation of castoff armor signals the peace brought about by this sensual reconciliation between the deities of love and war. When the critic and philosopher Denis Diderot saw this painting at the annual Salon exhibition of 1771, he remarked with disdain that the figures looked more like a "handsome country boy" and a "pretty trollop" than a god and goddess.[11] Critics like Diderot worried that mythological paintings which substituted scenes of love for depictions of glory and conquest, rather than elevating the minds and morals of the public, were awakening viewers' baser sensations. He wrote that he was tired of seeing so many "tits and asses" (*tétons* and *fesses*) in mythological painting: "These seductive objects upset the emotion of the soul by throwing the senses into turmoil."[12]

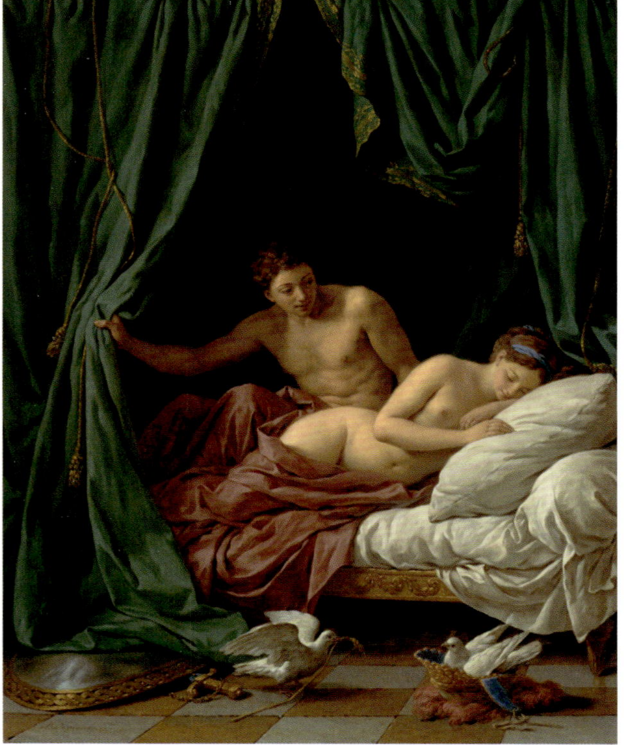

Fig. 70
Louis-Jean-François Lagrenée (French, 1725–1805), *Mars and Venus, Allegory of Peace*, 1770. Oil on canvas, 64.8 × 53.8 cm (25 ½ × 21 ⅛ in.)

Amorous mythological paintings evoked intimacy and desire not only through their subject matter but through their role in interior decoration. In Fragonard's *Aurora Triumphing over Night*, visible traces of the painting's original rounded upper edge and scalloped lower edge suggest that it was made to fit within ornamental paneling above a doorframe. The curvilinear shape likely harmonized with the furniture and other decorative objects that shared its space. Through the integration of the painting with the surrounding interior, the celestial world of the mythological figures becomes part of the material world of the senses.

The use of paintings as components of unified decorative schemes was characteristic of the Rococo era, also associated with the birth of architectural intimacy. When the French court moved from Versailles to Paris at the end of Louis XIV's reign, a building boom in the capital funded by wealthy financiers and aristocrats reflected a reconceptualization of domestic space. For the first time, architectural interiors sought to accommodate privacy, intimacy, and comfort. Rooms were designated for personal habits such as bathing, using the toilet, and sleeping. Bathing was rare until the end of the seventeenth century; by the middle of the eighteenth century, private bathrooms—often lavishly decorated—were a regular feature in upper-class homes. Interior spaces became smaller and were fitted with new types of furniture designed for specific functions as well as for the user's comfort. The Rococo decoration of these interiors followed principles of formal and chromatic harmony, creating an effect of sensuous unity between objects and, in turn, between people.[13]

Jean-François de Troy's painting *The Declaration of Love* shows how amorous mythological paintings could participate in the seductive effect of the Rococo interior (fig. 71). An elegantly dressed man performs a conventional declaration of love before an equally stylish woman, sinking to one knee and placing a hand on his heart. The woman appears to succumb to his advances: She relaxes into the sofa, her elbow resting casually on a well-stuffed pillow. On the wall above, a large painting depicts the embrace of a mythological couple whose image of ideal love has presumably emboldened the amorous exchange below. The sinuous shape of the painting echoes the gilded frame of the sofa, as well as the elaborate mount on the porcelain vase at right. The porcelain's red body, in turn, resonates with the crimson upholstery of the sofa, the velvet curtain at left, and even the man's jacket. As form and color merge in this space, the viewer loses sense of where one object ends and the next begins. This blurring of boundaries between objects anticipates the physical union of the couple.[14]

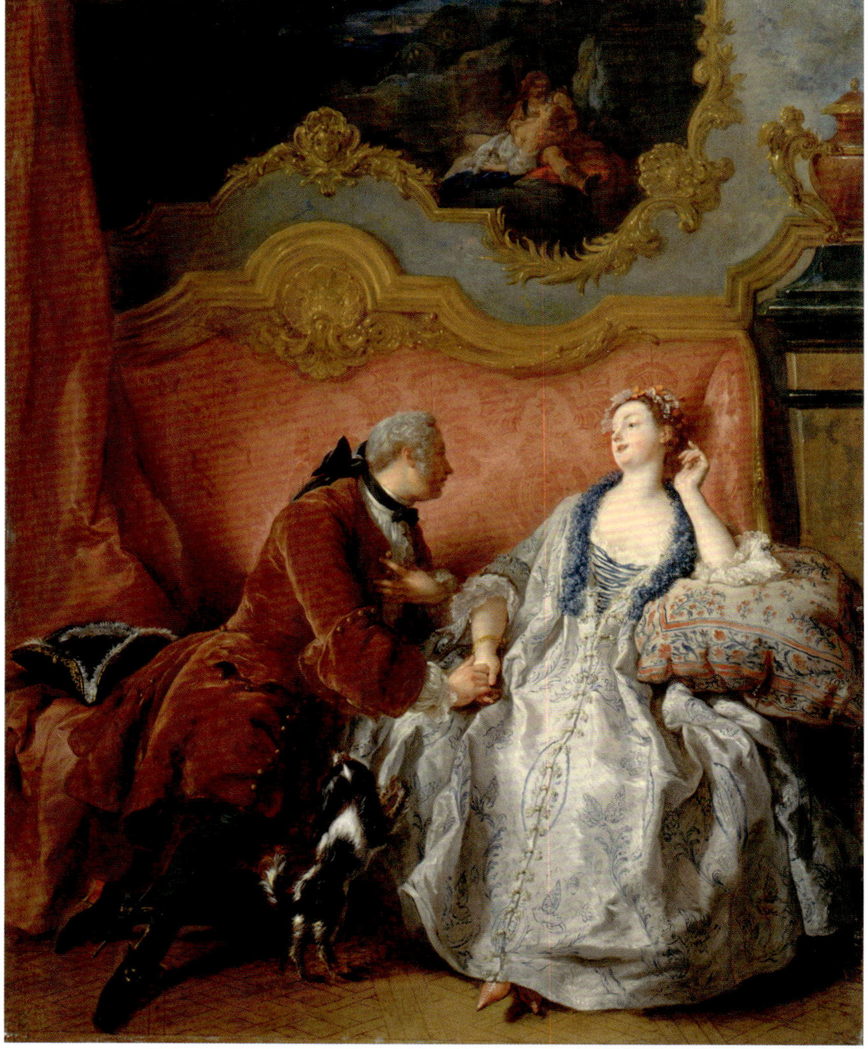

Fig. 71
Jean-François de Troy (French, 1679–1752), *The Declaration of Love*, 1724. Oil on canvas, 65.1 × 53.3 cm (25 × 21 in.)

Paintings depicting the loves of the gods were especially prevalent in the *petite maison*, a type of private "little house" akin to the Venetian *casino* that was kept for private assignations. The interiors of these houses were designed to encourage amorous conquests. At the start of Jean-François de Bastide's 1758 novella *La petite maison*, the lascivious marquis de Trémicour challenges the modest Mélite to test her virtue in the heady interior of his "little house." As she moves through the house, she gradually submits to the overwhelming sensuousness of its porcelains, lacquers, bronzes, and paintings, including "a circular canvas on which [the artist] Pierre had painted with all of his artfulness Hercules in the arms of Morpheus, awakened by love." Confronted with the alluring power of this interior decoration, Mélite begins to "fear that she was feeling."[15] Casanova evokes the seductive power of amorous painting in the *casino* he rents to entertain the nun M.M. Its opulent decor includes Chinese porcelain wall tiles painted with "amorous couples in a state of nature, whose voluptuous attitudes fired the imagination" (H 4:46).

Serial seducers like the marquis de Trémicour and Casanova are associated with the culture of gallantry, which changed considerably after the reign of Louis XIV. In seventeenth-century France, *galanterie* referred to a polite, agreeable, and honest sociability. In commerce between the sexes, the gallant man or woman demonstrated tenderness, mutual respect, and faithfulness, always with sincerity.[16] By the middle decades of the eighteenth century, however, gallantry had become corrupted. In the 1694 edition of the Académie française dictionary, *galanterie* was defined as "the obligations, respect, and service one renders to women," as well as "amorous relations." In the 1762 edition, the latter phrase was changed to "amorous and immoral relations." The genre of gallant pastoral painting explored this tension between chivalry and lust. Fragonard's *The Seesaw* depicts a young couple in a rustic clearing (fig. 72).[17] Their interaction is innocent enough: the boy uses the seesaw to raise the girl into the air, where she takes hold of a tree branch. But the rhythmic motion of the seesaw can allude to sexual activity.[18] The arc formed by the tree above the couple echoes that up-and-down motion.

François Boucher's gallant pastoral *Are They Thinking about the Grape?*, which shows a young boy and girl feeding each other grapes in a bucolic setting, introduces a hint of eroticism into a scene of naïve love (fig. 73).[19] The painting's source is usually identified as Charles-Simon Favart's 1745 play *Les vendanges de Tempé* (The Grape Harvest of Tempe), in which innocent love between a shepherd and shepherdess overcomes various obstacles. The conceit of the grapes—an attribute of Bacchus, god of pleasure—suggests that the couple's encounter is not entirely chaste. The entire painting seems to delight in the pleasures of artifice. The pristinely perfect landscape's colors are saturated beyond naturalism. The figures themselves are doubly artificial: They are pictorial representations of theatrical characters, and Boucher has reversed their gender roles. In his *Autumn Pastoral* (The Wallace Collection, London), a painting of the same subject, the boy occupies the dominant position. Gender is further destabilized in *Are They Thinking about the Grape?* by the boy's effeminate facial features; in the play, his role was performed by a woman in cross-dress.[20] The painting's overt artifice underscores the notion that eighteenth-century courtship had become a pretense for sexual adventure.

The English artist William Hogarth's *Before* and *After*, created as a pair for a wealthy patron, parody the degenerated state of gallantry in French pastoral paintings (figs. 74, 75).[21] *Before* depicts a young couple

Fig. 72

Jean-Honoré Fragonard (French, 1732–1806), *The Seesaw*, about 1750–52. Oil on canvas, 120 × 94.5 cm (47 ¼ × 37 ¼ in.)

Fig. 73

François Boucher (French, 1703–1770), *Are They Thinking about the Grape?*, 1747. Oil on canvas, 80.8 × 68.5 cm (31 ¾ × 27 in.)

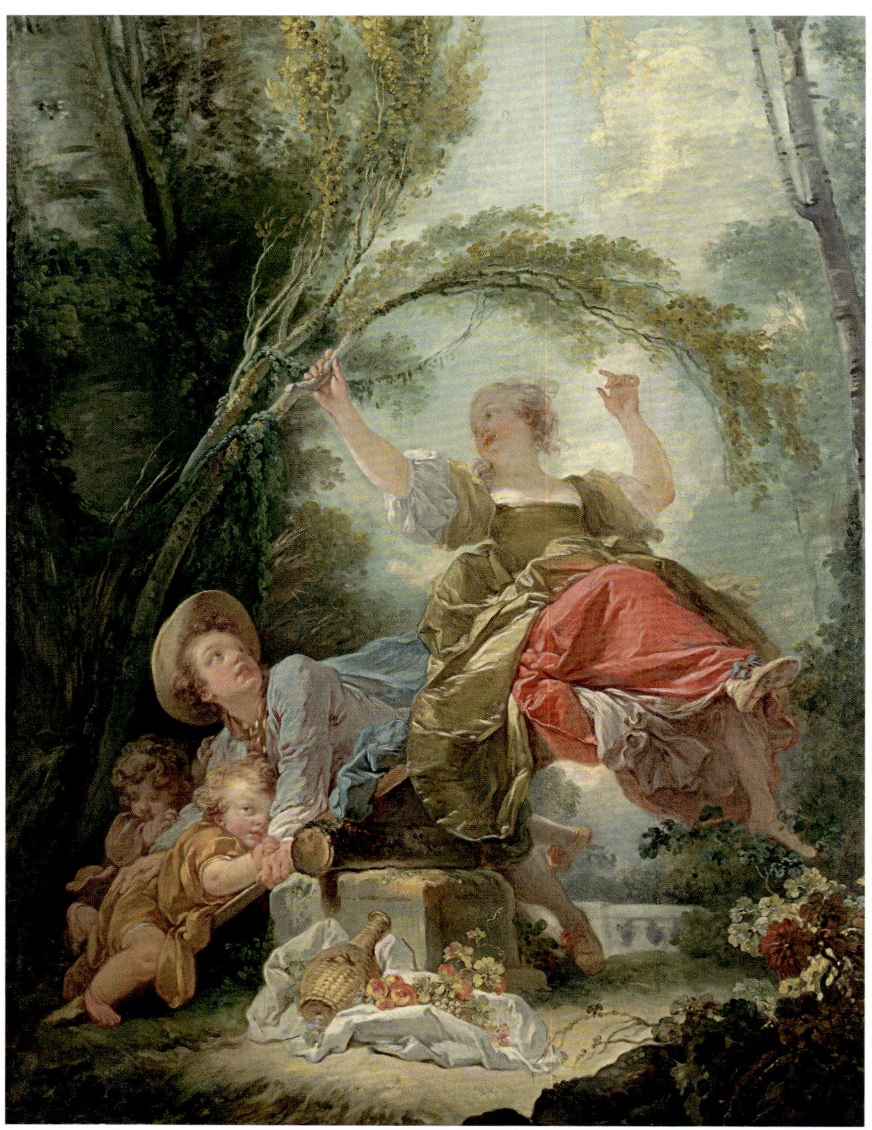

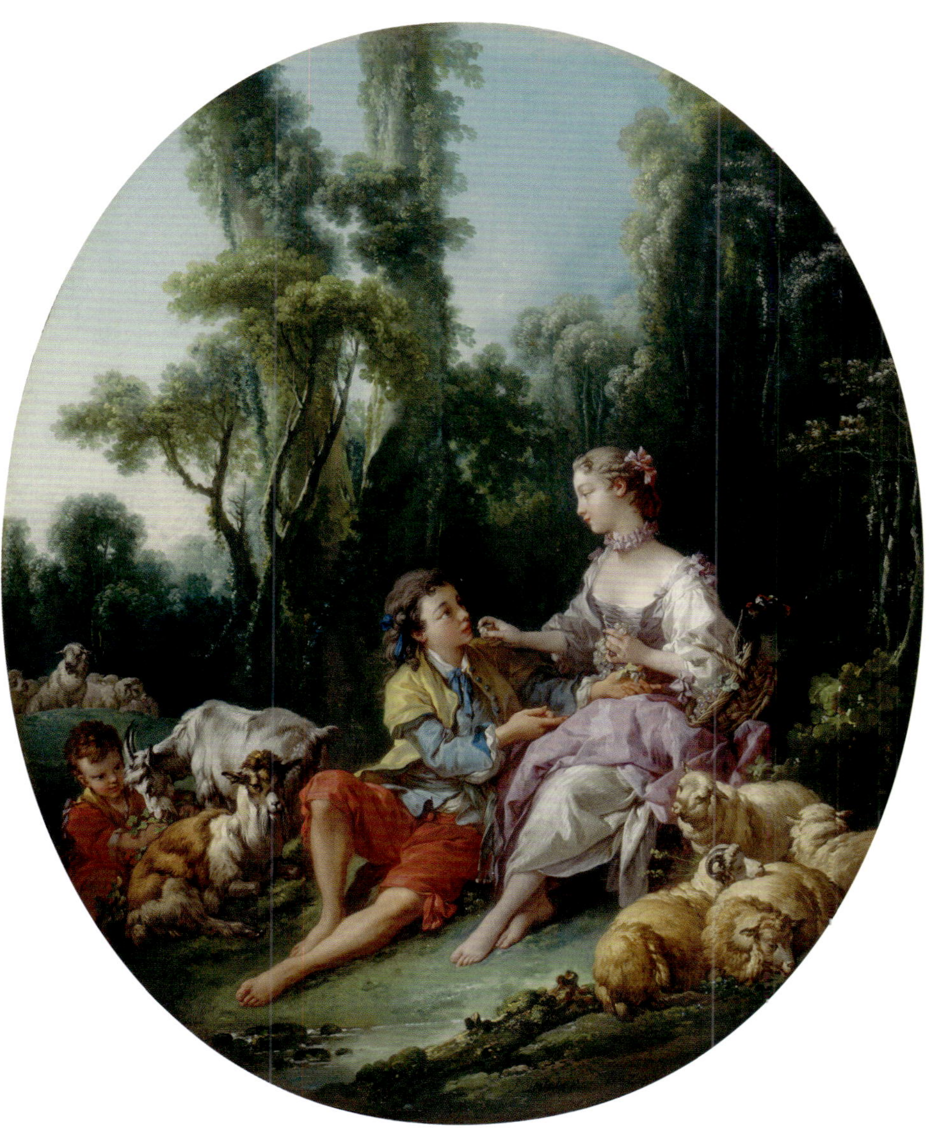

in a secluded grove. The young man gestures to his heart with one hand and takes the woman's hand with the other. She leans away, apparently expressing modest uncertainty, as she raises her hand to her ear. The integrity of this seemingly polite declaration of love, however, is called into question by the brazen penetration of the man's left leg into the folds of the lady's skirt. *After* presents the debauched aftermath of the courtship. The woman's bonnet is gone, the couple's faces are flushed, their hair is in disarray, and their disheveled dress reveals not only the woman's bare thighs but also the man's still-engorged penis. Even the

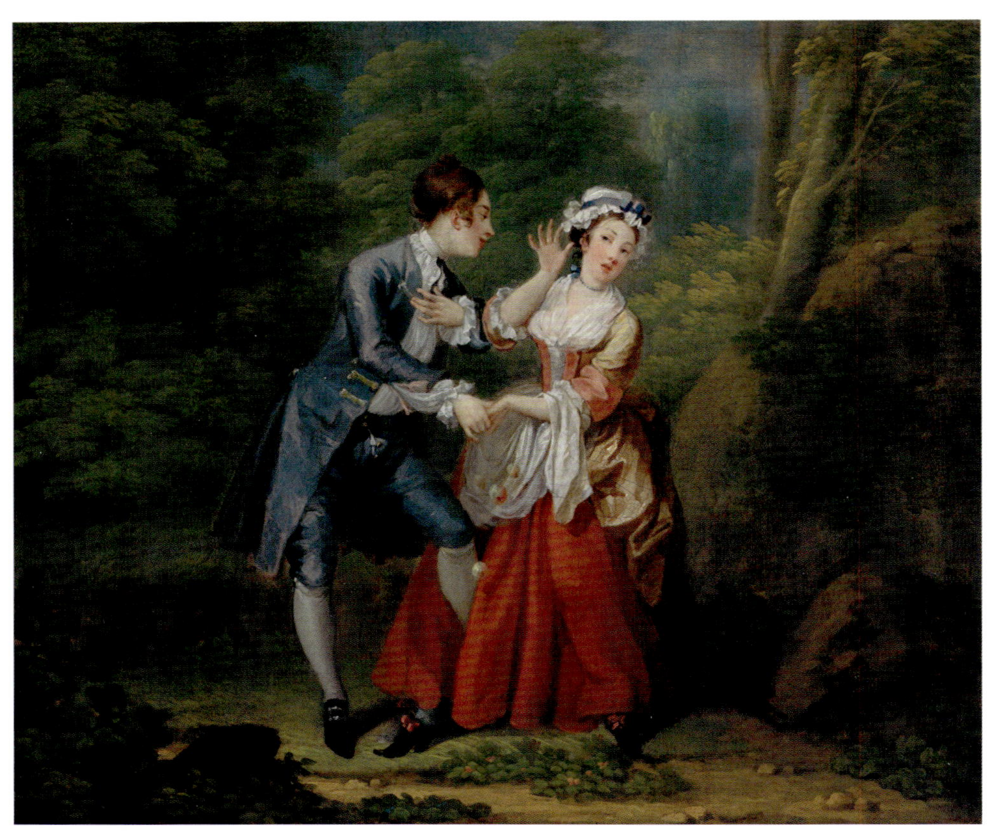

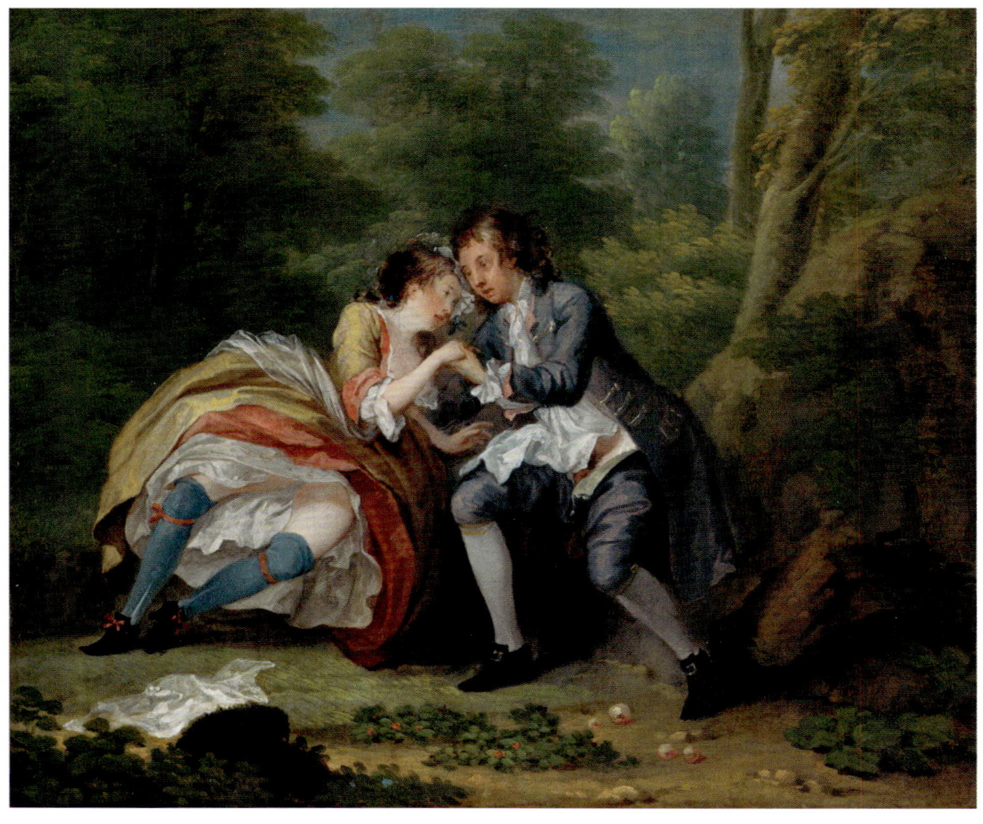

wooded setting now appears less green and lush, evoking the post-Edenic wasteland into which Adam and Eve were cast out following the commission of original sin.

The couple depicted in *Before* and *After* might be mutually complicit in the corruption of gallantry, but this was not always the case. The codes of gallantry were co-opted by dishonest men as a path to sexual conquest. By 1762 the Académie française dictionary used *gallant* informally to describe "a wily man, in whom one should not put much trust." The gallant man was associated with the distinctively eighteenth-century figure known as the libertine, driven by the desire for sex and freedom from polite conventions.[22] In 1757 the *Encyclopédie* warned: "*Galanterie* is nothing other than libertinism hiding under an honest name."[23] Libertines viewed marriage, the condemnation of adultery, and the cultivation of female virtue as deviations from nature and perversions of individual liberty. Eighteenth-century writers commented on the prevalence of libertinism, particularly in London and Paris, inveighing against its detrimental effects on society. By abstaining from marriage and procreation, the libertine was not only wreaking havoc on the virtue of young women, but was also interfering with the fundamental social and economic institutions of marriage and the family.

The age of libertinism required sophisticated contraception. Condoms appeared only in the late seventeenth century, and even in the eighteenth century they were relatively rare and found mainly in London.[24] Casanova was something of a condom connoisseur: he describes one example as "a little jacket of very fine, transparent skin, eight inches long and closed at one end, and which by way of a pouch string at its open end had a narrow pink ribbon" (H 7:11). Pink ribbon also appears on the condoms pinned to the wall in Johann Zoffany's *Self-Portrait* (fig. 76).[25] The artist is depicted in his studio with an array of artistic tools and sources of inspiration behind him, including a palette, a small print after Titian's *Venus of Urbino*, and the condoms, just to the right of Zoffany's head. Condoms were used not only as contraception but as precaution against venereal disease, an increasingly common problem in the age of license. One satirist wrote that fops saw such ailments as proof of "luck in love," adding that sexually transmitted disease "is the public subject of conversations and of a thousand jokes... doctors owe it a large part of their fortune!"[26] The French physician Jean Astruc, author of the

Fig. 74
William Hogarth (English, 1697–1764), *Before*, 1730–31. Oil on canvas, 37.2 × 44.7 cm (14 ⅝ × 17 ⅝ in.)

Fig. 75
William Hogarth (English, 1697–1764), *After*, 1731. Oil on canvas, 37.2 × 45.1 cm (14 ⅝ × 17 ¾ in.)

first significant treatise on venereal disease, doubted the effectiveness of prophylactics: "It is said that in England, debauched individuals recently have begun to use a thin and seamless skin in the form of a sheath with which they cover the penis... imagining that, so armed, they will be resistant to affliction.... But oh how they are sorely mistaken!"[27] Indeed, Casanova's worldly familiarity with condoms seems to have done little to shield him from sexual affliction. Whether he considered it lucky or not, his love life led to repeated bouts of infection and treatment.

Despite the libertine's disdain for social norms and laws, he did not flout them altogether. Instead, he conformed to the rules of polite courtship in order to exploit them. Even when a woman was willing to risk her reputation by having sex with a libertine, the libertine would help her play-act the role of virtuous woman. He would (falsely) profess his love and she would (falsely) resist, before finally giving in. An instance of this game of cat-and-mouse is depicted in Fragonard's *Useless Resistance* (fig. 77).[28] A young maid wearing a feathery white cap wrestles with her lover in a bedroom amply padded with large cushions in anthropomorphic shapes. The young man reaches toward the front of the woman's skirt with one hand and with the other firmly restrains her left arm; she pulls at his wig, revealing some of his natural hair. The maid's flushed cheeks, muted smile, and lack of concern that her breasts and thighs are exposed indicate that her resistance is indeed "useless"—it is a performance enacted despite a foregone conclusion. The painting's sunny palette and ebullient brushwork suggest that the couple's adoption of these artificial roles has served to heighten their pleasure. Nonetheless, the tautly coiled energy of the struggle and tight compression of space lend the scene a sense of peril: one wonders whether a last-minute change of heart would register in this swirling vortex of libidinous energy.

The elliptical shape of *Useless Resistance*, like that of *The New Model*, simulates the voyeuristic act of peering through a peephole.

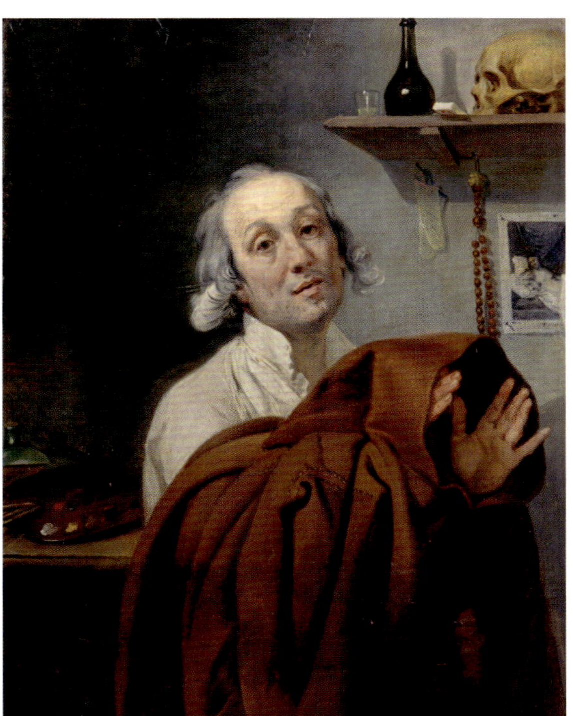

Fig. 76

Johann Zoffany (German, 1733–1810), *Self-Portrait*, 1770s. Oil on canvas, 43 × 39 cm (16 ⅞ × 15 ⅜ in.)

Fig. 77

Jean-Honoré Fragonard (French, 1732–1806), *Useless Resistance*, about 1770–73. Oil on canvas, 45 × 60.5 cm (17 ¾ × 23 ⅞ in.)

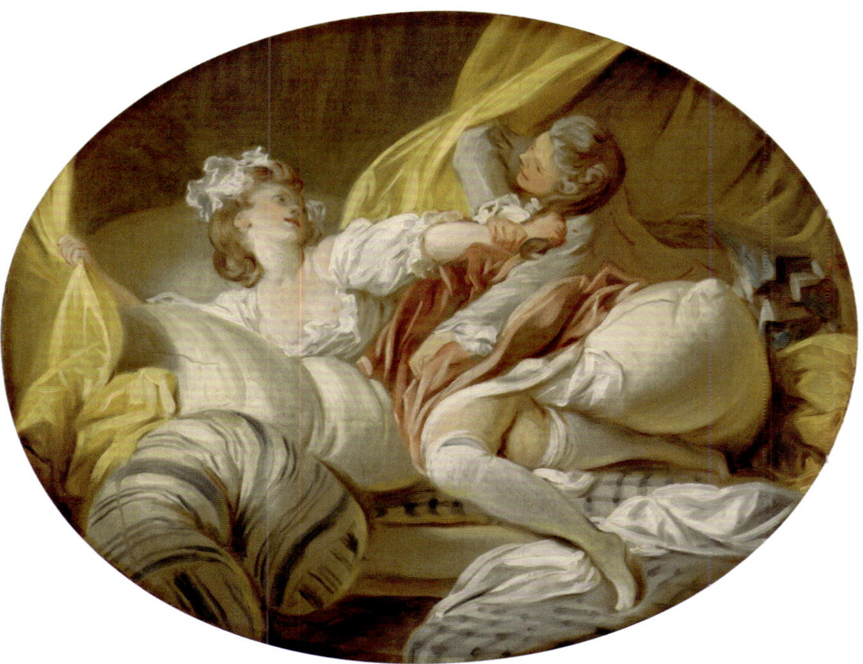

Voyeurism was not unfamiliar to Casanova, who made love to the nun M.M. while the abbé de Bernis watched through peepholes in the walls of his *casino*. Eighteenth-century pornographic literature frequently employed voyeurism as a device to heighten the narrative's erotic appeal.[29] Novels told from the point of view of inanimate objects—a popular eighteenth-century genre now known as the "it-narrative"—lent themselves especially well to the exploitation of voyeuristic fantasy. Claude Prosper Jolyot de Crébillon's *The Sofa: A Moral Tale*, for example, is narrated by a man whose soul has been sentenced to reside in various sofas—a punishment that grants him undetected access to episodes of ostensibly private lovemaking. Fragonard's *Curiosity*, an image of two young girls peering out from behind curtains, carries the voyeuristic gaze to an extreme (fig. 78).[30] On the broadly painted surface, forms are hardly legible. As the viewer's gaze fumbles across the surface, the image gradually begins to cohere: a hand at left holds a few rose petals, and their pink hue leads the eye to the pink nipple of a breast below, revealed through a gap in the curtains. A basket with more rose petals is visible at lower right. The creases of the curtains and the oblong shape of the central hole, which opens on to a dark void, are strongly suggestive of female anatomy. But as soon as the gaze penetrates that innermost space,

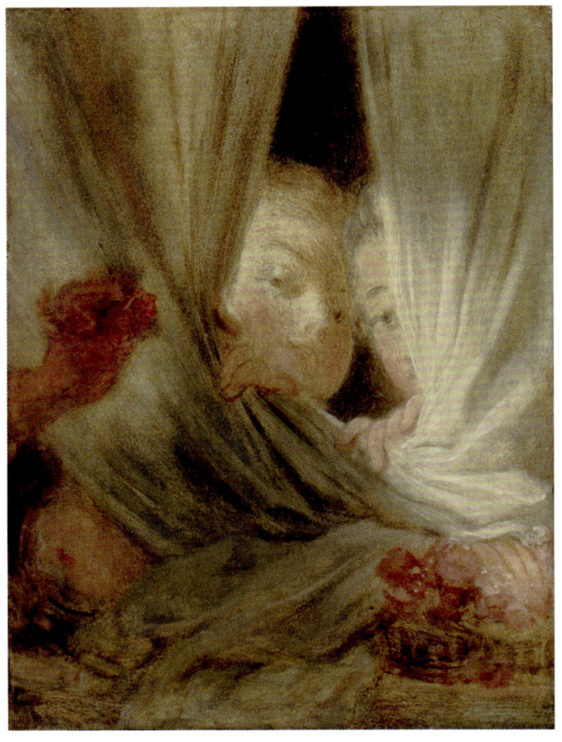

the illusion of secrecy is charmingly countered by the two faces looking back at the viewer. The painting's small scale and licentious subject suggest that it was commissioned for a wealthy patron's private cabinet.

While the eroticism of *Curiosity* turns on the girls' awareness of being watched, Fragonard's *The Desired Moment* offers a different kind of voyeuristic pleasure (fig. 79).[31] Two lovers embrace so ardently and with such mutual absorption that they appear completely unaware of being watched. Frenetic marks of ocher pigment radiate out from their bodies, as though the room were pulsating with red-hot energy, ignited by their passion. In this utopian image of pure bodily pleasure, the artful deceptions of courtship and flirtation have been displaced by natural, carnal desire. In a related drawing by Fragonard known (like the painting) as *Useless Resistance* (about 1770–73, Philadelphia Museum of Art), the couple's embrace is inverted, with the woman occupying the dominant role.[32] The two versions suggest that this composition depicts equality in love—a rejection of the conventional gender roles performed in courtship and marriage.

This granting of privilege to natural bodily impulses over conjugal duty extended beyond libertine culture. Anecdotal and statistical evidence suggests that fornication and adultery increased significantly during the eighteenth century, particularly among the upper classes in Paris and London.[33] In a discussion of Charles-Joseph Dorat's 1775 play *The Bachelor*, a critic noted that bachelorhood was "a vice particular to the eighteenth century" and that the term "bachelor" (*célibataire*) did not even exist in the previous century.[34] Another author (himself a bachelor) wrote in 1783 that there were a hundred thousand bachelors in Paris—a seventh of the city's total population. He asserted that this "frightening number" was an indication of "how difficult marriages are [in Paris], and how susceptible individuals are to the love of liberty."[35] A report on the population of Paris in 1770 showed that, while the number

Clothes Make the Man

Clothes Make the Man

PAMELA A. PARMAL

Velvet: the word comes up often in Casanova's memoirs. He takes pride in acquiring his first velvet suit, causes consternation in Turin with a velvet dress, and then buys three men's velvet suits that he later cuts up and remakes into lavish peasant costumes for a masquerade. The most sensual of fabrics, silk velvets of the eighteenth century had a soft, luscious hand (fig. 84). They are among the few textiles that Casanova mentions by name in his memoirs, as his descriptions of dress often lack detail. Yet he places great importance on dress in his writing. For Casanova, clothing, and the textiles from which it was made, revealed status and identity—or, when worn by one of history's most famous conmen, could be used as a disguise to mask his humble origins or help establish himself in a new city or a new venture.

The value of clothing and textiles during the preindustrial age is difficult for us in the twenty-first century to understand. The yarns out of which textiles were made were hand spun and processed, and then hand woven on the loom; finally, the finished textile was hand sewn into garments. The often-quoted statistic that in mid-eighteenth-century England a woman's silk dress cost from £10 to £60 ($2,000–$13,000 current value), while a prosperous merchant's home was worth £500 ($100,000 current value), indicates the serious investment made to wear the latest fashions. Court dress was significantly more expensive.[1] Such an investment paid off, as the Anglo-Dutch philosopher and economist Bernard Mandeville wrote: "People, where they are not known, are generally honour'd according to their Cloaths and other Accoutrements they

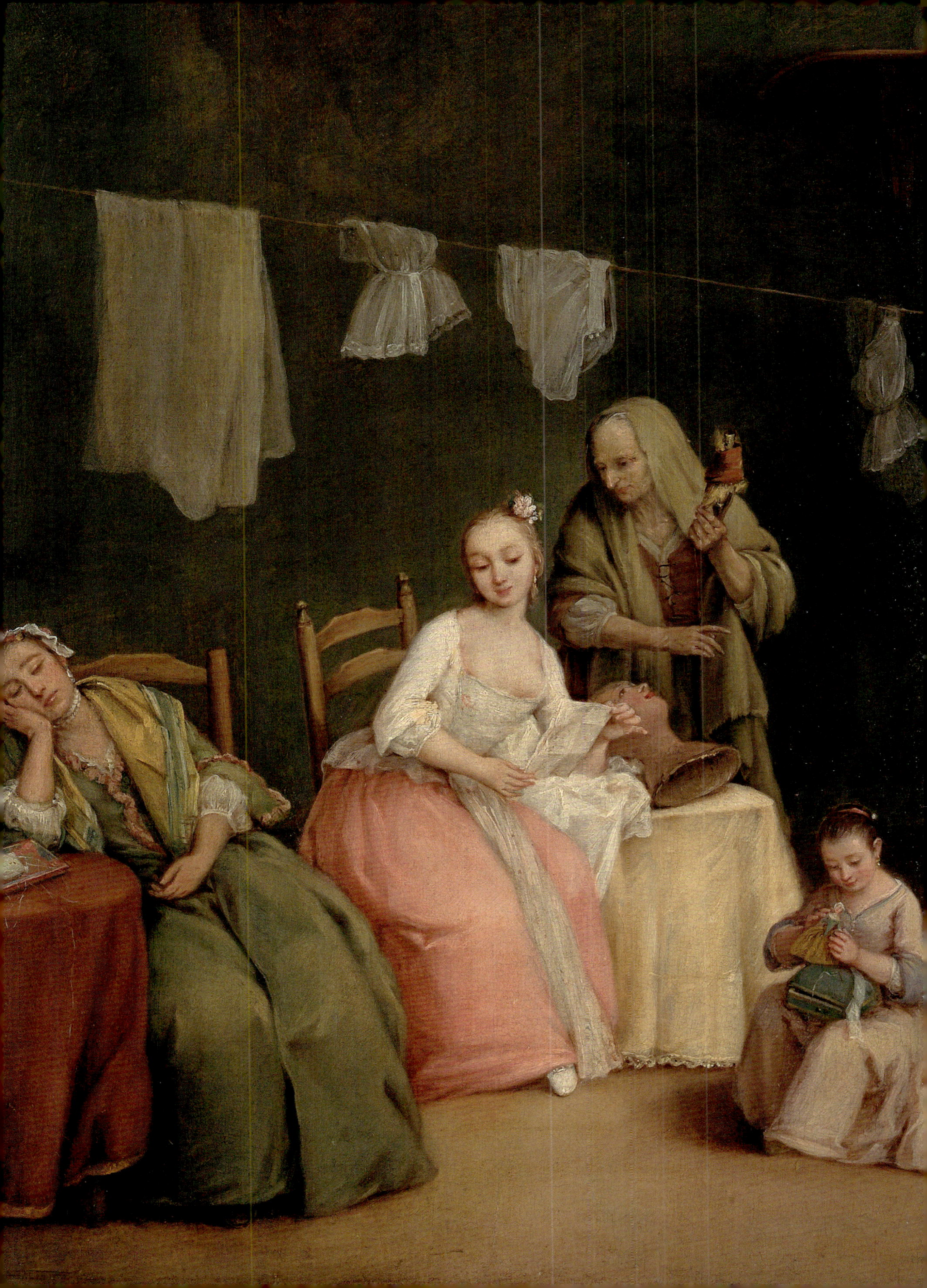

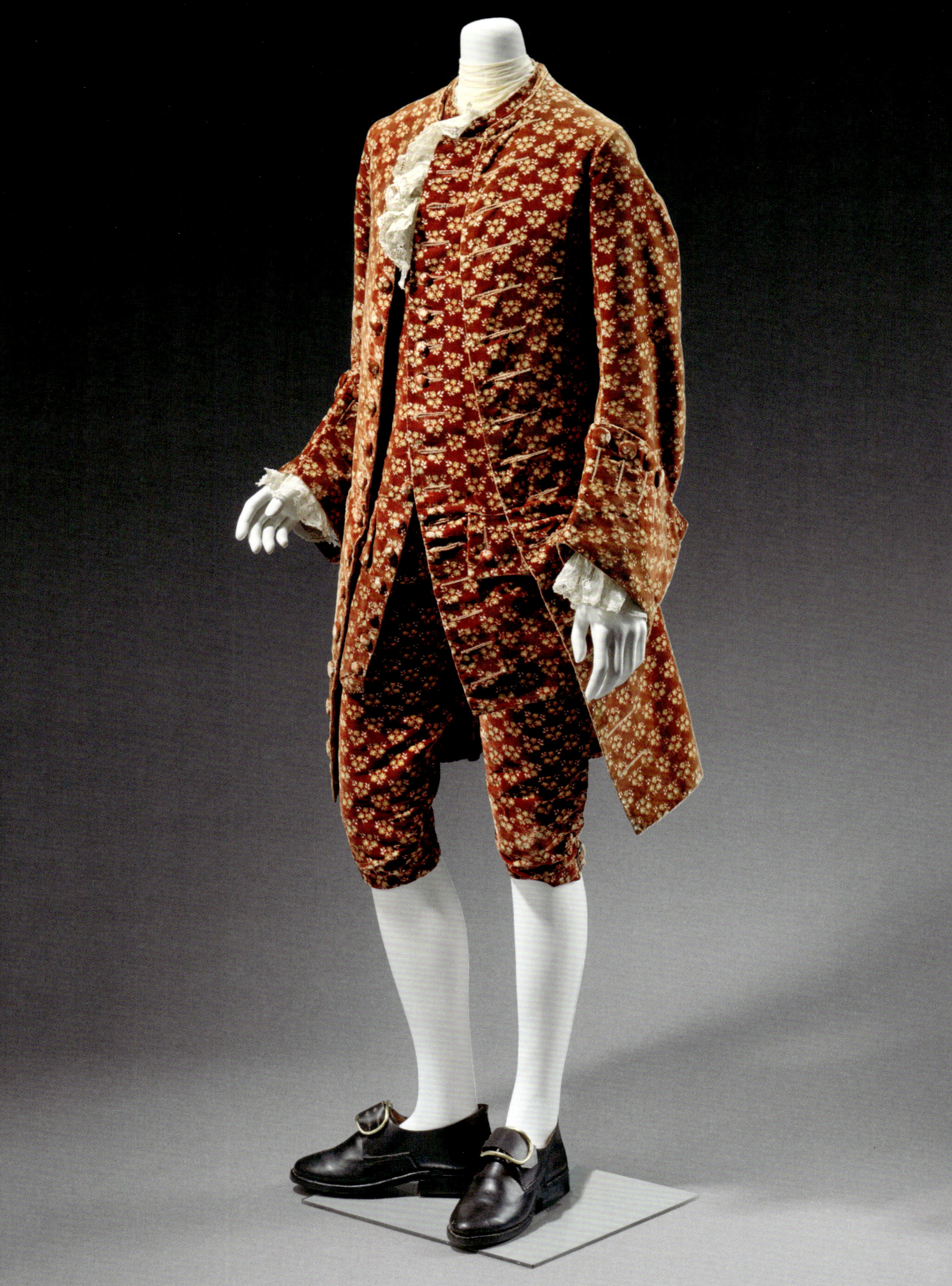

have about them; from the richness of them we judge of their Wealth, and by their ordering of them we guess at their understanding."[2]

Casanova understood this philosophy well. Throughout his memoirs, he reports that his clothing changed according to his circumstances. After finishing his studies in Padua at the age of sixteen, he was given a preacher's habit of black wool and sent to Rome to make his fortune (fig. 85).[3] When he decided that the preacher's life didn't suit him, he went to the tailors and had a uniform made up that would enable him to "impersonate a follower of Mars." The tailor created a military uniform that included a white wool drap jacket with silver and gold braid on the shoulders, and a blue vest. Drap was a heavy wool cloth that was closely woven and thick, making it warm—and expensive. Casanova also bought a long sword and a hat with a black cockade, had his hair cut "in side whiskers," and acquired "a long false pigtail" (H 2:45–46).[4] With his new finery, off he went to make a place for himself in the world. When he returned to Venice, at the age of twenty-three, he experienced a series of misfortunes and was forced to get a low-paying job as a violinist in the San Samuele Theater orchestra. Soon his fortunes rose again, after he saved the life of Senator Matteo Bragadin and eventually became his "adopted" son and protégé, a turn of events Casanova called "the whole story of my metamorphosis, and of the happy period which raised me at one bound from the base role of a fiddler to that of a nobleman" (H 2:200). Casanova does not specifically refer to the acquisition of clothes to match his improved social and financial status, but in recounting an escapade outside Venice in which he fell into a mud-filled ditch, he mentions that it spoiled his new velvet suit embroidered with gold spangles, his silk stockings, and his lace accessories (H 2:271).[5] Velvet, gold embroidery, and costly lace were marks of his improved standing.

Fig. 84
Suit, French or Italian, about 1750. Silk velvet, jacket center back length 95 cm (37 3/8 in.)

Fig. 85
Pietro Longhi (Italian, 1702–1785), *The Letter*, 1746. Oil on canvas, 61 × 49.5 cm (24 × 19 1/2 in.)

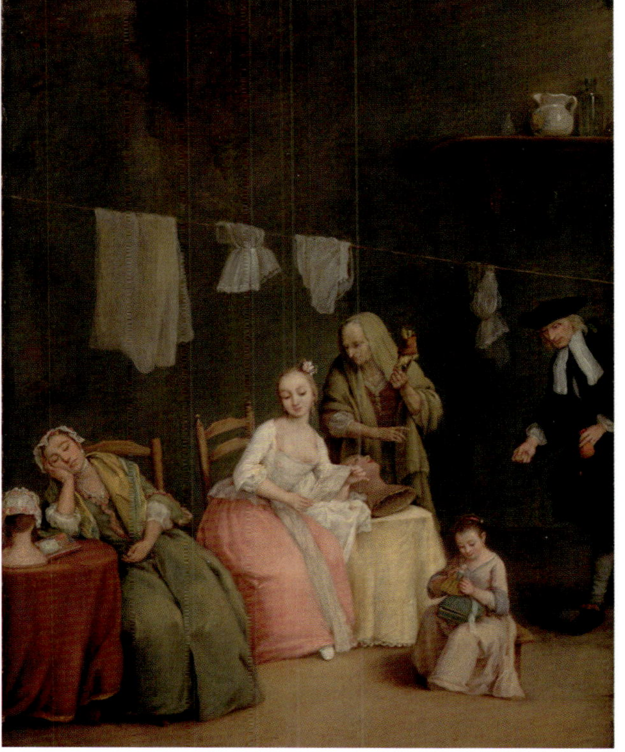

Fig. 86

Cloth of gold, French (Lyon), about 1760 (detail). Silk and metallic threads, fragment overall: 68.5 × 47 cm (27 × 18 ½ in.)

Fig. 87

Lace border, French (Argentan), about 1760 (detail). Linen needlelace, overall: 257.8 × 9.2 cm (101 ½ × 3 ⅝ in.)

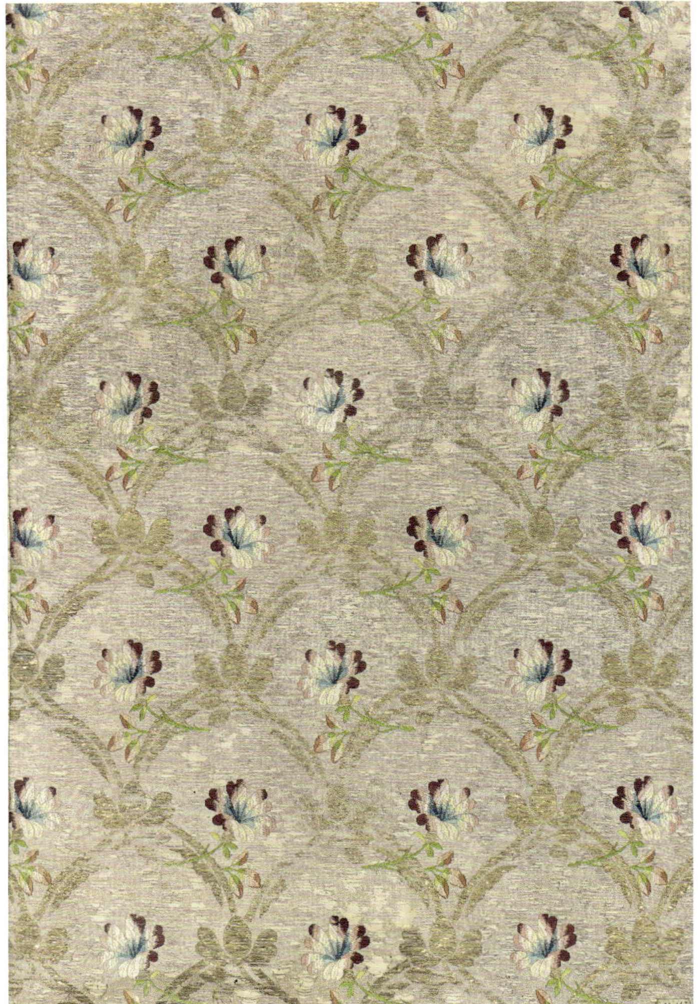

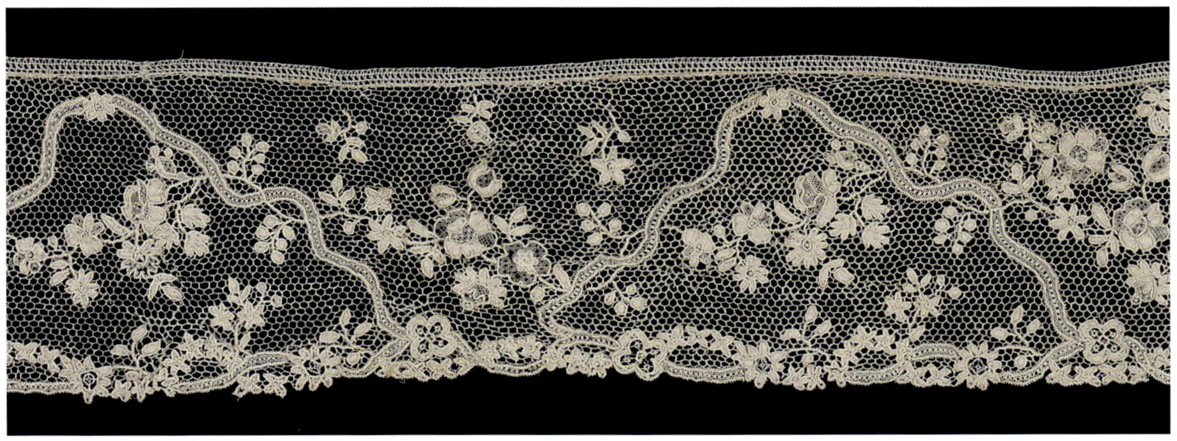

The progression of fabrics out of which Casanova's clothing was made, from wool to silk velvet, reflects the hierarchy of textiles during the eighteenth century. Upper-class men's attire, composed of three pieces—waistcoat, vest, and breeches—varied little, but people could easily distinguish drab wool cloth from fine broadcloth and understood that silk velvet was much more expensive than plain taffeta. Costly trims, such as metallic ribbons or lace, and embroidery of silk or metallic threads, also revealed the wealth of the wearer.

Casanova wears a velvet suit in his portrait attributed to Francesco Narice (see fig. 3). The waistcoat and breeches are of blue velvet, and the vest appears to be cloth of gold and silver. This type of cloth, probably the most expensive available at the time, was brocaded with silk and metallic-wrapped threads. The design of the silk is typical for the middle of the eighteenth century and was probably produced in Lyon, which led the fashion in silk design (fig. 86). Casanova himself comments on the importance of Lyon silks and attributes their commercial success to the high salaries that Lyon manufacturers paid textile designers (H 3:114). In the portrait, Casanova also wears lace ruffles on his sleeve cuffs and at his neck. The drape of the lace and the outlines of the pattern give the impression of needlelace from Flanders or France (fig. 87). Until nineteenth-century industrialization, lace was made by hand, using bobbins on a cushion to ply the threads, or building up one buttonhole stitch after another with a needle. This time-consuming process made it a very expensive commodity. In 1772, the duchesse du Berry purchased a set of French Argentan needlelace accessories for the large sum of 2,500 livres ($21,000 today). The set included a pair of sleeve ruffles, each with three tiers; a lace edging for the neckline; and borders for two neckerchiefs, or fichus.[6] By comparison, Louis XVI paid his tailor twelve livres to make a redingote (overcoat) and six livres each for making a pair of breeches and a vest in 1782.[7]

Casanova's acute awareness of the effect of dress on perceived status is evident in a youthful encounter he had with a Venetian noblewoman of an impoverished family. He originally met the young woman during his brief imprisonment at the Fort Sant'Andrea, located just outside Venice, in 1743. She arrived with her mother to visit her imprisoned father. Casanova describes her as elegantly dressed in the current fashion of young unmarried Venetian noblewomen, with wide side hoops (H 1:190;

fig. 88). When he returned to Venice, he paid a visit to her home and was surprised that her mother greeted him wearing "a dress which was all tatters and that her shift was dirty" (H 1:194). When the young woman appeared, he remarks on her "wretched dishabille"; he didn't even recognize her as the same girl he had met at the fort, and he now found her ugly. The young woman went on to explain that because of their poverty, they were obliged to go without dinner so that they could get their clothing out of hock and appear in public properly dressed for their status. Ironically, if they didn't appear at church on Sundays, the curate would erase their names from the list of those receiving alms from the Confraternity of the Poor. This story reveals the significance of dress in Casanova's valuation of others. During the visit he even remarks that had the young lady been a philosopher, she would have despised him, because he appeared to be interested in her only because of her fine apparel and the appearance it gave of nobility and wealth (H 1:195). The anecdote also reveals the importance of wearing the right clothing in public, even at the cost of other necessities of life.

After a series of further adventures, imprisonment, and escape from the Leads prison, Casanova eventually made his way to Paris, where he

Fig. 88

Francesco Guardi (Italian, 1712–1793), *The Parlatorio*, 1746 (detail, fig. 26).

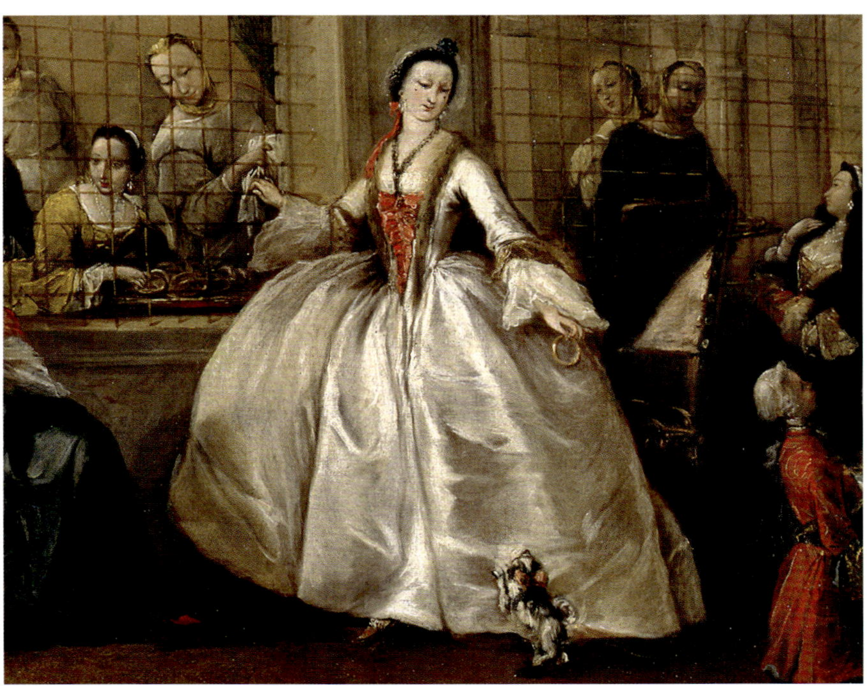

Fig. 89

William Hogarth (English, 1697–1764), *A Rake's Progress*, Plate 1, *The Heir*, 1735. Engraving, 35.4 × 40.6 cm (13 ⅞ × 16 in.)

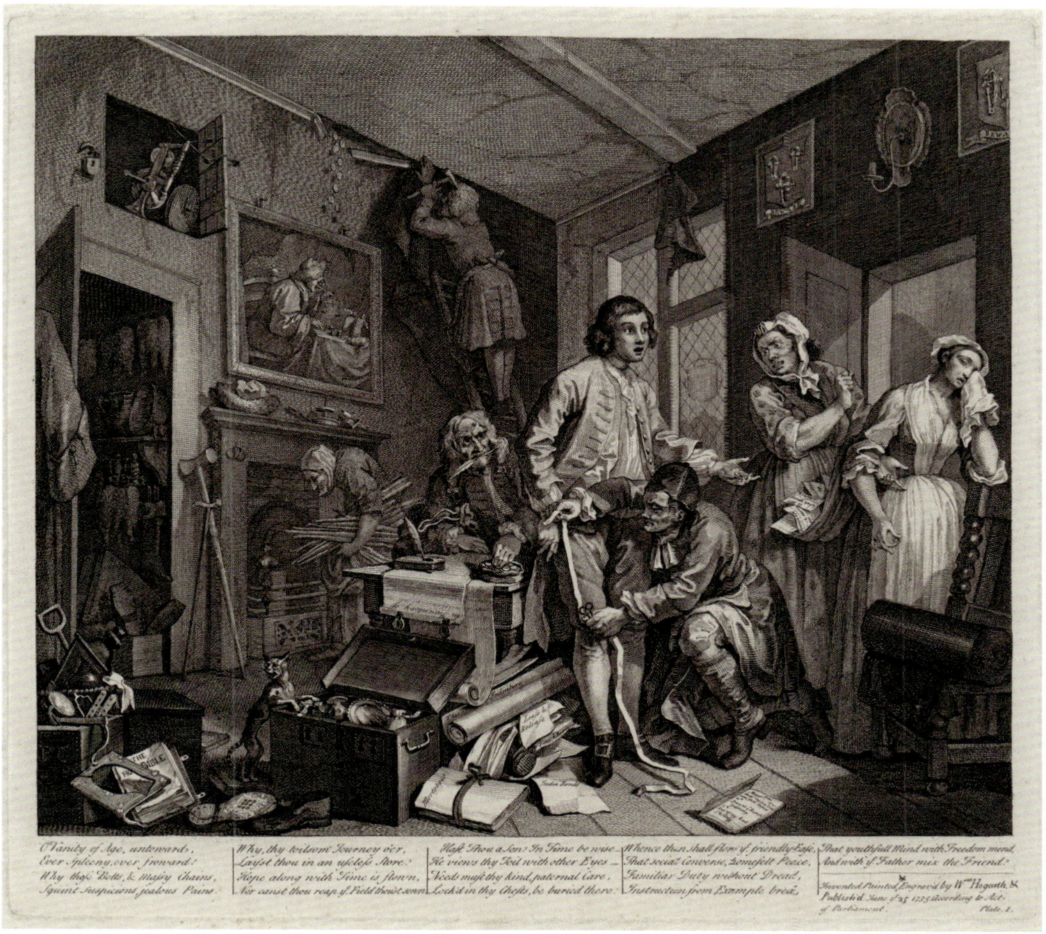

reconnected with the abbé de Bernis, the former French ambassador to Venice. The abbé, now a favorite of King Louis XV's mistress Madame de Pompadour, was appointed secretary of foreign affairs in 1757. Bernis, a writer and wit of some note, gave Casanova two hundred louis d'or soon after his arrival in the city. Upon receiving the sum, Casanova's first act was to acquire a suit of presentable clothes. Like Tom Rakewell in Hogarth's *Rake's Progress*, whose first order of business upon inheriting his miserly father's wealth was to invite a tailor to his home for a proper set of clothes, Casanova knew that the right clothes opened doors and proclaimed wealth and status (fig. 89). With the right clothing, he was ready to enter society and embark on a number of different financial ventures, eventually becoming wealthy by establishing the French state lottery system.

Fig. 90
Pietro Longhi (Italian, 1702–1785), *Lady at the Dressmaker's*, 1760. Oil on canvas, 61 × 52 cm (24 × 20 ½ in.)

With an upgraded wardrobe and business opportunities, Casanova began a new chapter in his life. His interest in women continued, along with his generosity to them in the form of gifts of clothing. An earlier encounter with the adventuress Henriette, who escaped from her husband and father-in-law wearing a man's military uniform, shows how he could turn his intimate familiarity with female dress to advantage when acquiring fashionable garments. Casanova met Henriette and her current protector, a Hungarian captain, in Mantua after he had fled Venice because of scandal in 1748. Our hero proceeded to save the couple from a scam perpetrated by the local clergy and police, and soon gained Henriette's affections and became her protector. One of his first acts in his new role was to procure a woman's wardrobe for her when the two reached the Spanish-held city of Parma. He began by visiting the shop of a linen seller, or *lingère*, and ordered what he felt was appropriate for a French woman of good birth, which included enough fine linen to make twenty-four chemises, dimity for stays and petticoats, and muslin and cambric for handkerchiefs. He also asked for the recommendation of a dressmaker, who would come to their rooms to make up the garments (fig. 90). He then stopped at the hosier to buy silk and linen stockings and at the shoemaker (*cordonnier*), who paid a visit to take Henriette's measurements. A milliner was also engaged, from whom Casanova instructed the young woman to order any caps, bonnets, and dress trims (*garnitures*) she wanted. Finally, a silk mercer arrived with samples of fabrics from which four dresses were made (H 3:41–45).

The clothing trades at this time were characterized by specialization. At the top of the hierarchy were the mercers, who sold silk fabrics, and the drapers, who trafficked in woolens. Clients would buy the fabrics and trims necessary for their garments and take them to tailors or dressmakers to have them made up. During the eighteenth century, tailors specialized in men's suits as well as tailored garments for women, such as riding habits. Tailors also made stays, or women's corsets. These stiffly boned foundation garments were made of layers of cloth into which fine casings were stitched to hold narrow strips of whale baleen that shaped the upper-body garment. Inserting a needle through the many layers of cloth and placing the baleen strips required hand strength, so the making of stays was reserved for tailors, who were predominantly male. Dressmakers were just that, specialists in the making of dresses. The cut

were better than those from China. A locally made product could be sold at a third of the price of imports and still yield a large profit. Casanova asked the man to produce several test samples, which he carried around with him for a few days. The samples were brightly colored, well designed, and as durable as promised.

Taken with the idea of owning a business, Casanova put up the funds to start the factory and appointed the designer as director. He found space near the Temple gardens in the third arrondissement of the city, an area to this day associated with the textile and dress trades, and set up shop in three weeks' time. The twenty young women, all between the ages of eighteen and twenty-five, who were hired to paint the silks eventually contributed to his financial ruin. Casanova treated the staff as his personal seraglio, establishing one young woman after another in her own household and buying gifts of furniture, clothing, and jewels (H 5:243–44). The business did well until the Seven Years' War (1756–63) caused the market to collapse, and Casanova was left with four hundred lengths of painted cloth in his warehouse and no market for his silk. He eventually lost the shop—along with much of his fortune—when he sold a portion of its shares to a man named Garnier, and members of the staff ran off with the money. This led to a series of encounters with the law, a brief imprisonment, and his eventual flight from Paris.

Even after his departure, Casanova continued to dress as he had when he was enjoying financial success in Paris. During his stay in Lyon in 1763, he met a party of Venetian ambassadors traveling from London to Venice and was invited to dine with them. He made an effort to impress his hosts by dressing in his best suit of gray velvet, embroidered with gold and silver paillettes, along with a shirt and lace accessories worth at least 50 louis d'or ($10,000). He was also decked out in diamonds, which he valued at more than 20,000 ecus ($200,000), that had been set into accessories such as his watch, snuffbox, rings, and the cross of his order (H 9:109).[8] The total value of his dress was a huge sum, equivalent to Marie Antoinette's annual wardrobe allowance just before the Revolution.[9] Casanova's clothing and accessory choices were the key to making the proper impression.

Casanova spent the next fifteen years wandering through Europe until finally taking up the position of librarian for Count Josef Karl von Waldstein at his palace in Duchcov, now in the Czech Republic. Casanova

Fig. 93
Suit, French, about 1780. Silk velvet embroidered with gold paillettes and glass and metallic thread; jacket center back length: 110.05 cm (43 ½ in.)

remained in Duchcov for the rest of his life and there composed his memoirs, which end in 1774. Because the memoirs do not cover his life at the palace, we do not have a direct record of the style of dress he may have adopted during this final period.

Although even in the years covered by his *History* Casanova does not devote much ink to the subject of his dress, it is possible to trace his professed identities as well as his rise and fall in society by the clothing he does describe. Before he is out of his early twenties, he appears in a preacher's black wool suit, then a military uniform, and finally, when he has achieved wealth and the status of a gentleman, velvet suits embroidered with silk and gold (fig. 93).Throughout his life he seems to have formed opinions about the status of people he met based on their dress. He was also a knowledgeable and exacting purchaser of clothes and accessories for the women in his life, sometimes with the aim of changing their perceived social standing, and he even dabbled in the trade. Although his descriptions of apparel in the memoirs are not detailed, they provide enough information to ascertain the cost of the garments, which would have been immediately recognized by his contemporaries as well. In Casanova's world, clothing and the materials of which it was made spoke volumes about the wearers' places in society, their wealth, and their taste. Casanova understood and used this principle to his advantage throughout his life.

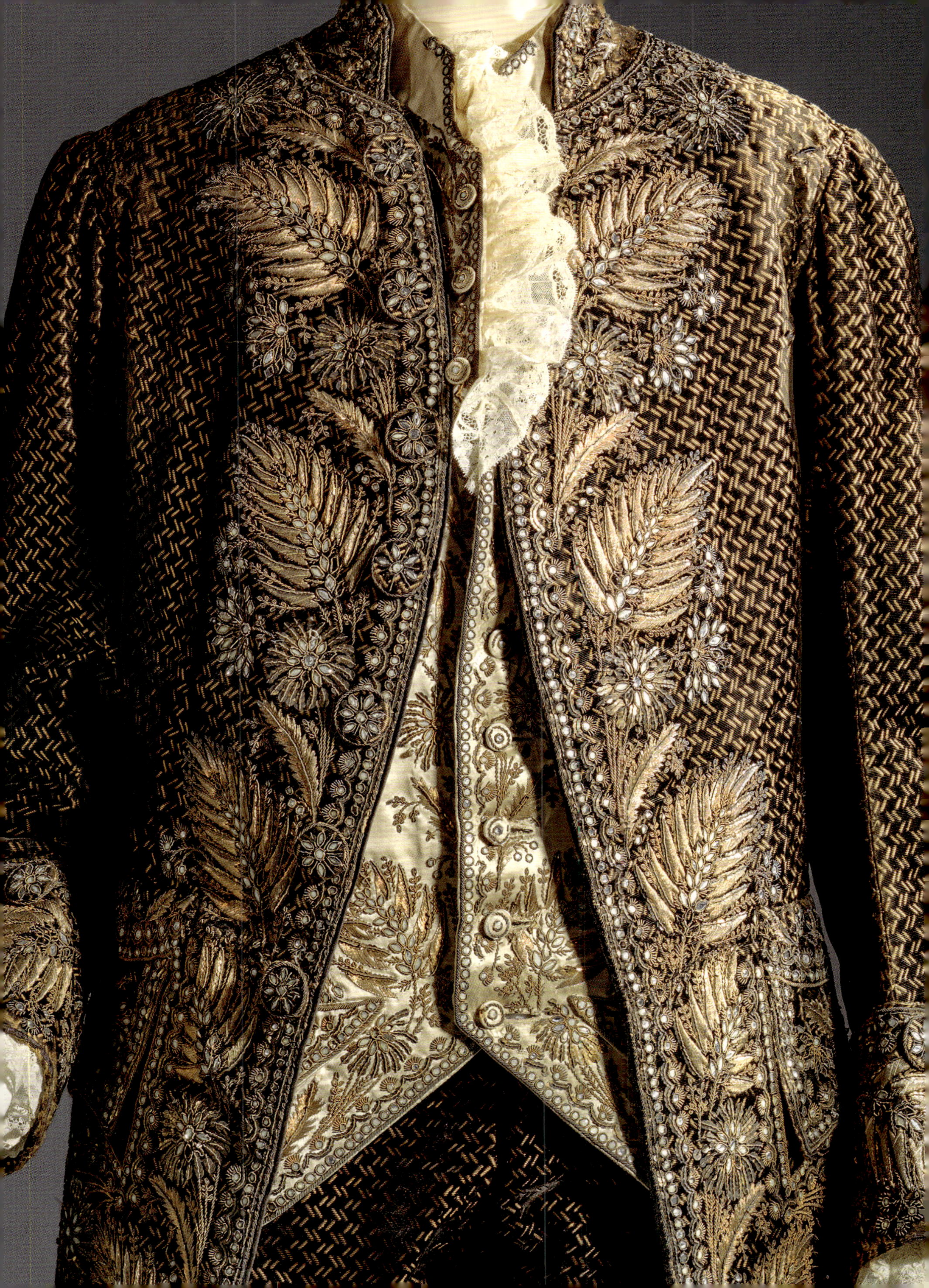

London

London

THOMAS MICHIE

Casanova's London was especially foreign to a Venetian who regarded Paris as his adopted home and Parisian society as his preferred social milieu. The time Casanova spent in London was brief, only the nine months from June 1763 to March 1764. Nevertheless, the London chapters of *History of My Life* are predictably crowded with accounts of places he went and people he met, with his presentation to George III and Queen Charlotte at one end of the social scale and numerous dalliances with Covent Garden prostitutes at the other. True to form, Casanova's amorous pursuits also spanned England's social spectrum.

Unique in his memoirs, however, is the sexual and financial humiliation he endured at the hands of Marianne de Charpillon, a "scheming wench," as well as the physical violence she suffered at his (H 9:298). "La Charpillon" was his nemesis: a professional courtesan who worked in league with her mother, aunts, and grandmother as part of an extended network of card sharps and swindlers.[1] Her immunity to Casanova's powers of seduction, even while accepting money from him to support her entire family, eventually drove him from rage to the brink of suicide. Perhaps because he had met her family a decade earlier in Paris and remembered Marianne as a strikingly beautiful teenager, Casanova assumed that he could pick up where he left off. In London, however, the mature Marianne was in full control. The Earl of Pembroke had cautioned Casanova about her, and Marianne herself warned that she would make him fall in love with her and then treat him so he "suffered the pains of hell." Casanova later rued the day "on which I had the misfortune to make her

paper currency rather than gold. As he grumbled to his fellow libertine Lord Pembroke, "I do not speak English, I like soup, French dishes, and the best wines; so I cannot put up with your taverns" (H 9:193).

A satire of tavern life, *A Midnight Modern Conversation*, after a lost painting by William Hogarth, is the archetypal drinking scene from early Georgian England (fig. 95). The absence of women in the room would have made the gathering less appealing to Casanova, who was unlikely to have been at ease among the cast of characters—tradesmen, clergy, and professionals—shown in various states of intoxication. As one modern critic has observed, this is a scene of "non-conversation," certainly not Casanova's idea of sociable company.[5] A later conversation piece (a genre of painting perfected in England that combines portraiture with narrative) of a similar scene by John Hamilton Mortimer includes several identifiable individuals, including himself seated at the far left, and is generally less moralizing than Hogarth's biting satire (fig. 96). It depicts an oyster supper with members of the Howdalian Society, an association of younger artists and architects who belonged to the Society of Artists of Great Britain, a precursor to the Royal Academy of Arts.[6] Unlike Hogarth's inebriated characters gathered around a punch bowl and surrounded by discarded wine bottles and an overturned chair, the Howdalians evidently shared Casanova's love of oysters and clearly enjoyed each other's company. The tall figure with his shirt open as he clasps his

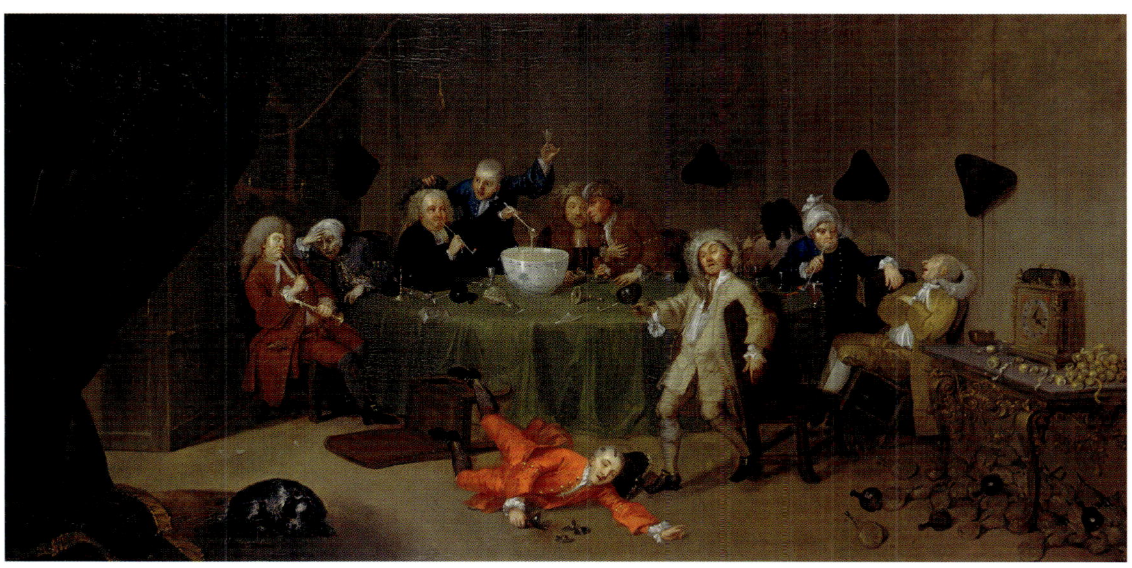

Fig. 95
Unknown artist, after William Hogarth (English, 1697–1764), *A Midnight Modern Conversation*, about 1732. Oil on canvas, 76.2 × 163.8 cm (30 × 64 ½ in.)

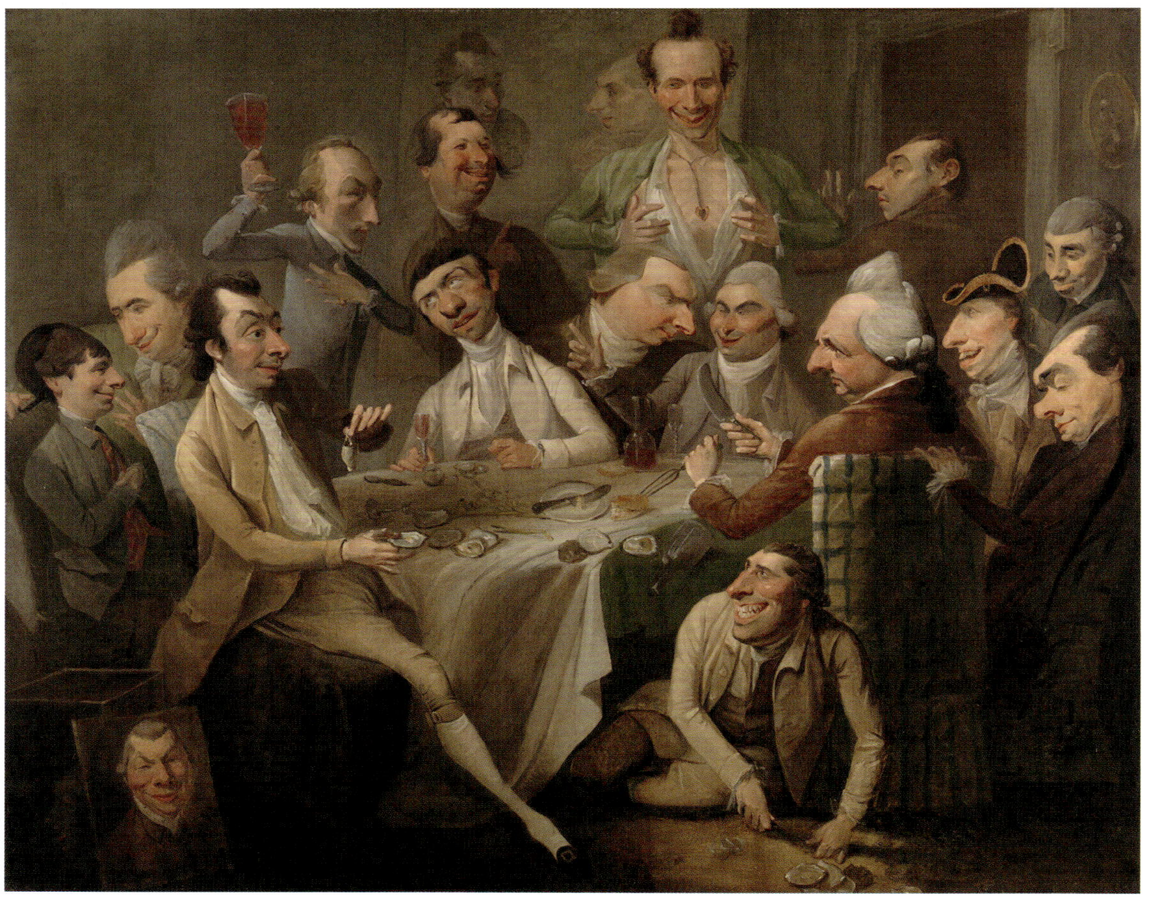

chest and displays a heart-shaped pendant confronts the viewer directly, although his identity and the significance of his gesture remain ambiguous. In Georgian England, taverns, coffeehouses, and assembly rooms were important centers of cultural life. In contrast to the lavish spending by absolute monarchs on the Continent, the purse of England's constitutional monarchs was overseen by Parliament. As a result, their residences were more domestic than palatial, and the social orbit of the Hanoverian kings was much more modest than most royal courts.[7] Compared with France, where Casanova flourished within court circles at Versailles, the social life of England's nobility residing in London must have been a disappointment.

As soon as Casanova arrived in London, he went to see Teresa Imer-Cornelys, an opera singer who had been a childhood friend in Venice and was the mother of a ten-year-old girl, Sophia, whom he believed to be his daughter. After moving to London in 1759, Teresa established herself initially as a successful impresario of concerts and eventually as a renowned hostess of lavish parties for paying subscribers. An important reason for Casanova's journey to England had been to deliver Giuseppe D'Aranda-Trenti (known as Joseph Cornelys in England), Teresa's son, whom Casanova had taken under his wing and raised at his own expense during six formative years in Paris. When Teresa failed to receive the travelers immediately, brusquely put them off until much later in the evening, and then directed them to overnight lodgings he considered unsuitable, Casanova concealed his indignation and instead set out on foot to explore the city. Not surprisingly, he soon landed in the company of another Italian, at the Prince of Orange Coffee House in the Haymarket, which he described as "notorious for those who frequented it, who were the dregs of all the scoundrelly Italians who were in London" (H 9:164).

Once settled more comfortably in furnished quarters he rented on Pall Mall, Casanova quickly graduated from the coffeehouse milieu to more upscale settings. The continuing saga of his failed rapprochement with Teresa Cornelys and her determination to prevent him from assuming the role of father to her daughter plays out against the backdrop of Carlisle House, Teresa's four-story mansion on Soho Square, whose assembly rooms she was continually expanding and renovating. Casanova's time in London coincided with the height of Carlisle House's fame, if not the fortunes of its hostess. Like Casanova, Mrs. Cornelys was a successful adventuress with a great flair for entertainments that included masked balls, concerts, and banquets for as many as four hundred guests. The novelty and exclusivity that enhanced the allure of Carlisle House were costly, and within a decade Teresa Cornelys had bankrupted herself, as she commissioned more and more lavish interiors, including two rooms in the Chinese taste and "proper furniture in an elegant and grand manner" supplied by Thomas Chippendale.[8] One cabinetmaker's accounts refer to a "Concert Room," "Great Supper Room," "Yellow Waiting Room," and a "Green Waiting Room with Octagon Glass Doors" at Carlisle House. Large mirrors with carved and gilded frames included one "with a bird at top," a second with "sheep in the China taste," and a third with "a pair of palms gilt branches."[9] These are consistent with contemporary descriptions of Carlisle House's elegantly

Fig. 96
John Hamilton Mortimer (English, 1740–1779), *A Caricature Group*, about 1766. Oil on canvas, 83.8 × 106.7 cm (33 × 42 in.)

Fig. 97
Covered vase, Chinese, Qing dynasty, Kangxi period (1662–1722). Porcelain with blue underglaze decoration, 51.5 × 20.3 cm (20 1/4 × 8 in.). Vase stand, English (London), about 1755. Mahogany, 45.7 × 27 cm (18 × 10 5/8 in.)

furnished interiors in the most up-to-date Rococo style (fig. 97). Fanny Burney, as an eighteen-year-old guest, declared that "the magnificence of the rooms, splendour of the illuminations and embellishments and the brilliant appearance of company exceeded anything I ever before saw."[10]

Gambling was a standard diversion at Carlisle House, whose card rooms attracted both men and women. The popularity of betting extended to every level of English society in the eighteenth century—from private social gatherings and public sporting events to government-sanctioned lotteries. Every kind of contest provided an opportunity for wagering, and tragic tales abound of family fortunes lost in a single evening. Whereas blood sports such as cockfighting, bear-baiting, and prize fighting were mostly favored by men of the lower classes, the aristocrats who patronized Carlisle House were apt to find themselves winning and losing at a games table, playing faro, piquet, whist, quadrille, or loo, among other popular card games. According to one English observer in 1751, there was "no nation in Europe so much addicted to Play as we are, nor any City where there are greater Sums lost" than London.[11] One of Hogarth's last major conversation pieces quickly came to be known as *The Lady's Last Stake*, although the artist gave it the slightly less risqué title *Piquet, or Virtue in Danger*. Probably inspired by Colley Cibber's comedy *The Lady's Last Stake, or The Wife's Resentment* (first performed in 1707), Hogarth's painting of the same title underscores the perils of high-stakes gambling (fig. 98). In Cibber's comedy, a well-to-do woman, having lost one too many hands of cards to a young army officer, debates whether to accept his wager allowing her either to recoup her fortune or to forfeit her last remaining asset—her virtue. Hogarth's painting depicts the fateful game, with the young officer proffering jewels and the woman steadying herself on a fire screen and leaning toward him as she appears to ponder his proposition. In Cibber's play, the lady is saved by her friends; in Hogarth's version, the outcome is more ambiguous.[12] Hogarth sets the scene in a grand room with a carved marble mantelpiece. Behind the players, the tall three-part window is the signature element of Palladian architecture, which dominated Britain in the first half of the eighteenth century. Based on Venetian models adapted for English building types, the neo-Palladian style was well suited to patrons who prized classical stability over more frivolous, if fashionable, architectural styles such as the Rococo.[13]

Champagne and Oysters

Champagne and Oysters

MEREDITH CHILTON

In the preface to his memoirs, Casanova confesses that "cultivating whatever gave pleasure to my senses was always the chief business of my life." First among these pleasures was his love of women; next he admits he was "extravagantly fond of good food." Casanova's passions for food and women are intrinsically linked:

> *I have always liked highly seasoned dishes: macaroni prepared by a good Neapolitan cook,... high game on the very edge, and cheeses whose perfection is reached when the little creatures that inhabit them become visible. As for women, I have always found that the one I was in love with smelled good, and the more copious her sweat the sweeter I found it.*
>
> *What a depraved taste!* (H 1:31–32)

For Casanova, dining was more than a gastronomic experience or a way to heighten the senses before a seduction. He also used it as an illustration of his refined personal taste, his important connections, his ability to entertain, and his ingenuity.

Casanova dined all over Europe during his lifelong travels in search of patronage, or any means to maintain the luxurious lifestyle he had craved since he was a young man.[1] He was no snob, relishing meals taken with a troupe of actors as well as the "pure bliss" of eating local ingredients simply prepared for him on the Greek island of Vido (H 2:124). However, he understood the importance of dining with people of rank,

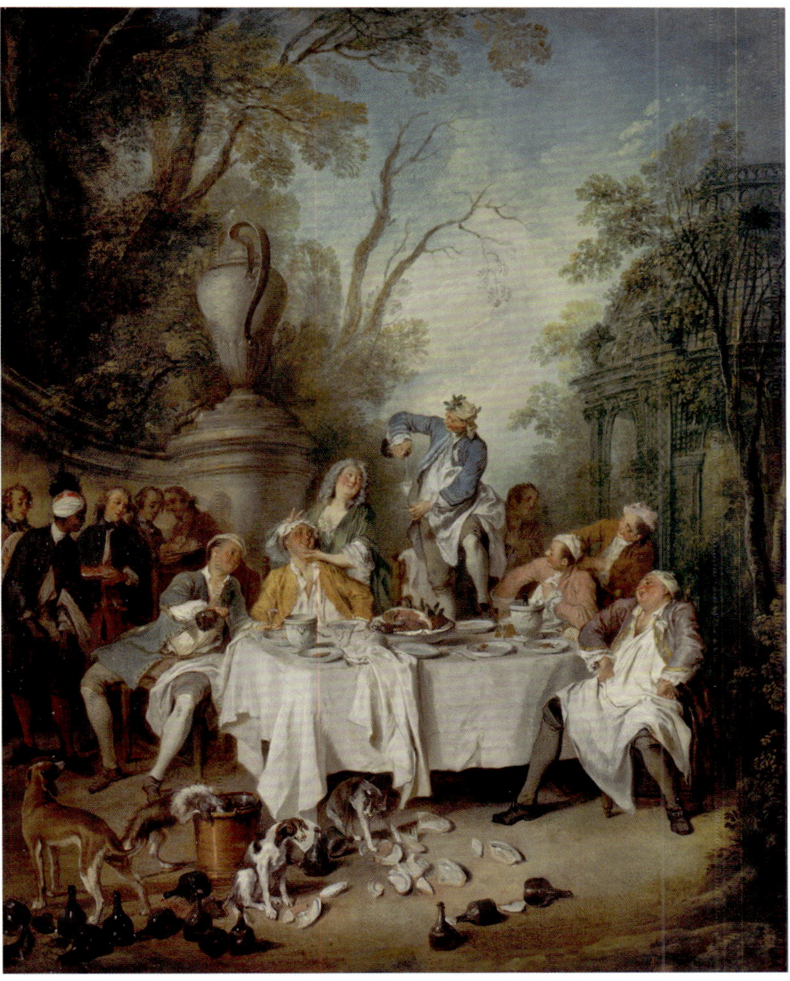

selves well in the honours of their table; that is to say in serving their guests and treating their friends agreeable to their rank and situation in life."[7]

Casanova also reminisces about the impression he made at meals he hosted at the house he rented in 1758–59 on the outskirts of Paris:

> *Everyone talked of the excellent table I kept. I had fowl fed on rice in a dark room; they were white as snow, with an exquisite flavor. To the excellence of French cuisine I added whatever the other cuisines of Europe offered to tempt the most refined palates. My* macaroni al sughillo, *my rice sometimes as pilau, sometimes* in cagnoni, *my* olla podridas *were the talk*

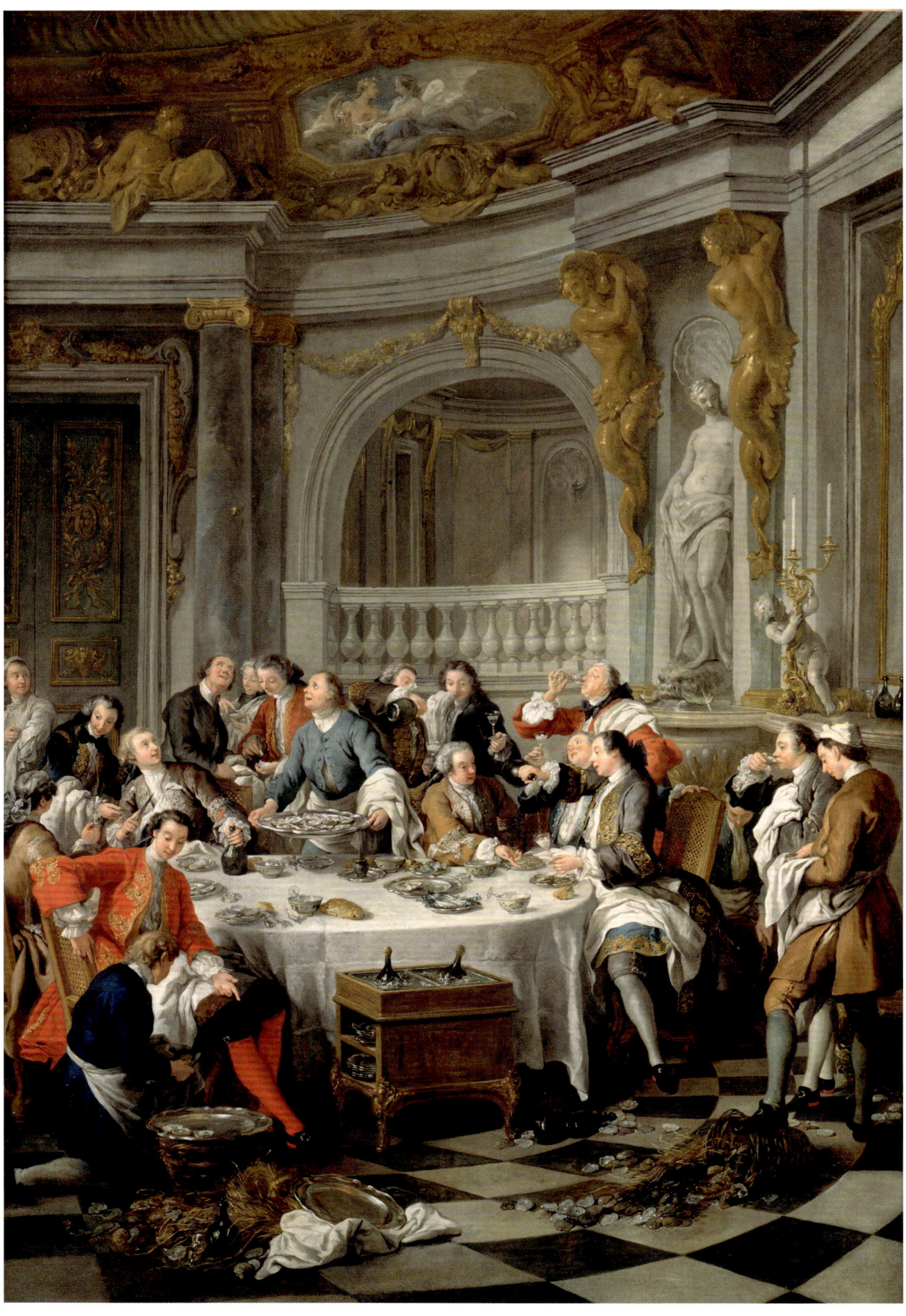

> *of the town. I matched well-chosen guests with exquisite suppers, at which my company saw that my pleasure depended on the pleasure I provided for them.*[8]

Learning these manners had not been easy for Casanova. As a young man, between 1744 and 1745, he had stayed in Corfu as the adjutant of Giacomo da Riva, governor of the Galleasses, a commander of the Venetian fleet. One evening at dinner he was instructed to carve a turkey—expert carving being an art expected of all gentlemen. Casanova carved the turkey badly into six pieces, and the "Signora F., who could not suppress her laughter, looked at me and said that since I was not sure I could carve it properly, I should have left it alone. Not knowing what to answer, I blushed, I sat down, and I hated her" (H 2:103–4). Introduced to Europe from Mexico in the sixteenth century, turkey became popular in high cuisine, and elaborate methods of carving and presenting the bird were spelled out in French culinary writings; there were even twenty-four named cuts recommended for carving fowl.[9]

Whimsical tureens in the form of turkeys, boars' heads, and cabbages as well as naturalistic serving dishes became the height of fashion in the mid-eighteenth century, advertising the host's taste in tableware (figs. 107, 108). They were part of the visual delights of dining and could also be entertaining: a life-size turkey-shaped tureen might sometimes surprise

Fig. 106
Jean-François de Troy (French, 1679–1752), *The Oyster Luncheon*, 1735. Oil on canvas, 180 × 126 cm (70 7/8 × 49 5/8 in.)

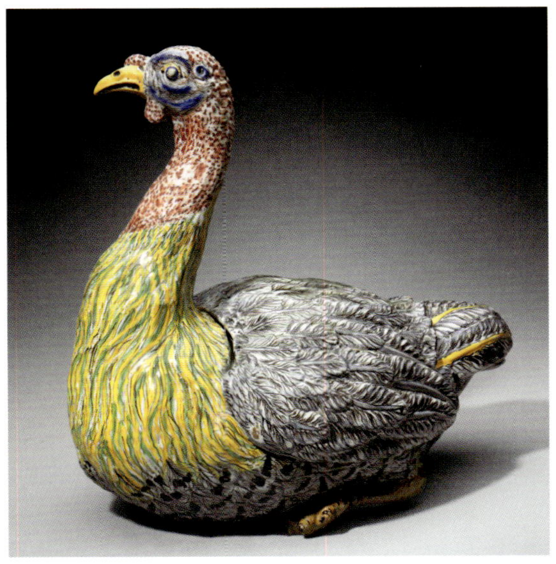

Fig. 107
Tureen in the form of a turkey, about 1760, made by the Holitsch Manufactory (Hungarian, founded in 1743). Tin-glazed earthenware, h. 39.4 cm (15 1/2 in.)

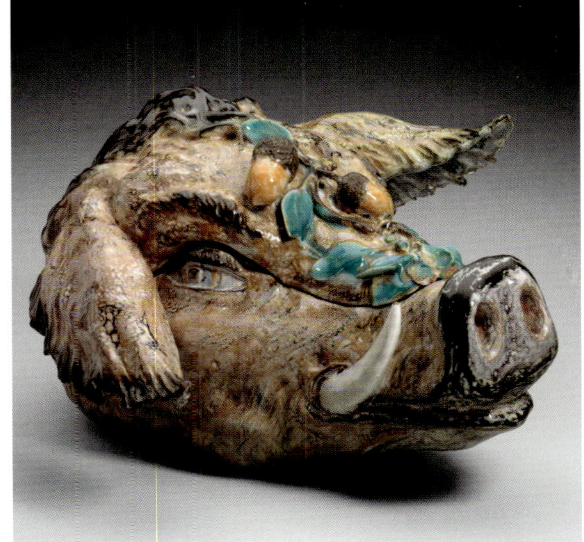

Fig. 108
Tureen in the form of a boar's head, about 1750, made by the Holitsch Manufactory (Hungarian, founded in 1743). Tin-glazed earthenware, enamel decoration; overall: 35.6 cm (14 in.)

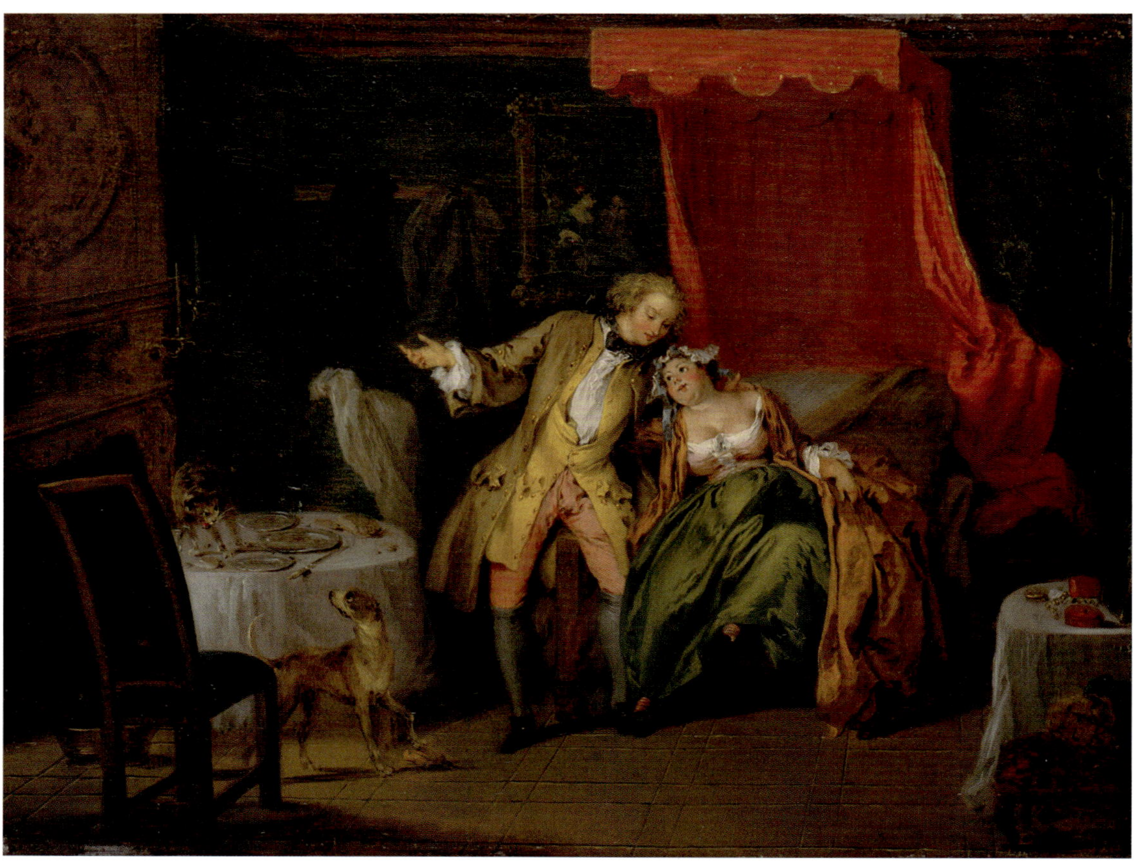

diners by containing something completely unexpected, such as a veal ragout. Alternatively, a cook could debone and roast a turkey, stuffing it so it retained its natural shape.[10]

In addition to using food to impress guests, Casanova recognized that food and choice wines heighten the senses, prompting him to include dining as an intrinsic element of seduction. For Casanova and his lovers, gustatory enjoyment intensified the pleasurable anticipation of an amorous encounter. The intimacy of a bedroom was perfect for a little dinner for two, as can be seen in another scene by Pater from the *Roman comique*, where Madame Bouvillon is attempting to seduce the hero (fig. 109).

What seems to give Casanova the most pleasure is staging an evening of the greatest refinement—one where all the senses are engaged, the seduction is much more than sex, and dinner or an intimate supper plays an important role. He describes a private Venetian apartment, or *casino*, that he rented as having "five rooms, furnished in exquisite taste.

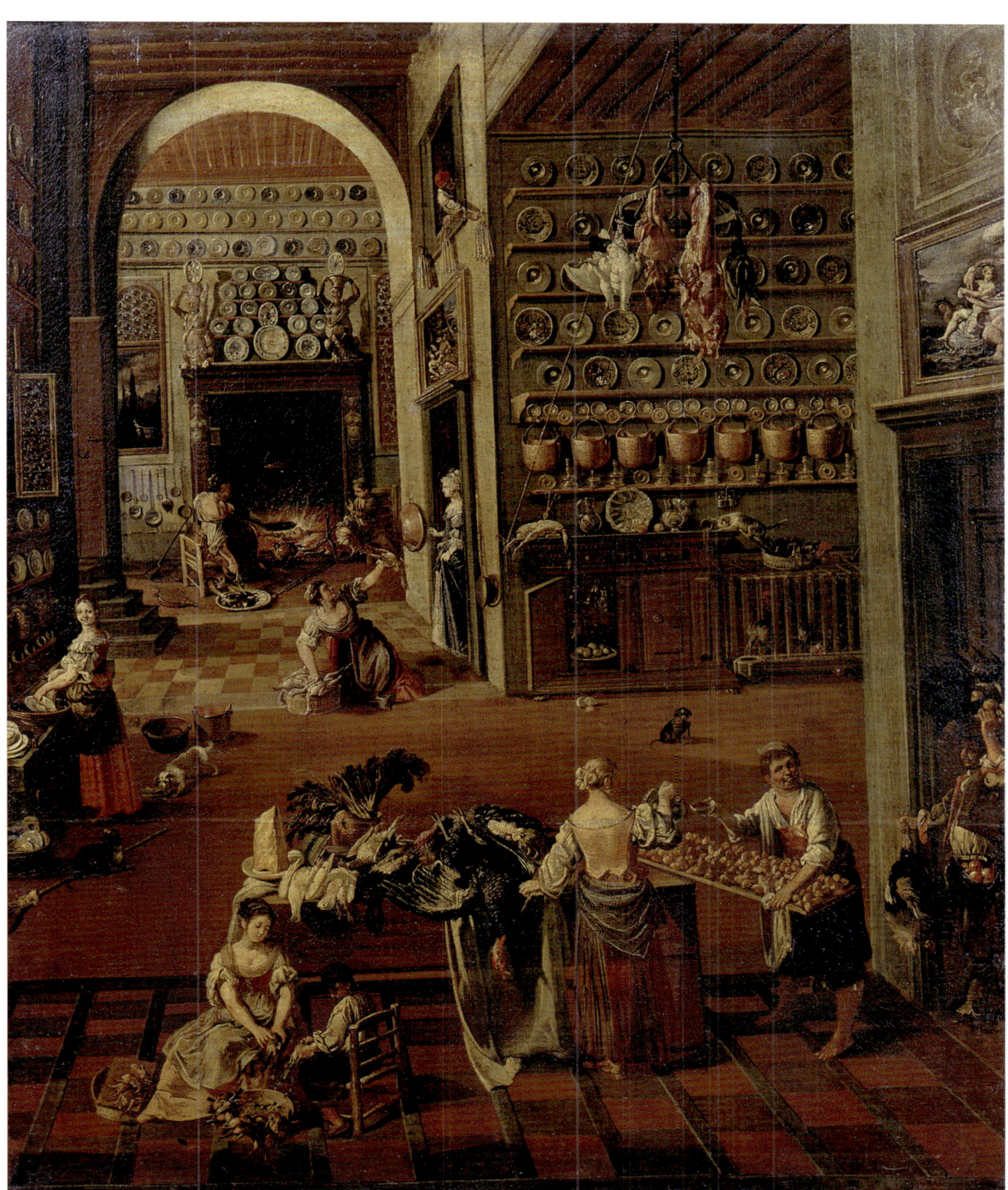

Dresden to Duchcov

Dresden to Duchcov

MICHAEL YONAN

By the time that Giacomo Casanova's wanderings led him to Central and Eastern Europe, the more sexually, financially, and socially adventurous chapters of his life had passed. The final volumes of the *History of My Life* describe romantic exploits in Berlin and Saint Petersburg, but say nothing about Vienna or Prague, cities that were the center of his world in the 1780s and 1790s. Indeed, we know little of his private life after 1774, the year in which his chronicle abruptly ends, and there may not be much to know. The uneventful years Casanova spent as librarian to Count Joseph Karl Emanuel von Waldstein in the rural Bohemian outpost of Duchcov gave him little opportunity to advance his social standing or add to his amorous reputation. For this reason and others, Casanova's Central European exploits seem an anticlimactic epilogue to a life filled with celebrity, intrigue, and pleasure.[1]

Contributing to the difficulty in understanding Casanova's years in Central and Eastern Europe is the profound transformation of its cities after the eighteenth century. The World War II bombings of Berlin, Dresden, and especially Warsaw diminished and in some cases totally erased their Baroque splendor. Furthermore, for long stretches of the twentieth century, Casanova's North American readers were unlikely to have a firsthand acquaintance with Prague and Saint Petersburg. Although Central and Eastern Europe have been perceived as peripheral spaces in Casanova's life, these regions are crucial to understanding the historical figure who fascinates us today. A closer look at Casanova's experiences in Germanic and Slavic Europe reveals how well suited he was to their

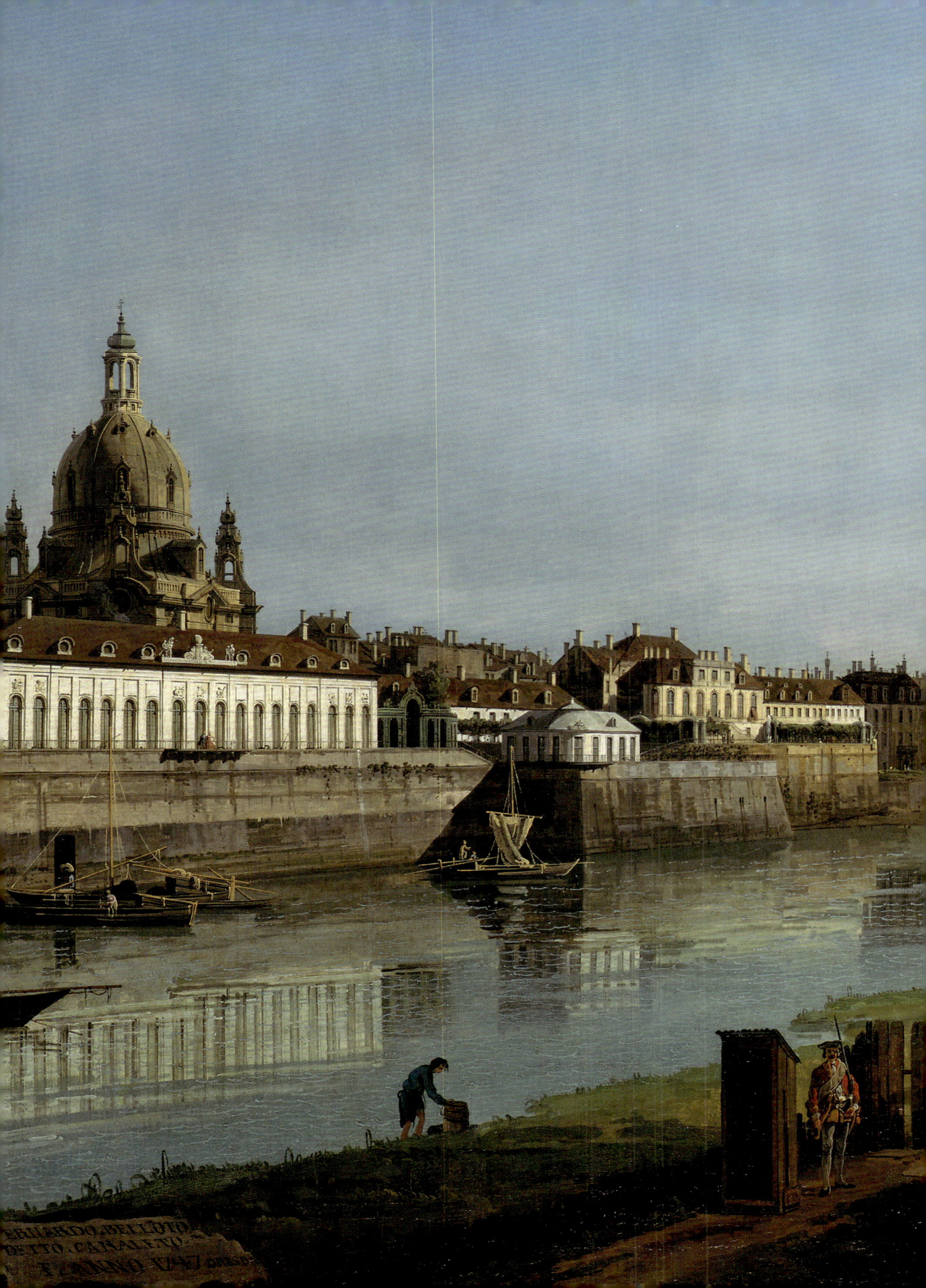
ERNARDO. BELLOTO
DETTO. CANALETTO
F. ANNO 1747 DRESD.

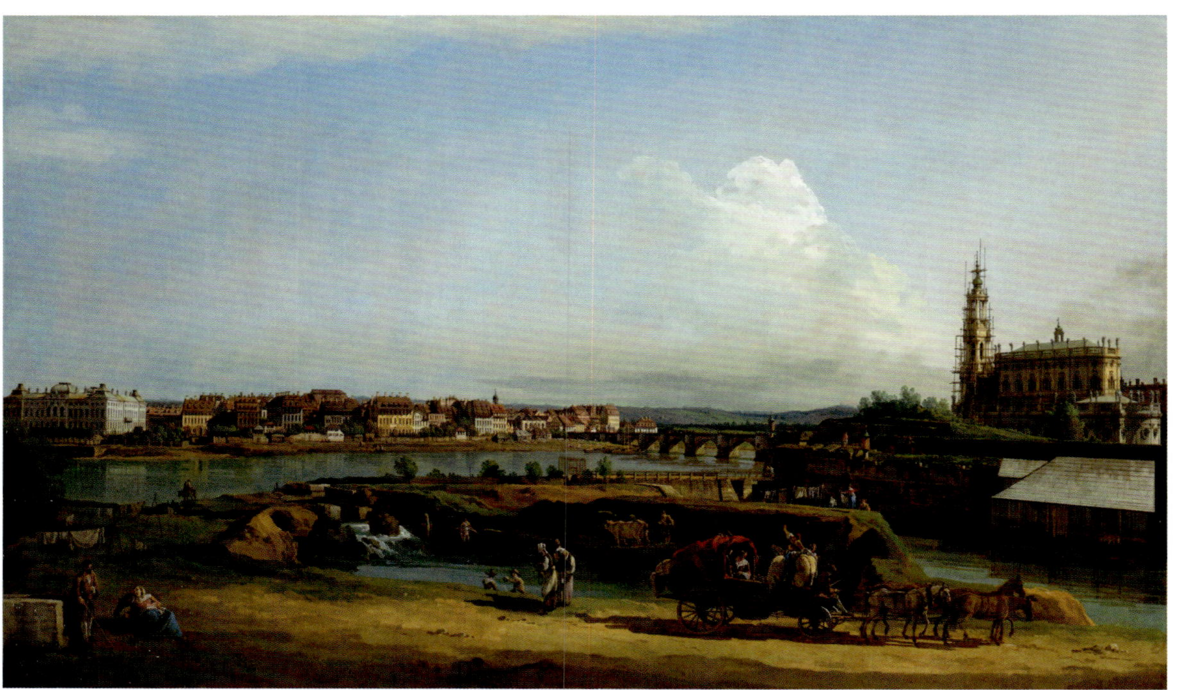

he cultivated to a greater degree than most eighteenth-century *veduta* painters. In the foreground of both paintings are figures whose activities convey the spectrum of daily life in Dresden, from washerwomen and guards to nobles and theatrically dressed courtiers, some of whom may portray known individuals.[9] Bellotto's mix of the grandiose and the mundane, the splendid and the rough, reflects the nature of the eighteenth-century city, which was at once elegant and earthy. Perhaps Bellotto's pictures are a kind of pictorial parallel to Casanova's writings: he too describes a world populated by kings and innkeepers, by scientists and dancers—a society containing every imaginable social type.

The Dresden public appears to have taken a liking to Casanova, just as it did to Bellotto and other Venetian transplants. Casanova wrote a highly successful play for the Dresden Theater, *La Moluccheide*, which was based on Racine's *Thebaid*.[10] His reimagining of the great French tragedist's work as a ribald farce became hugely popular with Dresden audiences. In appreciation, Augustus rewarded Casanova with a generous cash stipend, and it is likely that he could have attained a court post had he sought it. But apparently our hero thought his destiny lay elsewhere, and in 1753 he left Dresden to return to Italy.

Casanova next stepped foot on German soil in 1764, when, again in search of patronage, he traveled to Berlin. There he sought the attention of one of Europe's most magnetic monarchs, Frederick the Great, who had impressed the Continent with his intellectual brilliance and military demeanor. Frederick's skill on the battlefield transformed Prussia almost overnight from a regional principality of little significance to one of Europe's most authoritative and influential powers, with Berlin becoming an increasingly magnificent capital city as a result.[11] Casanova's meeting with Frederick is the first of two remarkable monarchical character studies in his *History*. After observing Frederick at the opera and briefly discussing with him the possibility of a Prussian lottery, Casanova waited for the king one day in his gardens at the Sanssouci summer palace to engage him in further conversation. As Casanova retells it, their encounter was awkward. They spoke briefly, and as their conversation concluded, Frederick looked the Italian over from head to toe and remarked, "You are a very fine figure of a man" (H 10:70). Knowing readers would recognize a reference to Frederick's homosexuality. The monarch's sexual identity was widely speculated about in the eighteenth century and even approached the status of an open secret, but rarely did it assume the personal dimension Casanova gives it here. Whether Casanova's retelling is accurate is impossible to say, but the passage suggests he knew his recollections might be read to provide insight into the personalities of Europe's famous personages. An alternative to this literary portrait, indicating something of Frederick's demeanor, can be seen in a painting by Johann Georg Ziesenis made about a decade before their encounter (fig. 115). Frederick wears the blue Prussian military uniform and holds a baton and map, very much identifying him as a battlefield strategist. The king later offered Casanova a job as tutor at an academy for Prussian officer cadets, a proposal the Italian found insultingly low-paying and well beneath his social stature.

Soon thereafter, Casanova traveled to Saint Petersburg, once more in search of patronage, but this time from the court of Catherine the Great of Russia. He arrived there on December 21, 1764, sharing a coach with a German mathematician whom he found fascinatingly boring. Casanova hoped his connections would enable him to set up a lottery in nearby Riga. In Saint Petersburg he found that the main language spoken was German, a tongue he had never mastered. Linguistic diffi-

Fig. 114
Bernardo Bellotto (Italian, 1721–1780), *View of Dresden with the Hofkirche at Right*, 1748. Oil on canvas, 135.9 × 233.7 cm (53 ½ × 92 in.)

culties notwithstanding, he insinuated his way into the city's elite class and quickly befriended several individuals close to the empress. He visited many of Catherine's palaces, including Tsarskoe Selo, Peterhof, and Kronstadt, all of which were famous for their architectural splendor and sumptuous decor (H 10:138). A drawing by Louis-Nicolas Lespinasse of the Grand Menshikov Palace at Oranienbaum gives a sense of what Casanova encountered in Russia (fig. 116). Oranienbaum was a complex of palatial buildings and gardens located just outside the city proper. It had originally been developed by the statesman Aleksandr Danilovich Menshikov, who lent his name to the site's main building. Designed by

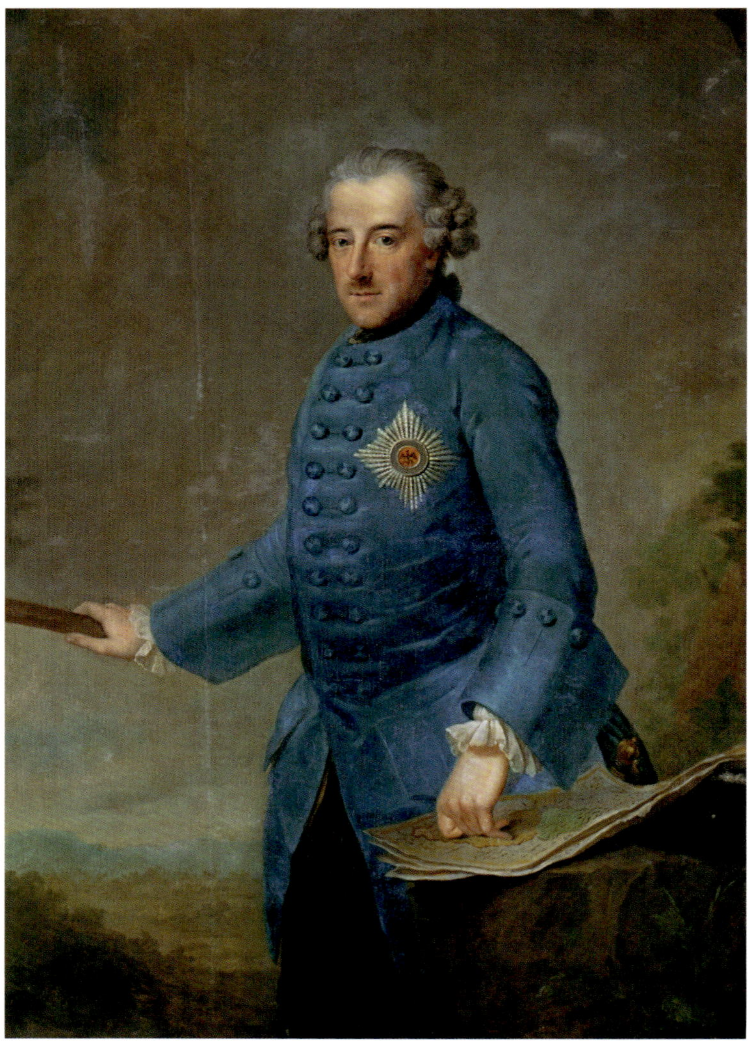

Fig. 115

Johann Georg Ziesenis (German, 1716–1776), *Frederick II of Prussia*, 1763. Oil on panel, 142 × 98 cm (16 ½ × 38 ½ in.)

Fig. 116

Louis-Nicolas Lespinasse (French, 1734–1808), *View of the Oranienbaum, Saint Petersburg*, about 1783. Watercolor, pen with brown ink, brush with gray wash, and graphite on cream laid paper, 21.8 × 65.3 cm (8 ⅝ × 25 ¾ in.)

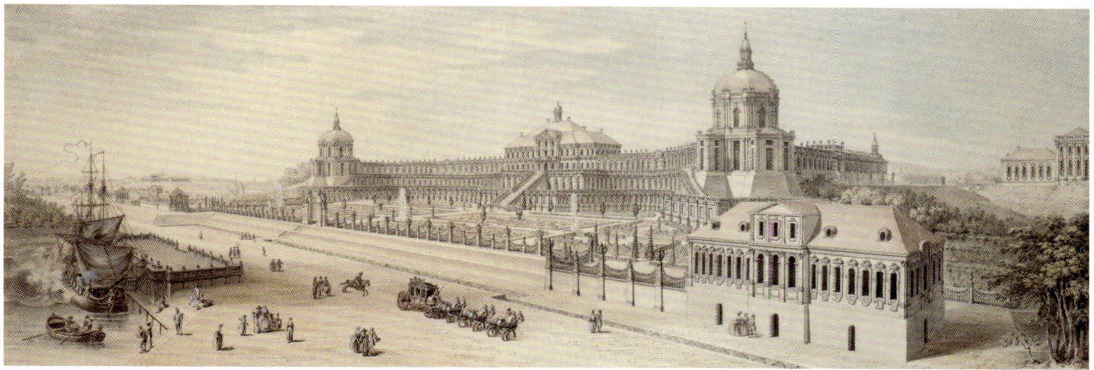

the Italo-Swiss architect Giovanni Maria Fontana in 1710 and expanded by Francesco Bartolomeo Rastrelli some decades later, the palace's two large colonnaded galleries flanked by domed pavilions exemplify Italian architectural influence, although its interiors offered a combination of Italian, English, French, and Asiatic styles typical in eighteenth-century Central and Eastern Europe.[12]

Through his contacts, Casanova received an invitation to a masked ball where he caught a glimpse of Catherine in disguise (H 10:101). He was able to approach the empress more directly a few weeks later in the Summer Garden near the Mikhailov Palace, a spot where she liked to take afternoon walks. On that occasion Catherine asked Casanova what he thought of her Italianate garden sculptures and, conversing in French, they began an exchange in which they spoke of Catherine's love of Venice and the Venetian style.[13] Though the monarch had never visited the city in person, she threw Venice-themed balls, including several held at Oranienbaum, and had recently asked her close political advisers the brothers Orlov to create a Venetian-style court ceremony to honor her reign.[14]

Casanova's description of Catherine is concise yet unusually evocative: "Of medium stature, but well built and with a majestic bearing, the sovereign had the art of making herself loved by all those who she believed were curious to know her. Though not beautiful, she was sure to please by her sweetness, her affability, and her intelligence, of which she made very good use to appear to have no pretensions. If she really had none, her modesty must have been heroic, for she had every right to have them" (H 10:141). This description matches remarkably well the portrait of Catherine by Pierre-Étienne Falconet painted a few years

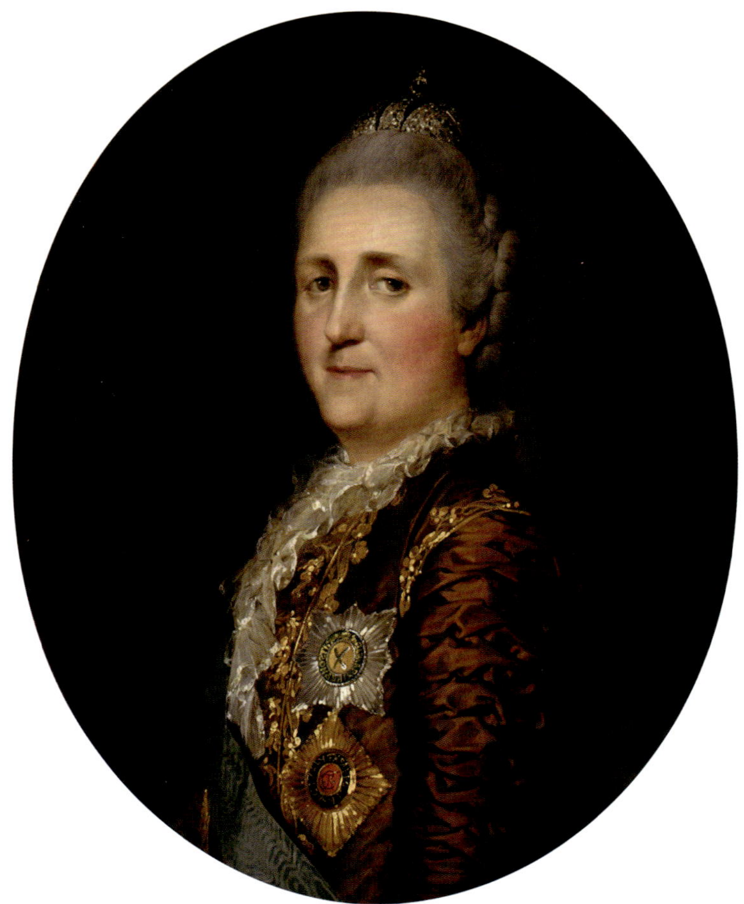

Fig. 117
Pierre-Étienne Falconet (French, 1741–1791), *Catherine the Great*, 1773. Oil on canvas, 68.6 × 55.9 cm (27 × 22 in.)

later (fig. 117).[15] Using the dynamic oval format so beloved among late eighteenth-century portraitists, Falconet shows a monarch who is indeed majestic, but with a pleasing, approachable countenance. And it is true that for all her majesty, this person could not be called conventionally beautiful. The portrait strikingly conveys the empress's intelligence, which comes across in her focused, intense, yet sympathetic gaze. It is interesting to imagine, as Casanova did, that this combination of intensity and kindness was a calculated effect Catherine cultivated to win over others. Perhaps Falconet's painting reveals just a hint of that self-conscious social artifice.[16] Casanova would speak with the empress on one later occasion in the Summer Garden, this time discussing the differences between the Russian and Venetian calendars.

Casanova hoped to gain employment in Saint Petersburg as a mathematician and calendar reformer, but this never came to be. Given the positive tenor of their interaction, it is notable that Catherine did not appoint Casanova to a court position. Perhaps she saw in the widely traveled Italian a potential publicity agent, someone who would spread word of her intelligence and appealing demeanor to interested parties across the Continent. Be that as it may, in late summer 1765 Casanova departed Russia for yet another Central European capital, Warsaw. He found in Poland a culture in the midst of profound political and social upheaval, and he quickly realized the literary potential in the nation's recent political troubles.[17] Upon arriving in Warsaw, he spent several weeks on a fact-finding mission, traveling among the city's elite and interviewing learned subjects to better understand Poland's national character and recent political history. He found the Poles a polite people, but still bearing the traces of their nation's rough, warlike origins. His time there was cut short after he took part in a duel with one Count Xavier Branicki over an offense to Anna Binetti, a former lover of Casanova's who had become prima ballerina at the Warsaw ballet. Binetti appears to have felt slighted when Casanova visited another ballerina before calling on her, and she voiced her displeasure to Branicki, her current protector, who approached Casanova and reprimanded him. Their exchange quickly escalated into insults and then to a duel with pistols in the early morning of March 4, 1766.[18] Although Casanova was only lightly wounded, and his opponent survived, the event generated much gossip in which it was revealed that the self-styled chevalier de Seingalt was nothing more than a common actress's son. This blow to Casanova's reputation caused him to flee Warsaw in embarrassment, but he retained his affection for Poland for the rest of his life. In 1774 he published a three-volume history of Polish politics, *Istoria delle turbolenze della Polonia* (History of the Turmoil in Poland), which was well received by Polish readers.[19] Somewhat later he wrote a satirical pamphlet on the Venetian nobility, *Ne amori ne donne* (Neither for Love nor for Women), which he dedicated to his onetime rival Branicki, who had since become a good friend. Just a year after Casanova left Warsaw, another prominent Venetian arrived there: once again, the painter Bellotto, who like Casanova was traveling north to seek work from Catherine the Great. Bellotto never made it to Saint Petersburg, since Poland offered him ample patronage and a friendly environment for his talents. During the thirteen years he lived there, he produced many *vedute*, which are notable for the increased

Fig. 118

Bernardo Bellotto (Italian, 1721–1780), *View of Krakowski Street*, 1778. Oil on canvas, 107.5 × 83.5 cm (42 3/8 × 32 7/8 in.)

scale he gives to human figures.[20] His *View of Krakowski Street* suggests something of the bustling city that Casanova encountered in Warsaw a few years earlier (fig. 118).

Upon leaving Poland, Casanova passed through Dresden again as he commenced a decade of travel that took him to Germany, Flanders, France, Spain, and back to Italy. The scandal attending the publication of *Ne amori ne donne* in 1783 prompted him to leave Italy permanently, once again turning his attention north and east to Dresden. The city had become home to several members of the Casanova family. Casanova's mother had died there in 1778, after living in Dresden for nearly four decades. Likewise, his brother Giovanni, after studying in Rome with the German painter Anton Raphael Mengs, had become the director of the Dresden Academy of Arts, and his sister Maria Maddalena had also relocated permanently to the city.[21] This family presence in Dresden does not seem to have resulted in a permanent position for Giacomo, and he wandered on to Vienna and then Berlin and Prague. In the last city, he finally landed a post as secretary to Sebastiano Foscarini, Venetian ambassador to the Holy Roman Empire. Not long thereafter, Count Waldstein offered Casanova a position as librarian at his country estate, which he declined.[22] But when Foscarini died unexpectedly in April 1785, Casanova found himself without an income once again.

After trying unsuccessfully to secure a post in Berlin, he finally relented to Waldstein and relocated to Duchcov (fig. 119).[23] Known in German as Dux, Duchcov is a small town in northwestern Bohemia, located not far from the modern border with Germany. In the eighteenth century this region was mostly a German-speaking area, part of the Holy Roman Empire and governed from Vienna. The Waldstein dynasty had first established a presence there in the sixteenth century and between 1675 and 1685 charged the Dijon-born architect Jean-Baptiste Mathey to build a sprawling Baroque palace adjacent to the village. The Waldsteins used Duchcov Castle as a retreat and a base for hunting expeditions in the region's forests.

Undoubtedly Casanova's life at this country estate fell short of the excitement he had once known. Waldstein was often absent and when in residence insulted his librarian by paying minimal attention to him. Casanova fought regularly with the castle's staff, whom he judged to be irritating, uncivilized provincials. They, in return, found him a hilariously antiquated relic of a bygone era.[24] He held back little in describing Duchcov's torpor in letters to friends. In 1795 he made an effort to leave, traveling to Weimar to seek a literary position from its duke—who was unimpressed, as he already had in his service none other than Johann Wolfgang von Goethe.[25] So Duchcov remained Casanova's home until his death, in 1798.

Although unexciting, Casanova's existence at Duchcov was not as bleak as the writer himself sometimes made it out to be. The nearby fashionable spa town of Teplice was home to a small court. Among its regular summer visitors was Charles-Joseph, seventh prince de Ligne, Waldstein's uncle. The prince, a decade younger than Casanova, was a former field marshal in the Austrian army, erstwhile *philosophe*, and something of an international playboy.[26] Like Casanova, the prince de

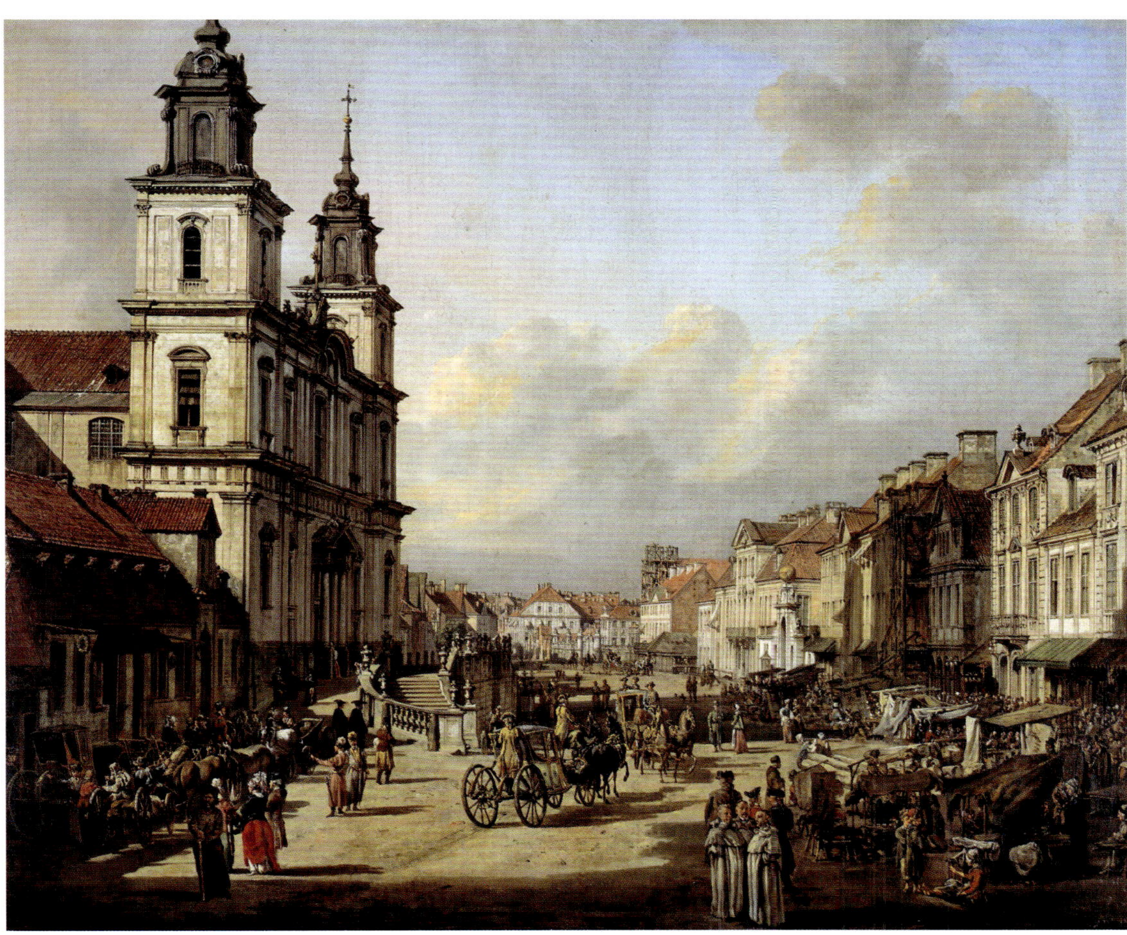

Ligne had flitted from court to court across Central Europe for decades, along the way befriending Joseph II of Austria and Frederick of Prussia, and even accompanying Catherine the Great on her 1787 journey to Crimea. Like Casanova, the prince wrote many books and pamphlets, including works for the stage and treatises on military strategy. He was also a legendary charmer and lover. With so many comparable life experiences, the prince and Casanova became fast friends.

At Duchcov Casanova had at his disposal a library of forty thousand books and ample time to write. He made regular trips to Prague to attend balls, operas, and the theater. We know that in 1787 he heard one of the premiere performances of Wolfgang Amadeus Mozart's opera *Don Giovanni*, held at the Estates Theater in Prague, and he likely also was in attendance for the initial run of the composer's *La clemenza di Tito* in 1791.[27] The years at Duchcov were the most literarily productive of his life. There he wrote the *Histoire de ma fuite* (Story of My Flight), his riveting account of escape from prison in Venice. He also completed a sprawling, bizarre, nearly unreadable science-fiction novel called *Icosameron*.[28] And it was at Duchcov that Casanova began putting on paper his expansive *History of My Life*, the text for which he is best known.

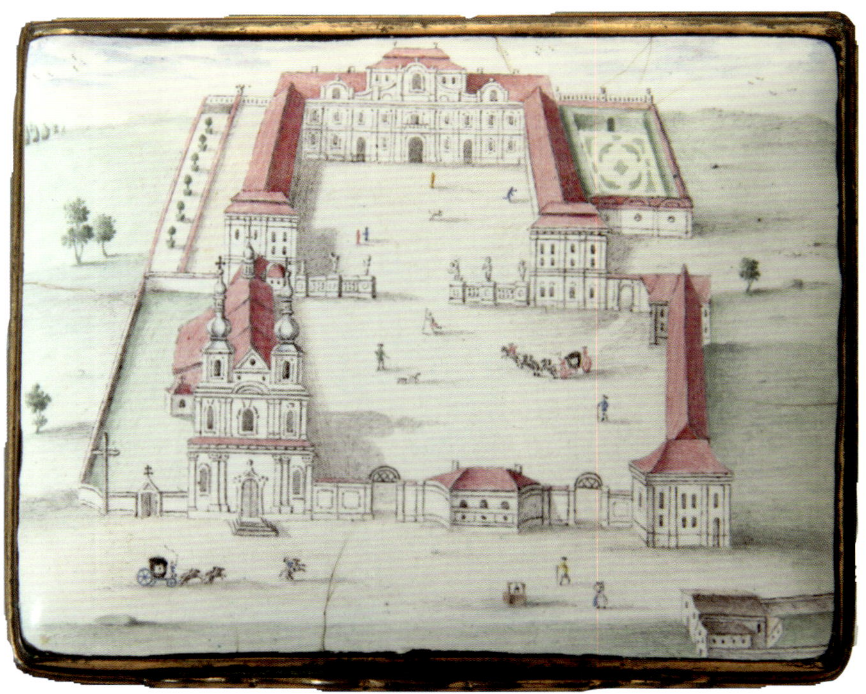

Fig. 119
Snuffbox showing the view over Duchcov Castle with French garden and Baroque hospital, 18th century. Copper, enamel, glaze, 4.5 × 10 × 7 cm (1 ¾ × 3 ⅞ × 2 ¾ in.)

How he came to write his memoirs is not entirely clear. One possibility is that it began as a joint project with the prince de Ligne. The prince tells us in his own memoirs that Casanova shared early drafts of the text with him, and that the two men found great entertainment in conjuring up the people Casanova had known and loved.[29] Another tantalizing suggestion is that the *History* was inspired, at least partly, by the experience of seeing *Don Giovanni*, an opera whose main character and incidents resemble Casanova and aspects of his life. Casanova was well acquainted with the opera's librettist, Lorenzo Da Ponte, yet another Venetian in Central Europe, having spent time with him in Venice, Vienna, and possibly also Prague.[30] Among Casanova's posthumous papers are two literary sketches of a scene in *Don Giovanni*, a moment in the drama that Casanova either helped Da Ponte write or, more plausibly, tinkered with after the premiere to improve.[31] Although today we think of Casanova as a great lover, his own self-image was that of a man of letters. In that capacity, Central Europe served Casanova extremely well as a region where he was able to write the works that would secure his posthumous fame.

Whatever the origin of the *Don Giovanni* notes, they suggest that Mozart's opera about a manipulative libertine dragged down to hell had more than a superficial effect on the aging Venetian. After seeing it, Casanova would begin writing the detailed narrative of his personal, financial, and erotic exploits, his own counterpart to Leporello's catalogue aria of Don Giovanni's romantic conquests. It was in Central Europe that he had the time and space to reflect on the substance of that life and form it into the multivalent portrait that has enthralled readers since its first publication. Although a bit anticlimactically, perhaps, the story surely ended more satisfactorily for Casanova than it did for Mozart's protagonist.

Man of Numbers

Man of Numbers

NINA L. DUBIN

How did the lowly progeny of a family of actors and the grandson of a shoemaker appear to join the ranks of the nobility? In the second volume of his memoirs, Casanova tells the story of his "metamorphosis" into a member of high society. Like nearly every notable episode in his autobiography, the event owes as much to chance as to the author's self-described capacity for "honest cunning" (H 1:232). When the Venetian patrician Bragadin, who suffered an apoplectic fit while sharing a gondola with our narrator, is informed of Casanova's assistance in his rescue, he concludes that his savior possesses supernatural healing powers. Rather than "offend" his patient's "vanity" by correcting him, Casanova relates that he has access to the formula of an oracle—a "numerical calculus," as he puts it, "which, when I put it a written question which I reduced to numerals, returned me an answer, likewise in numerals, which gave me the information I wanted and which no one on earth could have imparted to me." Before long, Bragadin's two closest companions, persuaded that Casanova holds the key to a divine "cabala," swear "eternal brotherhood" to him; as for the nobleman, he adopts Casanova as his son and confers upon him an apartment, a servant, a gondola, and a monthly allowance. Such luxuries fade, however, in comparison with the immaterial riches that Casanova accrues from the allegiance of his powerful devotees: "With the friendship of these three eminent persons, I became a man who would enjoy consideration and prestige" (H 2:195, 199–200).

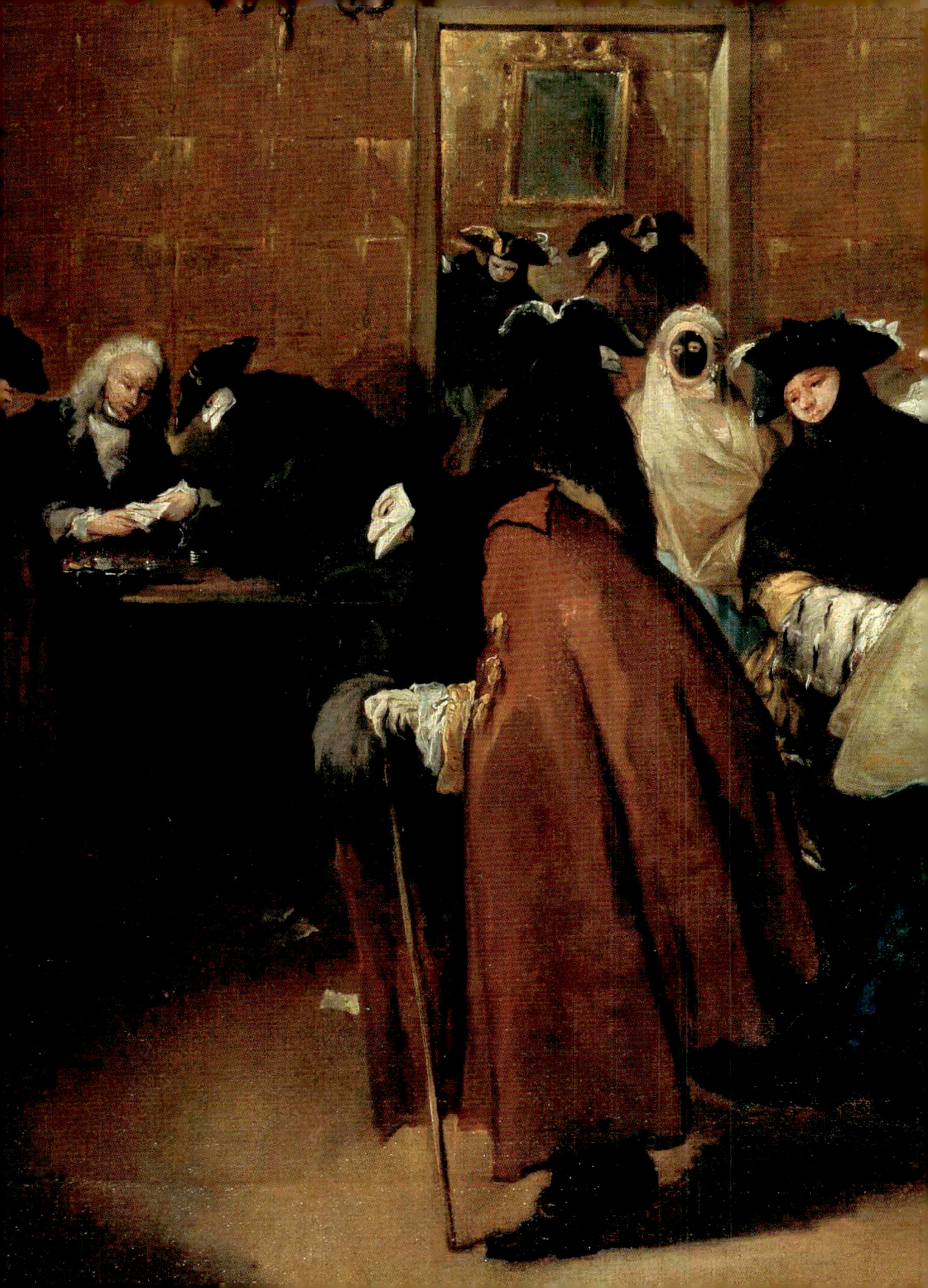

Casanova's spontaneous fabrication of a miraculous numerical device launched his rise to the highest echelons of European society. It not only secured him access to Bragadin's credit for the remainder of his patron's life; it also brought him approbation from the likes of Louise Henriette de Bourbon, duchesse de Chartres, who depended on Casanova's oracle for medical advice; a prominent Amsterdam merchant, identified only as Monsieur D.O., who entrusted it with the question of whether to insure a ship feared missing at sea; the lieutenant-general of Lyon, François de la Rochefoucauld, marquis de Rochebaron, who sponsored Casanova's initiation into Freemasonry; and the eccentric Jeanne Camus de Pontcarré, marquise d'Urfé, who placed her fiduciary trust in Casanova in addition to believing him capable of fulfilling her wish to be reborn as a boy. Literally and figuratively, Casanova's ascendancy was founded on a confidence game masquerading as mathematical infallibility, thus highlighting his age's peculiar fusion of occult knowledge and numerical truth.

Perhaps most meaningful about Casanova's use of a fictive calculus to induce investor confidence, so to speak, is that it encapsulates the workings of credit. In eighteenth-century Europe one's credit—defined as a reputation for trustworthiness—was not necessarily related to one's actual financial holdings.[1] Unstable markets and the growth of speculative ventures made durable, dependable fortunes increasingly a relic of a precommercial world. Casanova himself cheerfully admits that his fortune, "though apparently ample, had no solid foundation" (H 7:134). Indeed, in contemporary French parlance, the expression *à crédit* denoted the lack of a firm financial base.[2] Casanova's cabala, emblematic of a credit economy whose currency was trust, exemplifies what critics fearfully perceived as a mass habit of buying into illusions sustained by the crafty manipulation of numbers. Indeed, when Casanova observes that "strength without confidence is useless," he channels the existential dilemma of today's hedge fund managers, whose businesses depend on client trust and whose assets can consequentially vanish should their reputations take a hit.[3] Casanova, whose favored refrain is "Trust me," specialized in compelling the credence of others, often by dazzling them with his charismatic performance in the role of a numbers man.

Nowhere did Casanova reap more benefits from this persona than in Paris, the "only city in the universe," he remarks, "in which the Blind

Goddess dispensed her favors to those who trusted in her completely." In this lair of Fortuna, "there is no reality... everything is mere appearance" (H 5:13, 18). Only here could a peddler of mediocre snuff become the most sought-after dispenser in town by receiving a few visits from the duchesse de Chartres. "Ex liquidis solidum" (from liquids, a solid) reads the Latin inscription that graces the house of a tavern keeper who became rich when word spread that the king had been spotted drinking in his establishment (H 3:129–31). The motto aptly summarizes the potential for spectacular and sudden reversals of fortune in a city that worshipped at the altar of "novelty and fashion"; it also reflects the alchemy that enabled the conversion of financial insolubility into the most substantial riches.[4]

How appropriate, remarks Casanova, that a capital city associated with the rise and fall of reputations would feature a ship on its coat of arms. After all, Paris resembles "a vessel which only asks to move and which demands wind, and whatever wind may be blowing is good" (H 5:18). The observation, of course, applies no less to the author himself, who early in his memoirs declares, "The only system I followed... was to let myself go wherever the wind which was blowing drove me" (H 1:26). In Paris, Casanova's surrender to uncertain fate, his courtship of risk, paves the way for one of his career's most triumphant episodes: his role as midwife in the birth of the French royal lottery.

Casanova stumbles into the venture when Joseph Pâris-Duverney, first intendant of the École militaire, mistakes him for a financier and solicits advice on how to raise funds for the construction of a new school. Rather than disillusion the brother of one of the country's most renowned bankers, Casanova gambles on his own wits. He intimates a plan for building costs to be covered five times over at no expense to the state, letting Pâris-Duverney come to his own conclusions. Casanova goes on to receive credit for the idea of a national lottery after Giovanni Antonio Calzabigi, the true mastermind behind the venture, fails to inspire confidence in the operation despite having drawn up mathematical proof of its soundness. Recognizing Casanova's powers of persuasion, Calzabigi furnishes him with his tabulations, and following Casanova's masterly pitch before the Council of the École militaire—joined by no less than the mathematician, philosopher, and Encyclopedist Jean Le Rond d'Alembert—the lottery wins approval.

Fig. 120
Jean-Honoré Fragonard (French, 1732–1806), *The Charlatans*, about 1775–76. Oil on canvas, 49.5 × 38.7 cm (19 1/4 × 15 1/4 in.)

Casanova emerges from these maneuvers as the premier supplier of lottery tickets in town, and hordes of Parisians—fancying him a modern Midas—pay him to divine a winning set of numbers. "The other collectors did not have this privilege," the author reports. "Only I went about in a carriage of my own; it gave me a reputation and unlimited credit" (H 5:36).

For all the singularity of his brand, the cult of Casanova was symptomatic of a golden age of rogues and of the widespread credulity that permitted a new breed of adventurers to flourish. Scheme-peddling rakes wandered from one European court and gaming table to the next. Con artists donning false identities shared Casanova's perpetual itinerancy and his plainly stated modus operandi: "Arousing astonishment was my passion" (H 8:272). Tricksters and their susceptible audiences joined the stock-in-trade of eighteenth-century genre painters. In Jean-Honoré Fragonard's *The Charlatans*, two actors and a monkey captivate a small crowd, verifying—along with the painter's otherworldly landscape—a contemporary observer's contention that "the love of the marvelous ceaselessly seduces us" (fig. 120).[5] Quacks and their gullible customers recur in Pietro Longhi's casually cutting portrayals of contemporary Venice: *The Fortune Teller* and *The Alchemists* inventory two types of scams that lay in wait for naïve visitors to the Carnival (figs. 121, 122). A drawing by Pierre-Antoine Baudouin depicts another instance of the fad for things paranormal: consorting with a medium. In an alchemist's studio—replete with animal specimens, glass vials, and signs of the zodiac—a young female client gazes into the mirror at the likeness of a man whose spirit the exotically dressed proprietress has ostensibly summoned.[6]

Such depictions offer glimpses of pastimes practiced by Casanova himself. Gambling on his own uncanny ability to prognosticate, if not to shape, the fates of others (including a young woman from Grenoble who, on his word that she was destined to be the king's mistress, followed Casanova to Paris), he cultivated the affect of a visionary soothsayer. Earlier in his career, Casanova had styled himself an alchemist in an effort to augment his meager fortune. Persuading a wealthy Greek that he possesses the secret to increasing the volume of mercury by a fourth while retaining its purity, he then withholds the recipe until his starry-eyed acquaintance assures him of his good credit by supplying Casanova with a bill of exchange.[7] Ultimately, the Greek, having purchased the secret and realized no rewards, rather than risk public scrutiny of his miscalculation, genially pays off Casanova, who congratulates himself on being "free, rich and certain of appearing... a well-turned-out youth instead of a tramp."[8]

Casanova's credit reaches its peak in Paris, which "is and will always be the city in which imposters will succeed" (H 3:203). In the wake of the lottery's launch, he wins the confidence of the state's comptroller-general, who deputizes him to raise the value of France's declining

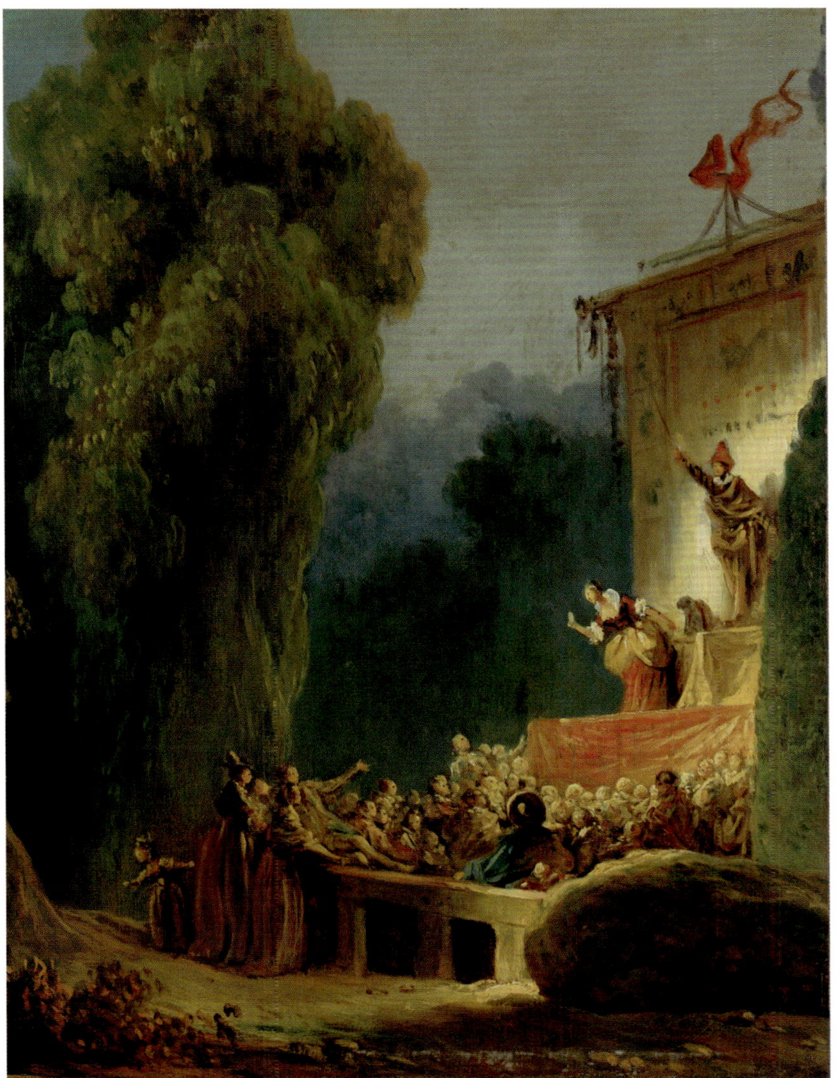

Fig. 121

Pietro Longhi (Italian, 1702–1785), *The Fortune Teller*, 1752. Oil on canvas, 59.1 × 48.6 cm (23 1/4 × 19 1/8 in.)

Fig. 122

Pietro Longhi (Italian, 1702–1785), *The Alchemists*, 1752. Oil on canvas, 61 × 50 cm (24 × 19 5/8 in.)

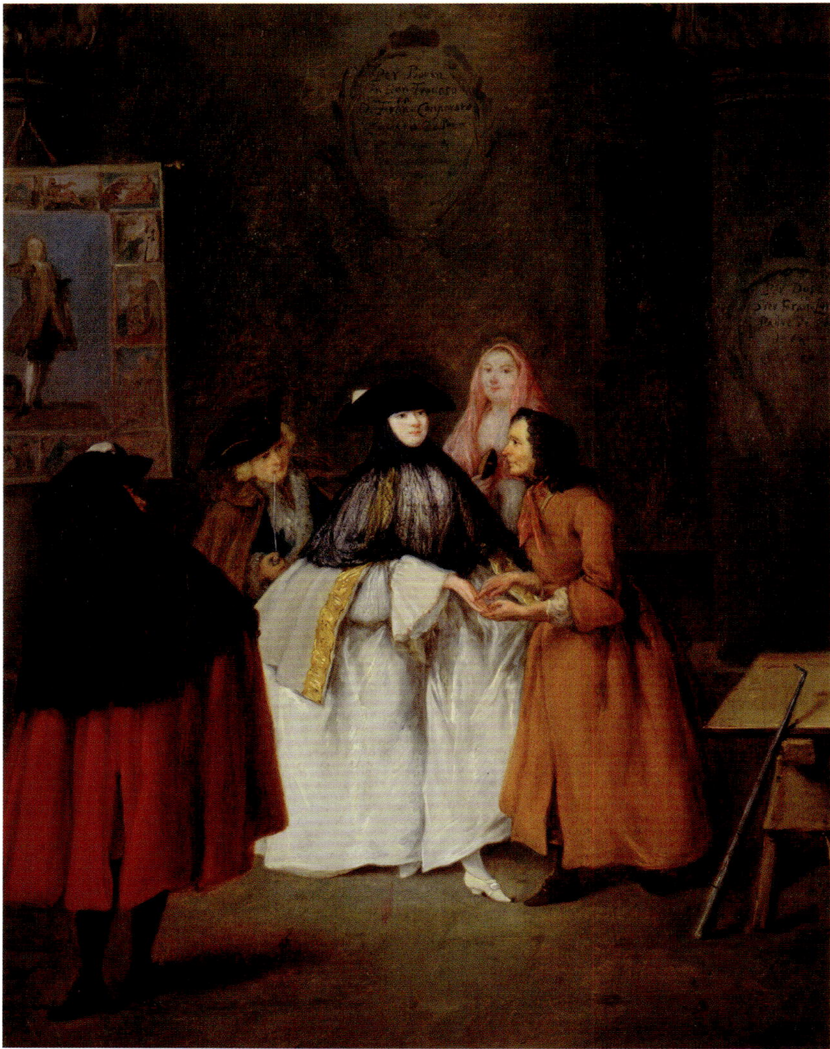

currency by trading it on the Amsterdam stock exchange. Determined to overcome the mission's unfavorable odds, Casanova, with the help of his trusty cabala, unleashes a charm offensive that ensures the project's success. He returns to Paris a hero, fêted for having resuscitated French securities. Though rumors of his financial windfall abound—fueled by the lavish parties he hosts at his newly acquired country estate—Casanova's sole payoff for having enhanced the state's credit is the rise of his own stock in the eyes of the public. Hiding his descent into bankruptcy beneath the cover of a profligate lifestyle, he enjoys his celebrity until a failed silk manufactory venture sends him packing.

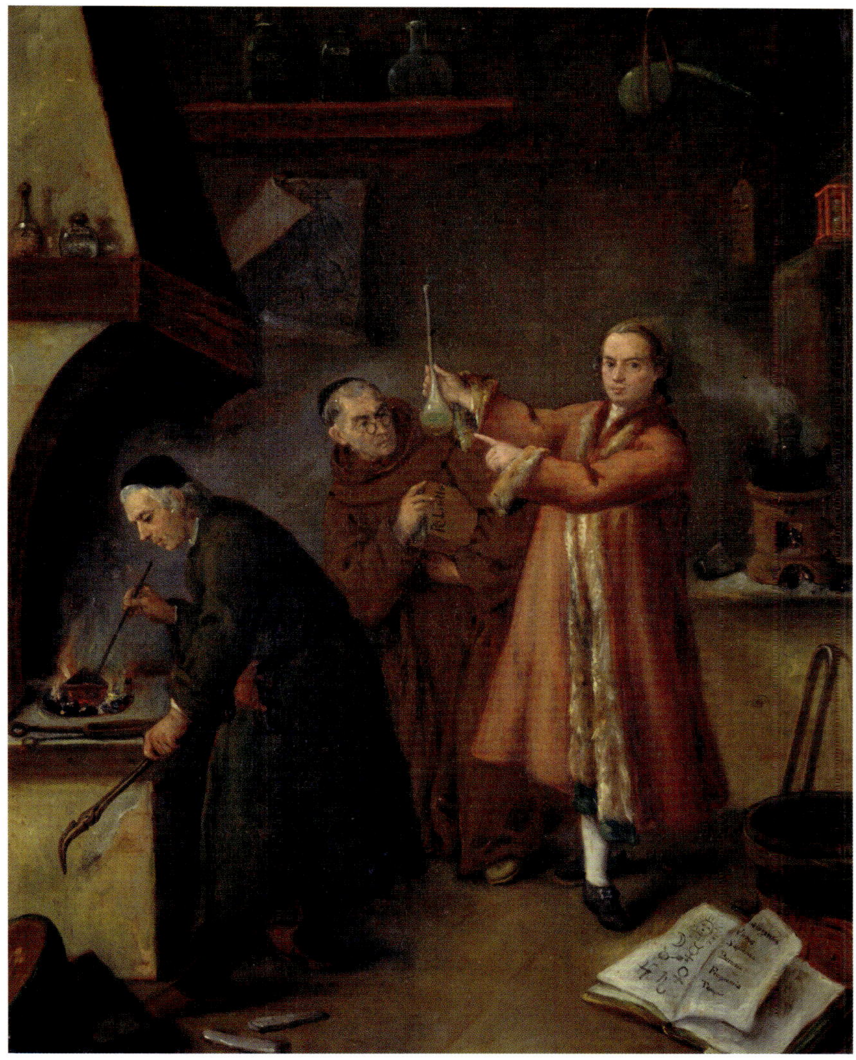

Casanova's self-portrait as a windblown adventurer, fated like a sailing vessel to a life of unmoored flux, recalls the unlikely protagonists of the era's new and thriving genre of "object narratives"—fictions recounted from the point of view of things on the move. Examples include *The Adventures of a Bank-Note* (Thomas Bridges, 1770) and *The Adventures of a Rupee* (Helenus Scott, 1782), both narrated by units of currency whose unpredictable meanderings mirror their changeable worth. Casanova may well have appreciated the comparison of his memoirs to such monetary escapades. He came of age at a time when the fluctuating value of metal and the use of credit contributed to a shift in perceptions of money as no longer a thing of intrinsic worth, but rather as an instrument whose worth was assigned.[9] In adopting the pseudonym of the chevalier de Seingalt, Casanova inscribes himself within this nominalist economy. Asked by an official in Augsburg why he uses a false name, he pointedly replies by asserting his financial credibility: "My name is not false. Inquire of the banker Carli, who paid me fifty thousand florins" (H 8:38).[10] Similarly, the sole constant in Casanova's otherwise unstable existence—the one ritual that he faithfully performs upon arrival at every new destination—is a visit to the local banker to withdraw currency against a bill of exchange. It is striking that his memoirs so faithfully commemorate this quotidian event; the repetition underscores the extent to which Casanova's identity—contingent and situational as it was, and partaking of his successive personas as priest, soldier, orchestra fiddler, theater troupe manager, and so on—internalized the precarious character of a monetary instrument.

"I must show you that I am worthy of a trust of which I know none higher, by treating you with a sincerity equal to your own," announces Casanova to one of his first loves, Teresa—a woman whose sincerity, in truth, he has cause to doubt, given her propensity for passing herself off as a male castrato singer (H 2:32). Moments later, he realizes he has misplaced his passport and is promptly arrested. The incident illustrates the elusive identity not only of Casanova, master of self-invention, but also of those in his preferred social orbit of actors and performers. Casanova's instinct for trading one improvised role for another is matched by his willingness to gamble on the uncertain trustworthiness of those he encounters, from cross-dressers to potential business partners.[11] At a time when misplaced trust could demolish one's face value and finances alike, Casanova consistently raises the stakes of such bets, as when he agrees to endorse a bill of exchange purportedly worth millions of *maravedis* (a Spanish coin whose value had steadily diminished) offered to him in payment for a gambling debt. He later learns that the bill is forged and that he faces arrest and possible execution.[12] It is all the more meaningful, then, that the disappearance of his passport leads to one of Casanova's first encounters with gambling: a game of piquet, to which his prison guard invites him (H 2:38). Casanova's missing identification serves as the appropriate entryway to a life of high-stakes gambling, for succeeding in such endeavors, as he later writes, requires the malleability of "a great dissimulator, impenetrable, obliging, often base, ostensibly sincere" (H 1:257).

Just such a chameleonic character—alternating between master and dupe of his own machinations—makes an appearance in an etching and engraving of an incident at a ball (fig. 123). A disguised visitor to a masquerade ball kneels to kiss the hand of his love interest, who tricks him by substituting for her own outstretched arm that of his former lover—a woman he had "betrayed." Redolent of the unexpected role reversals that recur in Casanova's memoirs, the verse concludes by suggesting the tendency of the duplicitous to fall victim to their own plots: "Very often one finds shame where one expected to find pleasure."[13]

Casanova's portrait of the "great dissimulator" similarly evokes the masked revelers who flocked to the ridotto at Palazzo Dandolo, a popular subject of Venetian painting. A work by Francesco Guardi—one of a handful of the artist's depictions of Venice's state-operated casino—typifies the genre, by emphasizing less the dynamics of a round of faro (a fashionable card game) than the theatrical gestures and mannered postures of those assembled in the gambling den's utterly artificial world (fig. 124). Devoid of any sign of a natural order beyond its damask-lined walls, the spotlighted space provides a suitable stage for its elaborately costumed occupants.[14] Guardi's *Ridotto* displays the artist's characteristic sensitivity to the look of fleeting grandeur, exhibited in his views of the sun-speckled surfaces of Venice's dilapidated palazzi. Majestic, light-catching fabrics, like the playing cards on the floor, spell out the vanity of materialist ventures. The masqueraders embody the twilight of a conservative order that required the donning of masks to preserve distinctions among classes whose mingling was otherwise forbidden; only the dealer of the cards,

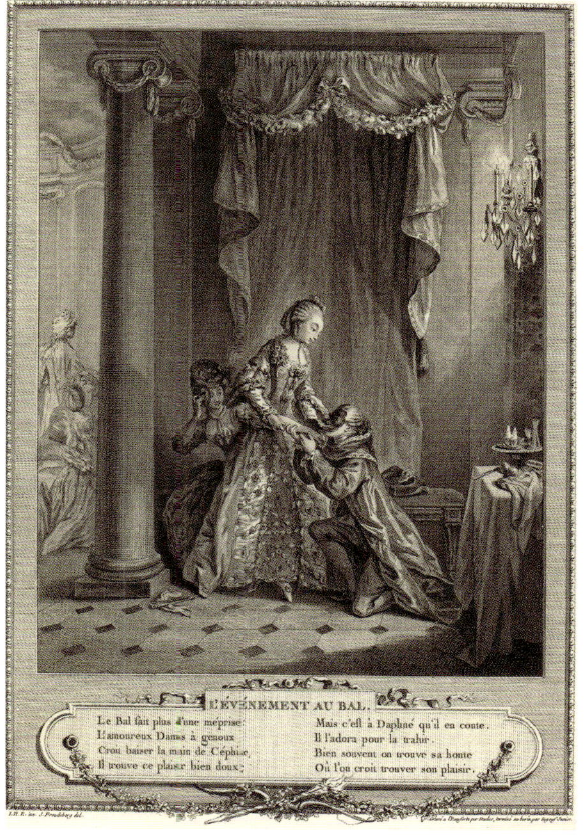

Fig. 123
Antoine-Jean Duclos (French, 1742–1795) and François-Robert Ingouf (French, 1747–1812), after Sigmund Freudeberg (Swiss, 1745–1801), *The Event at the Ball*, 1775. Etching and engraving, sheet: 40.8 × 29.3 cm (16 1/8 × 11 1/2 in.)

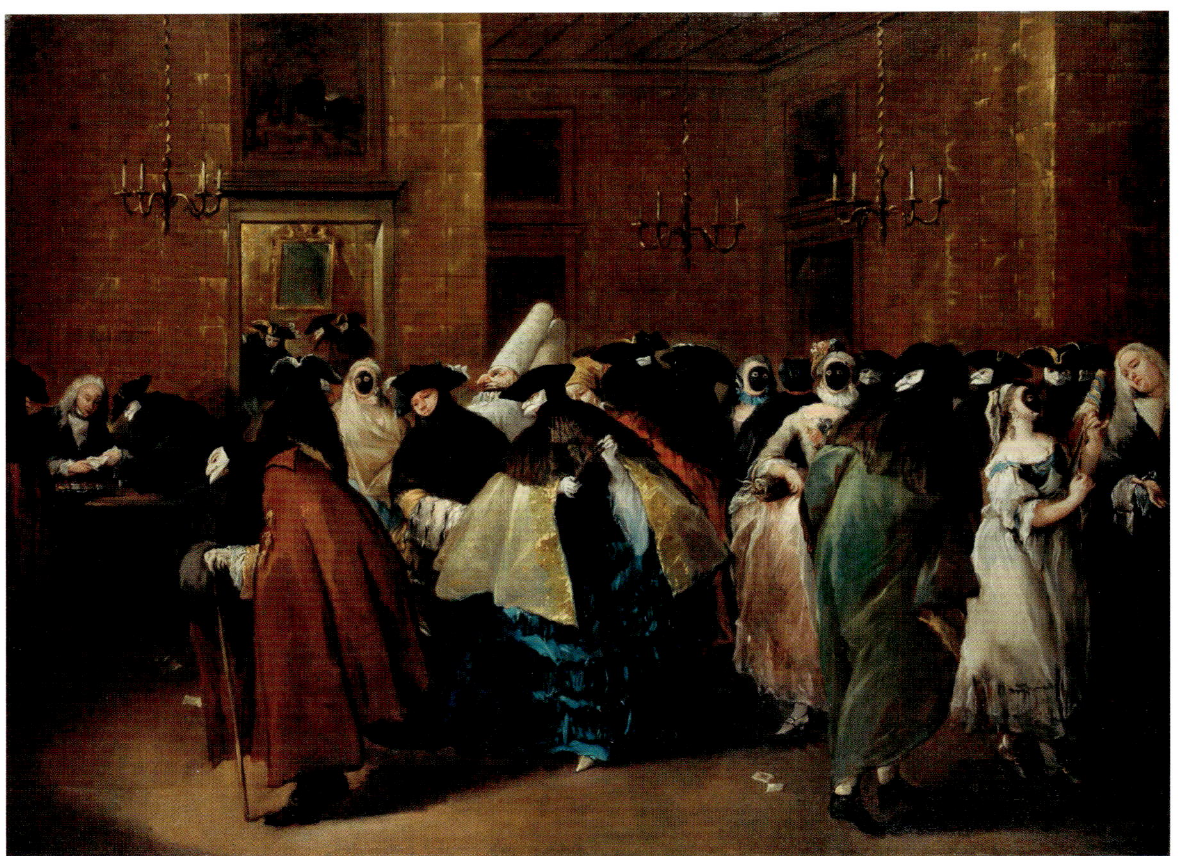

a role reserved for a member of the impoverished nobility known as the Barnabotti, was required to appear unmasked.[15]

Appropriately enough, some two decades after Guardi completed his painting, the state—wary of an establishment associated with iniquity and dishonor—ordered the casino's closure. Yet portrayals of the ridotto as a site of role-playing capture a fundamental aspect of the gambling frenzy that swept through eighteenth-century Europe.[16] Whether it involved dice, cards, wheels, or lottery tickets, gambling offered players the prospect of exchanging one identity for another, of ascending to an otherwise unattainable social status. If Casanova's ultimate talent was that of a performer, he rehearsed his skills at the gaming table: "I smiled when I was losing and looked unhappy when I was winning" (H 2:104). An artificial front—whether in the form of a mask or a controlled demeanor—was the hallmark of the gambler, if not an inescapable fixture of social life in the age of credit.

The evocation in Guardi's *Ridotto* of flirtatious encounters between disguised strangers captures another dimension of gambling that lies at the heart of Casanova's memoirs: namely, its associations with the erotic. Casanova himself promoted the reputation of the ridotto for amorous intrigue and secrecy—the name probably derived from *ridurre*, meaning "enclosed"—by casting it as an ideal venue for seduction. To put it mildly, our protagonist incarnated the symbiosis between gambling and gallantry. He declared that gambling was "a great palliative for a man in love" and love a domain in which "we run… risks willingly." His amorous pursuits—which, according to the tally he kept, added up to well over a hundred lovers—extended, while also heightening, the thrills and perils of the gaming table; whereas succeeding at games of chance often involved deceiving cheats and scoundrels, "when love enters in, both parties are usually dupes."[17] Like his cabala, bridging the mathematical and the mystical, Casanova's dual identity as gambler and lover rendered his financial dealings inseparable from the tumult of his passions. Two of his notable successes at the casino correlate with his consuming love affairs with a pair of nuns.[18] Conversely, a relationship with an infamous courtesan costs him his wealth and reputation (H 2:178). The economic and the erotic partake in a shared economy of risk: the flow of paper in Casanova's wake—letters of recommendation and credit, banknotes, bills of exchange, pawnshop and lottery tickets—has its counterpart in the spread of venereal disease, whose symptoms circulate no less efficiently. When a surgeon thanks Casanova for inadvertently enriching him, by contaminating the townsfolk with a sexually transmitted disease and thus expanding his client base, he evokes the caprices of fortune reigning over eros and money alike (H 2:63). What is more, the surgeon's profession of gratitude implicitly caricatures the logic of a paper economy: The circulation of wealth has parallels with an uncontainable outbreak of the love bug.

The risks inherent in both love and gambling found more refined expression in polite society. The vogue for gambling among the aristocracy promoted the design of intimate settings for games, replete with luxury accessories that often displayed the equally modish iconography of eros (fig. 125). A set of ivory counting chips for the card game of quadrille offers one such example (fig. 126). The vignette of a heart consumed by flames appears on several of the game pieces, including one

Fig. 124
Francesco Guardi (Italian, 1712–1793), *The Ridotto of Palazzo Dandolo at San Moisè with Masked Figures Conversing*, about 1750. Oil on canvas, 76.2 × 104.7 cm (30 × 41 ¼ in.)

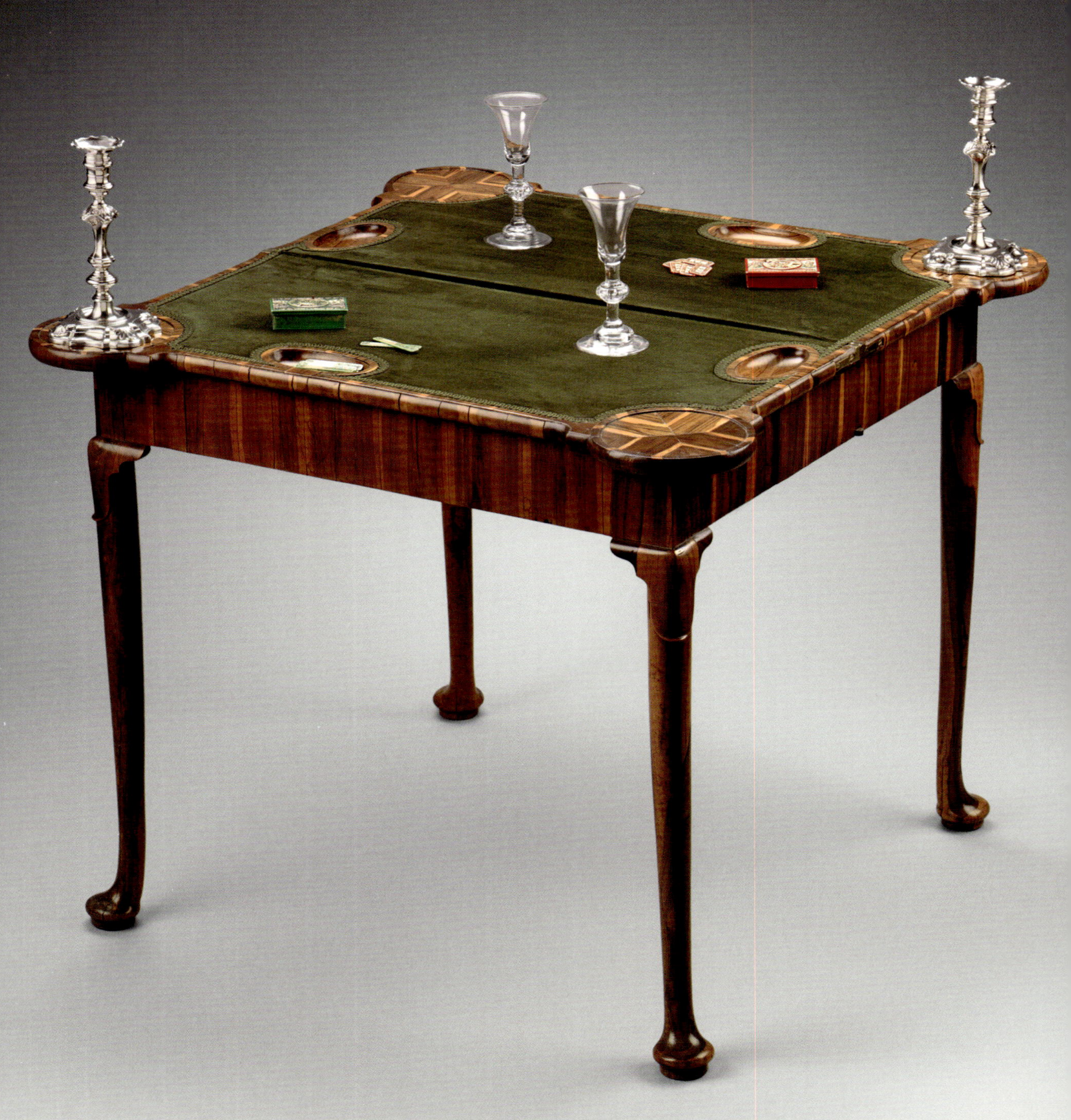

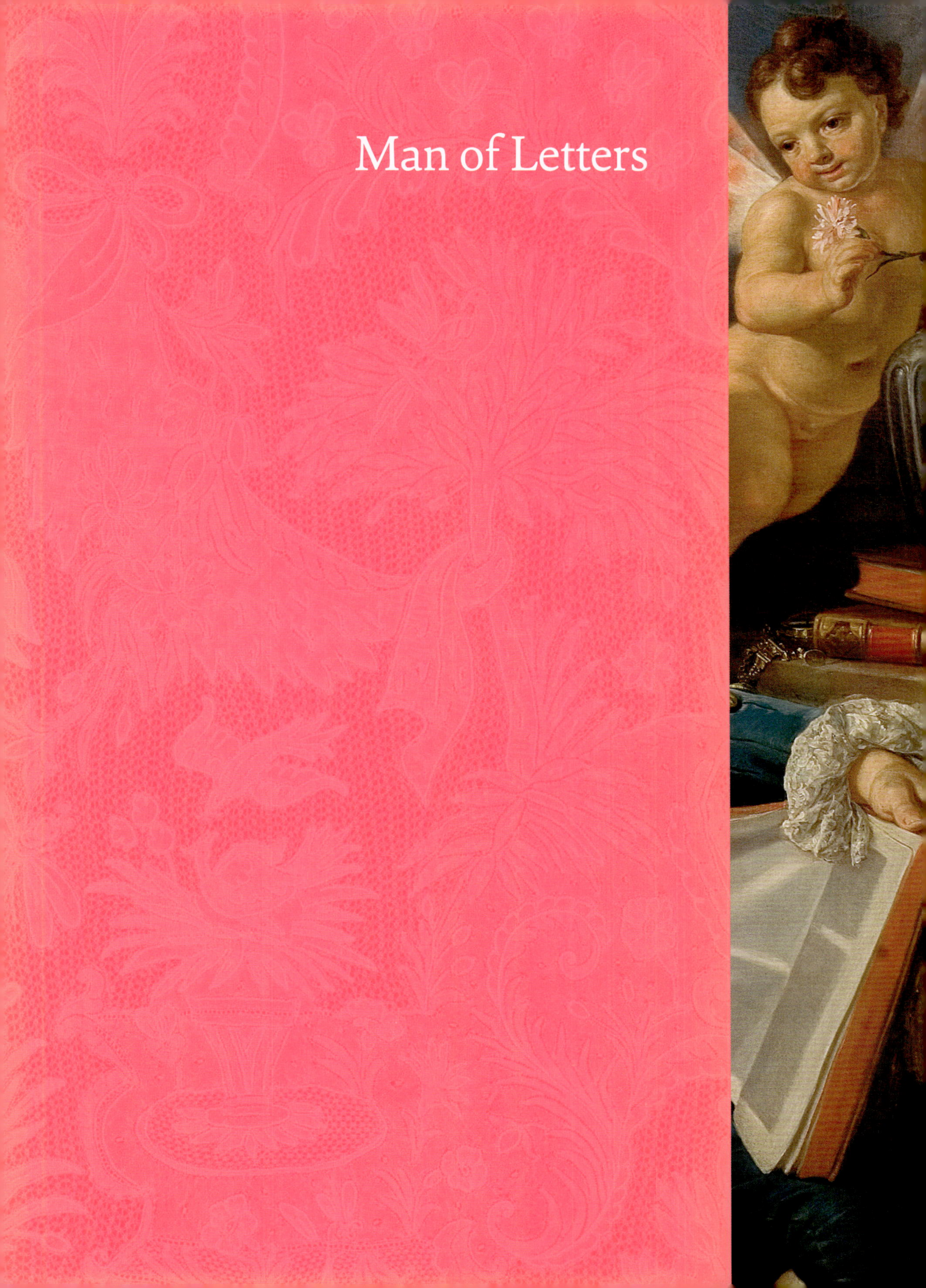

Man of Letters

Man of Letters

MALINA STEFANOVSKA

In 1770, as Casanova traveled through Pisa, a friendly abbé took him to a gathering hosted by two sisters. The younger was very beautiful, the elder a poet. Although Casanova deemed the literary sister unattractive, he responded when she approached him gently and asked him to recite a poem, and then reciprocated by declaiming a verse of her own. Doubting her authorship, he dared her to versify on the spot and soon discovered they belonged to the same literary Academy of the Arcadians. At that point, he became "fanatical" with admiration, which made "all her ugliness disappear." And even though no romantic idyll ensued, thirty years later he recounted this magical effect of poetry in his *Histoire de ma vie* (V 3:625; H 11:212).[1]

The anecdote combines the two passions that ruled his life and shaped his written account of it: women and literature. Casanova was a seductive interlocutor in all types of exchanges, from witty conversations to erotic encounters; his sociable character, enhanced by erotic attraction or simply by friendship, made his mind sparkle. "I only notice that I am witty when another person's wit provides the impulse," he wrote, likening the contact to electricity.[2] In his constant quest for pleasure, he developed a superior gift for erotic narratives that could make the woman he was courting "ardent" with desire. He also cultivated the art of telling fascinating stories about his adventures. His 1757 escape from the Leads prison in Venice produced such a narrative showpiece, delivered only to select audiences and in no less than two hours. It was to become the first published piece of his autobiography (fig. 129).[3]

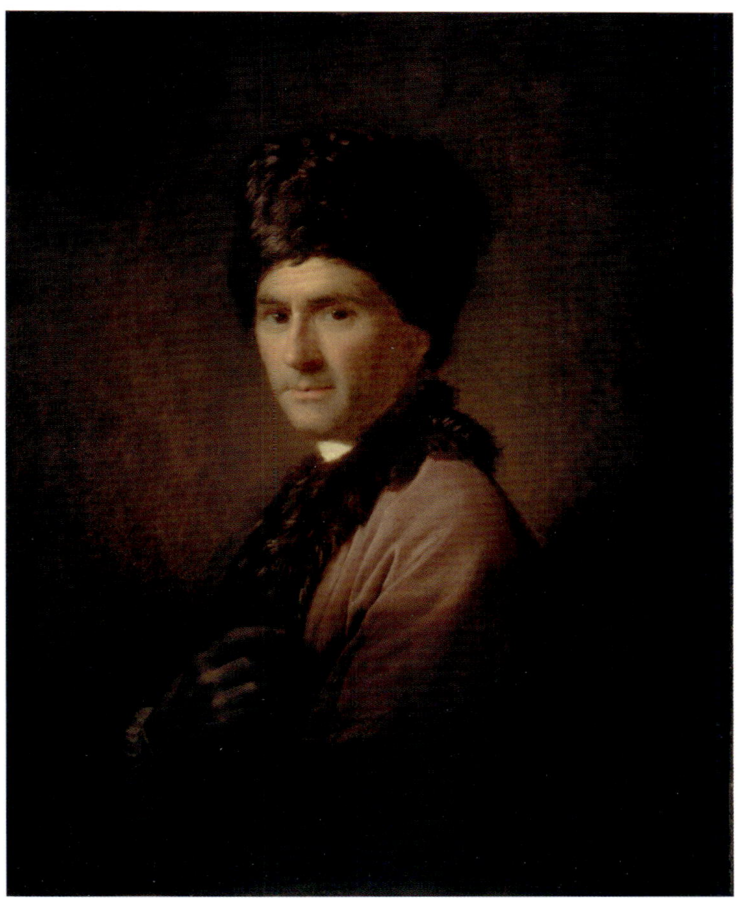

time to write. Evidence for this practice is found throughout his memoirs: When he first left Venice, his most precious possession, entrusted to his friend Signora Manzoni, was a trunk full of papers and forbidden books. Upon arriving in a new city, his first concern would be to procure "a large desk for writing" on which he would set "my papers and my books" (V 3:258; H 10:101). He sat at this desk every morning, and sometimes through the night as he hastened to record notable events, such as meeting Voltaire or Catherine the Great, on the same day, lest he forget the details. "The older I get," he declared, "the more I regret that I will part with my papers; they are the true treasure which attaches me to life and makes me hate death" (V 2:373; H 6:206). These papers accompanied him even to jail: Arrested in Barcelona in 1768 for getting involved with the army commander's mistress, he requested his trunk and astounded the guard by showing that it was "two thirds filled with

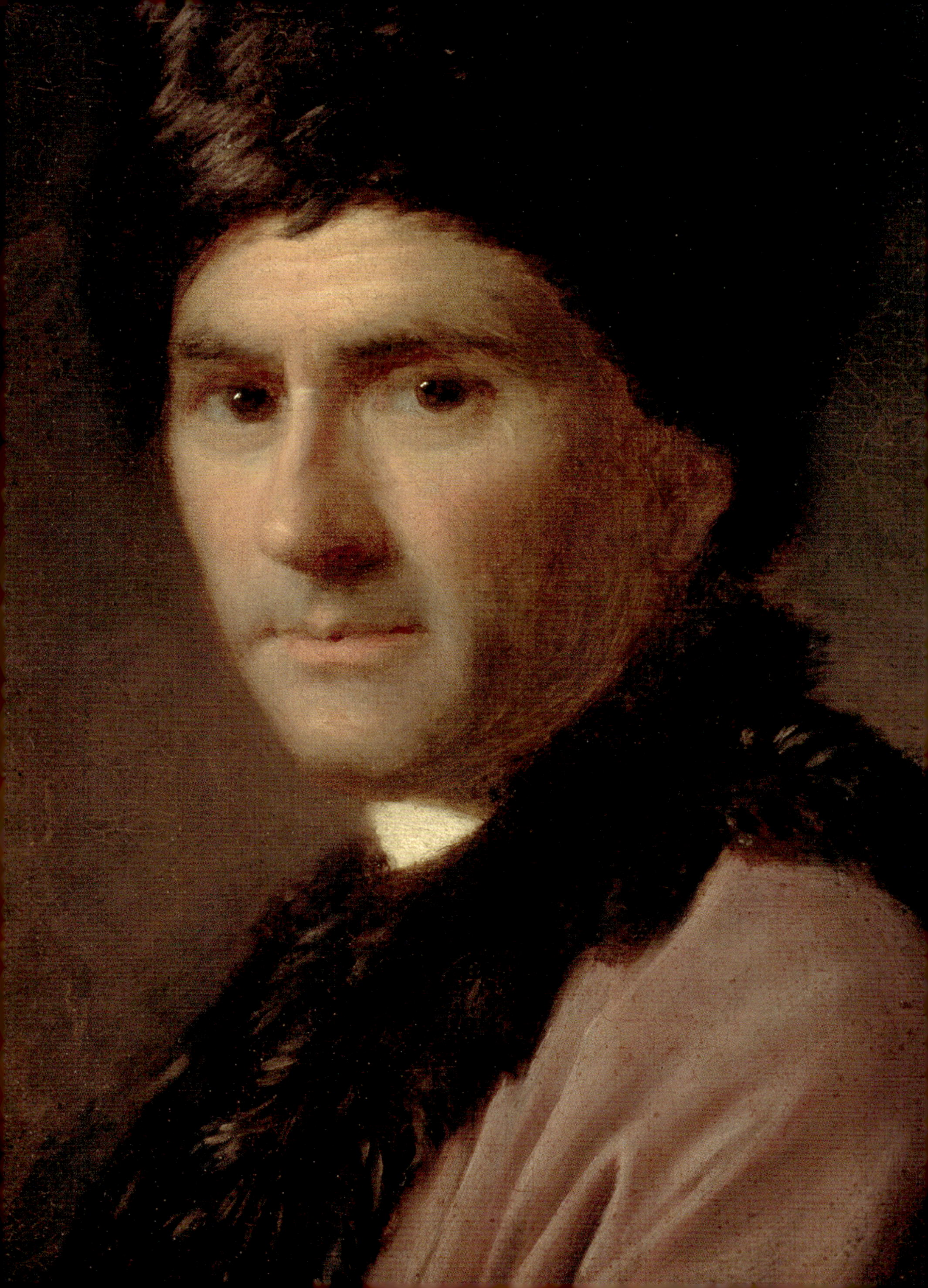

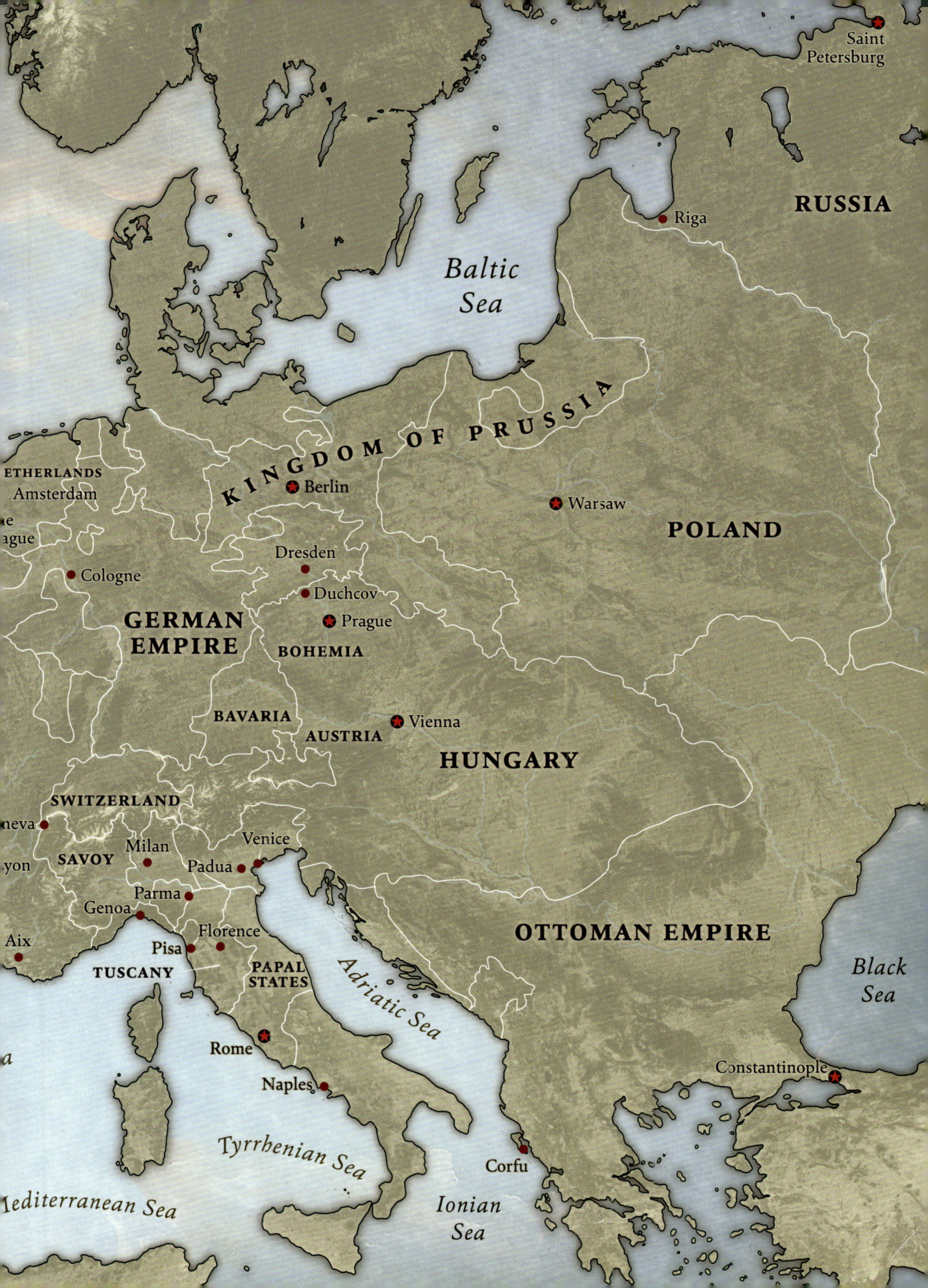
Saint Petersburg
RUSSIA
Riga
Baltic Sea
KINGDOM OF PRUSSIA
Berlin
Warsaw
POLAND
ETHERLANDS
Amsterdam
Dresden
Cologne
Duchcov
GERMAN EMPIRE
Prague
BOHEMIA
BAVARIA
Vienna
AUSTRIA
HUNGARY
SWITZERLAND
Venice
Milan
SAVOY
Padua
Parma
Genoa
Florence
Aix
Pisa
OTTOMAN EMPIRE
TUSCANY
PAPAL STATES
Adriatic Sea
Black Sea
Rome
Constantinople
Naples
Tyrrhenian Sea
Corfu
Ionian Sea

Chronology

COURTNEY LEIGH HARRIS

Casanova's *History of My Life* is at times imprecise in sequence, and some dates given in the memoir are inconsistent with historical fact.

1725

APRIL 2 Giacomo Casanova born in Venice to the actress Zanetta Farussi. Though Zanetta is married to Gaetano Casanova, an actor, her first child is believed to be the son of the theater owner, Michele Grimani.

1734

APRIL Sent to Padua for his health by his grandmother, Marcia Farussi, who has primarily raised him while his mother traveled around Europe.

1737

After studying with the Abate Antonio Gozzi in Padua, enrolls at the age of twelve at the University of Padua to study law.

1739

Returns to Venice briefly.

1740

Receives the tonsure at the Church of San Samuele.

1741

Inducted into the first four minor holy orders by the Patriarch of Venice.

Receives Doctorate of Law from the University of Padua.

MARCH 19 Preaches at San Samuele, by invitation of the Venetian senator Alvise Gasparo Malipiero.

Travels with the count and countess of Montereale to their country estate near Friuli for the summer.

Returns to Venice in the fall and has his first encounter with the sisters Nanetta and Marta.

1743

Zanetta, who is working in Poland, secures employment for her son with the Bishop de Bernardis.

MARCH 18 Marcia Farussi dies. Shortly thereafter, Casanova enrolls at the seminary of San Cipriano on Murano to await his summons to follow the bishop to Rome.

APRIL 2 The Grimani family has him arrested and imprisoned after he is expelled from the seminary. Spends his eighteenth birthday in the Santa'Andrea prison in Venice and is released from prison on the bishop's arrival in the city.

NOVEMBER Arrives in Rome, traveling via Orsana (on the Croatian coast), Pula, and Ancona. Fails to connect with Bernardis and travels on to Naples.

1744

Released from Bernardis's employment, goes to Rome, where he works for Cardinal Acquaviva.

Presented to Pope Benedict XIV in Rome.

1745

APRIL 2 Arrives in Venice as an officer on his twentieth birthday, having assumed military dress while traveling through Bologna.

MAY Arrives in Corfu after sailing there with a naval regiment.

JULY Arrives in Constantinople on the warship *Europa*.

Returns from Constantinople to Venice at the end of the year.

1746

MARCH Joins the orchestra at the Grimani theater.

Encounters Senator Matteo Giovanni Bragadin, who becomes his patron. His association with Bragadin and members of the nobility attracts the attention of the Venetian Inquisition.

1749

Early in the year, travels to Milan and Mantua, where he moves in theatrical circles. In Mantua, meets the runaway Henriette. Accompanies Henriette to Parma, where family members find her and force her to return to the south of France.

1750

Travels with Henriette as far as Geneva.

Returns to Venice briefly and sets up a small gambling casino.

Travels with his friend Antonio Balletti to Ferrara, Turin, and Lyon. Initiated into the Freemasons in Lyon.

AUGUST The pair arrives in Paris.

OCTOBER Joins Balletti and his family in Fontainebleau for Louis XV's hunting season and meets Madame de Pompadour at the opera.

1752

Leaves Paris with his brother Francesco.

OCTOBER Giacomo and Francesco arrive in Dresden, where their mother is an actress at the court of the Elector of Saxony, after traveling through Champagne, Metz, and Frankfurt.

1753

MAY 5 Casanova returns to Venice and falls in love with Caterina. By the summer, she is pregnant, and her father sends her to the convent of Santa Maria degli Angeli on the island of Murano.

While visiting Caterina, he is drawn into a relationship with another nun, M.M., who is the mistress of abbé de Bernis, the French ambassador.

DECEMBER Meets Bernis.

1754

Bernis leaves Venice early in the year. Casanova's assignation with the patrician M.M. attracts the attention of the Inquisition.

1755

JULY 26 Arrested and sentenced without trial to five years in the prison in the Palazzo Ducale known as the Leads.

1756

AUGUST 25 Moved to better accommodations in the prison at Bragadin's behest, causing him to abandon work on an escape hole in the floor of his cell.

OCTOBER 31 Escapes from his new cell with a fellow prisoner.

1757

Returns to Paris at the start of the year, after traveling through Bolzano, Munich, Augsburg, and Strasbourg. Falls in love with Manon, the younger sister of Antonio Balletti.

Performs lucrative clandestine missions to Dunkirk and Holland on behalf of the French regime.

Makes the acquaintance of the marquise d'Urfé.

1760

After Manon Balletti's engagement to the architect Jacques-François Blondel, embarks on extensive travels. Meets Voltaire in Geneva.

Begins to style himself the chevalier de Seingalt.

JULY Travels to Rome and Naples via Aix-les-Bains. In Rome, meets the new pope, Clement XIII, who confers on him the Papal Order of the Golden Spur.

1761

In Naples, is attracted to a young woman who turns out to be his daughter. Moves on to Turin.

1762

Travels through Paris and Aix-la-Chapelle while working for the marquise d'Urfé.

1763

Attends a peace conference in Augsburg with the Portuguese government.

JUNE 11 Arrives in London and stays for nine months. During the summer, has affair with a Portuguese woman who lodges in his house.

SEPTEMBER Falls for the scheming Marianne Charpillon, whose ill treatment drives him to the brink of suicide.

NOVEMBER Arrested on charge of attempting to disfigure Charpillon and subsequently released on bail.

1764

MARCH Out of money, ill, and in legal trouble, flees London for Brussels.

Travels to Prussia to meet Frederick the Great, who offers him a position as a tutor, which he turns down.

DECEMBER 21 Arrives in Saint Petersburg and meets with Catherine the Great on several occasions.

1765

Travels to Moscow, then Warsaw.

1766

MARCH 4 Fights a pistol duel with Count Xavier Branicki in Warsaw. The ensuing damage to his reputation forces him to leave town, traveling to Dresden and other Central European cities.

1767

Spends time in Augsburg, Cologne, Aix-la-Chapelle, and Spa, Belgium.

NOVEMBER Expelled from France by Louis XV.

1768

MID-JANUARY Arrives in Madrid, traveling via Bordeaux. Seeks refuge at the home of the painter Anton Raphael Mengs.

FEBRUARY 20 Is arrested and spends two days in the Buen Retiro prison.

Leaves for Valencia and Barcelona, where he is briefly imprisoned after he is accused of killing a man.

1769

Spends the first part of the year at the home of the philosopher marquis d'Argens in Aix-en-Provence. Moves on to Turin, where he publishes a treatise on Venetian government.

1770

Travels to Livorno at the beginning of the year, then on to Naples, where he spends time with his daughter, Leonilda.

SEPTEMBER Journeys with Leonilda to Rome and stays until July.

1773

Publishes a theatrical comedy while living in Trieste.

1774

Receives a pardon from the city of Venice in September and returns there for the first time in eighteen years.

The narrative of *History of My Life* stops in this year, when he is forty-nine.

1775

Publishes the first of three volumes of a translation of the *Iliad* into Italian.

1776

Begins working for the Inquisition in Venice.

NOVEMBER 29 Casanova's mother dies in Dresden.

1783

JANUARY 17 Leaves Venice, returning only briefly once more.

NOVEMBER 23 In Paris, meets Benjamin Franklin.

Travels with his brother Francesco to Dresden and then Vienna.

1784

Finds work as a secretary to Sebastian Foscarini, the Venetian ambassador to Vienna, through whom he meets Mozart's librettist Lorenzo Da Ponte.

1785

Following Foscarini's death, accepts a position as librarian at the Waldstein castle at Duchcov, in Bohemia.

1787

OCTOBER 29 Attends the first performance of Mozart's opera *Don Giovanni* in Prague. Consults with Da Ponte on the libretto, before or after the premiere.

Publishes the fantastical novel *Icosameron*.

1788

Publishes *Histoire de ma fuite* (History of My Flight), about his escape from prison in Venice.

1791

Travels to Prague for the coronation of Leopold II, king of Bohemia, on September 6.

1798

JUNE 4 Casanova dies in Duchcov.

Notes

References to editions of Casanova's memoirs are abbreviated as follows, in text and notes:

H Giacomo Casanova, *History of My Life.* Translated by Willard R. Trask. 6 vols. New York: Harcourt, Brace & World, 1966–71.

V Jacques Casanova, *Histoire de ma vie.* Edited by Gérard Lahouati and Marie-Françoise Luna. 3 vols. Paris: Gallimard, 2013–15.

A digitized facsimile of the original manuscript is available on the website of the Bibliothèque nationale de France, http://gallica.bnf.fr.

THE ART OF DISPLAY

1. Giacomo Casanova, *Histoire de ma vie*, ed. Jean-Christophe Igalens and Érik Leborgne, 2 vols. (Paris: Robert Laffont, 2013–15), 1: 1322.

2. For a similar revisionist approach focused on Casanova as philosopher, see Ivo Cerman, Susan Reynolds, and Diego Lucci, *Casanova: Enlightenment Philosopher* (Oxford: Voltaire Foundation, 2016).

3. For a recent interpretation of *The Bolt*, with emphasis on its libertine connections, see Guillaume Faroult, ed., *Fragonard amoureux: Galante et libertin*, exh. cat. (Paris: Réunion des musées nationaux, 2015), 208–10.

4. On Casanova and alchemy, see Guy David Toubiana, "Casanova: Magicien ou la fabrication d'un mythe?" *Romance Quarterly* 56 (2009): 217–25; Adeline Hargam, "Between Scientific Investigation and Vanity Fair: Reflections on the Culture of Curiosity in Enlightenment France," in *Women and Curiosity in Early Modern England and France*, ed. Line Cottegnies, Sandrine Parageau, and John J. Thompson (Leiden: Brill, 2016), 207–9.

5. For general biographical information on Bernis, see Marcus Cheke, *The Cardinal De Bernis* (New York: Norton, 1958); Serge Dahoui, *Le cardinal de Bernis, ou La royauté du charme* (Aubenas: Lienhart, 1972); Jean-Marie Mouart, *Bernis: Le cardinal des plaisirs* (Paris: Gallimard, 1998); Virginie Larre, "Le cardinal de Bernis ambassadeur des arts à Rome: Mécène et collectionneur," in *Collections et marché de l'art en France au XVIIIe siècle*, ed. Patrick Michel (Bordeaux: Centre François-Georges Pariset, 2002), 51–64.

6. For the report of the 200,000 francs, see François-Joachim de Pierre de Bernis, *Mémoires du cardinal de Bernis*, ed. Philippe Bonnet (Paris: Mercure de France, 1980), 68. For mention of the *valet de chambre tapissier*, see François-Joachim de Pierre de Bernis, *Mémoires et lettres de François-Joachim de Pierre, cardinal de Bernis (1715–1758)*, ed. Frédéric

Masson, 2 vols. (Paris: E. Plon, Nourrit et Cie, 1878), 1:418.

7. Only extracts of the inventory have been published, for which see Bernis, *Mémoires* (1878), 1:418–20n3.

8. On the collection Bernis formed in Rome, see Larre, "Le cardinal de Bernis."

9. About the law, see James H. Johnson, *Venice Incognito: Masks in the Serene Republic* (Berkeley: University of California Press, 2011), 135–40.

10. Cheke, *Cardinal De Bernis*, 56–57.

11. On courtiers and their role in the patron-client systems of the Ancien Régime, see Norbert Elias, *The Court Society*, trans. Edmund Jephcott (Oxford: Blackwell, 1983); Sharon Kettering, *Patrons, Brokers, and Clients in Seventeenth-Century France* (New York: Oxford University Press, 1986).

12. H 5:20. For Bernis's other apartments, see Dahoui, *Le cardinal de Bernis*, 135–36; and Larre, "Le cardinal de Bernis," 51.

13. Letter dated November 3, 1758; Bernis, *Mémoires* (1878), 2:326.

14. Emmanuel de Croÿ, *Journal inédit du duc de Croÿ (1781–1784)*, 2 vols., ed. Emmanuel Henri de Grouchy and Paul Cottin (Paris: Flammarion, 1906–7), 1:431.

15. Larre, "Le cardinal de Bernis," 51. The description leaves unclear whether the statues were marbles or bisque porcelains.

16. For Pompadour as patron of ceramics, see Donald Posner, "Mme. de Pompadour as a Patron of the Visual Arts," *The Art Bulletin* 72 (March 1990): 74–105, esp. 85–92; and Xavier Salmon, ed., *Madame de Pompadour et les arts*, exh. cat. (Paris: Réunion des musées nationaux, 2002), 406–525.

17. For the development of porcelains at Vincennes, see Sven Eriksen and Geoffret de Bellaigue, *Sèvres Porcelain: Vincennes and Sèvres, 1740–1800*, trans. R. J. Charleston (London: Faber and Faber, 1987), 60–88.

18. Although Pigalle first worked for Pompadour in 1748, and Falconet not until 1750, they were both well known to her earlier from their work for the court. See Posner, "Mme. de Pompadour," 94. On their relationship with her more broadly, see Salmon, *Madame de Pompadour et les arts*, 291–313.

19. Dahoui, *Le cardinal de Bernis*, 136.

20. See Mimi Hellman, "Furniture, Sociability, and the Work of Leisure in Eighteenth-Century France," *American Society for Eighteenth-Century Studies* 32, no. 4 (1999): 415–45.

21. About the location of the house, see *Histoire de ma vie*, 3 vols., ed. Francis Lacassin (Paris: Laffont, 2000–2002), 2:147n2.

22. For a romanticized account of the relationship, see Judith Summers, *Casanova's Women: The Great Seducer and the Women He Loved* (New York: Bloomsbury, 2006), 198–231. For the letters between the lovers, see *A Giacomo Casanova: Lettere d'amore di Manon Balletti ed Elisa von der Recke*, ed. Vittorio Orsenigo (Milan: Archinto, 1997).

23. For example, Xavier Salmon, ed., *Jean-Marc Nattier, 1685–1766*, exh. cat. (Paris: Réunion des musées nationaux, 1999), 276.

24. For the provenance, see ibid., 274.

25. For discussions of Casanova and his miniature portraits, see Isadora Rose de Viejo, "References to Jewelry in Casanova's Memoirs," *Intermédiaire des Casanovistes* 23 (2006): 5–6; and Bradley S. Reichek, "Rake Sentimentalism, or the Libertine Reformed: Re-evaluating Late Eighteenth-Century Libertinage, 1770–1812" (PhD diss., Northwestern University, 2008), 36–40.

26. For the most complete analysis of the story, see *François Boucher, 1703–1770*, exh. cat. (New York: The Metropolitan Museum of Art, 1986), 258–63.

27. In the salon *livret* (booklet), the Pierre is no. 56 and the Aved is no. 79. *Collections des livrets des anciennes expositions depuis 1673 jusque'en 1800: Exposition de 1750* (Paris: Liepmannssohn et Dufour, 1869).

28. About Francesco Casanova as painter, see Heinrich Leporini, "Francesco Casanova,"

Pantheon 22 (1964): 173–83; Brigitte Kuhn-Forte, "Der Landschafts- und Schlachtenmaler Francesco Casanova (1727–1803)," *Wiener Jahrbuch für Kunstgeschichte* 37 (1984): 89–118; and Roland Kanz, *Die Brüder Casanova: Künstler und Abenteurer* (Munich: Deutscher Kunstverlag, 2013).

29. About Giovanni Battista, see Kanz, *Die Brüder Casanova*.

30. One artist Casanova mentions, whom he may also have known personally, is Pietro Liberi; see the anecdote in which he comments on a painted copy of Liberi's *Adam and Eve* (H 1:191).

31. For speculation about the painter of the O'Murphy, see H 3:334n6, and *Histoire de ma vie*, ed. Lacassin, 1:622n1.

32. For a recent summary of the portraits with complete bibliography, see Corinne le Bitouzé in *Casanova: La passion de la liberté*, ed. Marie-Laure Prévost and Chantal Thomas, exh. cat. (Paris: Bibliothèque nationale de France, 2011), 68–71.

33. According to the prince de Ligne, Charles-Joseph Lamoral, "He would be a very handsome man, if he were not ugly." See *Histoire de ma vie*, ed. Lacassin, 3:1162.

34. The painting, which is unpublished, bears the inscription "[Ven]ezia / Pietro Longhi / [pin]xit 17[...]" and measures 46.6 × 38.5 cm (18 ⅜ × 15 ⅛ in.).

VENICE

For help on Casanova in Venice, I would like to thank Alberto Craievich, Luca Zentilini, Andrea di Robilant, Toto Bergamo, Thomas Michie, Courtney Harris, and Dulcia Meijers.

1. For Casanova and Venice, see Kathleen Ann González, *Casanova's Venice: A Walking Guide* (Venice: Supernova, 2013), and Riccardo Selvatico, *Cento note per Casanova a Venezia (1753–1756)* (Vicenza: Neri Pozza, 1997).

2. See Helmut Watzlawick, "House of Childhood, House of Birth: A Topographical Distraction," *Intermédiare des Casanovistes*, 16 (1999): 17–24.

3. For regulations, see Dennis Romano, "The Gondola as a Marker of Station in Venetian Society," *Renaissance Studies* 8, no. 4 (Dec. 1994): 359–74, esp. 362. For design and decoration, see Gianfranco Munerotto, *La gondola nei secoli: Storia di una continua trasformazione tra architettura navale e arte* (Treviso: Vianello Libri, 2010). According to the boat specialist Chris Mason, the watercraft in the painting's foreground are, from left to right, a *batelon* (far left, with barrel and tarp), a *sandalo* (with single oarsman, and closest to the viewer), a *sandalo a coda di gambero* (pointing to the gondola), a gondola with *felze*, and a *peata* (leaving the Grand Canal at far right). For this painting and its pendant, see William George Constable and Joseph G. Links, *Canaletto: Giovanni Antonio Canal, 1697–1768*, 2 vols. (Oxford: Clarendon Press, 1989), nos. 166, 200; Katharine Baetjer and J. G. Links *Canaletto*, exh. cat. (New York: Metropolitan Museum of Art, 1989), nos. 35, 36.

4. See Ian Kelly, *Casanova: Actor, Lover, Priest, Spy* (New York: Penguin, 2008), 26–27.

5. For recent confusion about the Palazzo Bragadin in question, see Adriano Contini, "Where Casanova Lived," *Intermédiare des Casanovistes* 28 (2011): 53.

6. For *The Grand Canal from Campo di San Vio*, see Constable and Links, *Canaletto*, no. 187, and Stanton Thomas in *Venice in the Age of Canaletto*, ed. Alexandra Libby, Marina Pacini, and Stanton Thomas, exh. cat. (New York: Prestel, 2009), no. 20.

7. For *View from the Molo*, see Constable and Links, *Canaletto*, no. 88, and George T. M. Shackelford in *European Treasures: International Gothic through Realism* (El Paso, Tex.: El Paso Museum of Art Foundation, 2010), 265–66.

8. For a summary of politics and elections, see Frederic C. Lane, *Venice: A Maritime Republic* (Baltimore: Johns Hopkins University Press, 1973), 89–97, 258–62, and John Julius Norwich, *A History of Venice* (New York: Vintage, 1989), 166–67. Ian Kelly asserts that Casanova first came to the attention of Venetian authorities for "class infraction" rather than his love life or gambling; *Casanova*, 110–13.

9. Casanova, *My Escape from Venice Prison*, trans. Arthur Machen (Venice: Lineadacqua Edizione, 2009), 128. See also H 4:304.

10. For Casanova's "Venetian" attitude to sex, see Kelly, *Casanova*, 130–32.

11. See Adriano Mariuz and Giuseppe Pavanello, "The Interior Decoration of Palaces in Venice: From Baroque Magnificence to Rococo Elegance," in *Venice: Art and Architecture*, ed. Giandomenico Romanelli (Cologne: Könemann, 1998), 582–639.

12. For Venetian palace design, see Deborah Howard, *The Architectural History of Venice*, rev. ed. (New Haven: Yale University Press, 2002), 96–110.

13. The sketch was preparatory to a ceiling vault in Palazzo Clerici in Milan. See Beverly Louise Brown, ed., *Giambattista Tiepolo: Master of the Oil Sketch*, exh. cat. (New York: Abbeville, 1993), no. 20.

14. The iconography is standard for the period, derived from Cesare Ripa's *Iconologia* and other Baroque emblem books. See William L. Barcham in *Giambattista Tiepolo, 1696–1770*, ed. Keith Christiansen, exh. cat. (New York: Metropolitan Museum of Art, 1996), 180, and Filippo Pedrocco, *Tiepolo: The Complete Paintings* (New York: Rizzoli, 2002), no. 245. More recent research by Enrico Maria Guzzo suggests the painting was probably commissioned for the Palazzo Orto agli Scalzi in Verona.

15. See Keith Christiansen, "Tiepolo, Theater, and the Notion of Theatricality," *Art Bulletin* 81, no. 4 (Dec. 1999): 665–95.

16. See Michael Levey, "Tiepolo's 'Empire of Flora,'" *The Burlington Magazine*, 99, no. 648 (March 1957): 88–91, and William L. Barcham, "Il 'Trionfo di Flora' di Giambattista Tiepolo: Una Primavera per Dresda," *Arte veneta* 45 (1993): 70–77.

17. For *The Music Lesson*, see Terisio Pignatti, *Longhi*, 2nd ed. (Milan: Electa, 1972), 96, fig. 54; and Adriano Mariuz, Giuseppe Pavanello, and Giandomenico Romanelli, eds., *Pietro Longhi*, exh. cat. (Milan: Electa, 1993), no. 49. For *The Concert (The Mandolin Recital)* see Pignatti, *Longhi*, 105, fig. 197.

18. See Pignatti, *Longhi*, 88, fig. 100.

19. See Philip Sohm, "Pietro Longhi and Carlo Goldoni: Relations between Painting and Theater," *Zeitschrift für Kunstgeschichte*, 45, no. 3 (1982): 256–73.

20. The description in Goldoni's memoirs implies that Zanetta was the playwright's lover. See González, *Casanova's Venice*, 17, and Judith Summers, *Casanova's Women: The Great Seducer and the Women He Loved* (London: Bloomsbury, 2006), 43.

21. Baetjer and Links, *Canaletto*, no. 30, and Constable and Links, *Canaletto*, no. 365a.

22. Willard Trask identifies the Murano convent as that of San Giacomo di Galizzia (H 4:326n 18), while Ian Kelly argues for Santa Maria degli Angeli (*Casanova*, 163). On M.M., see Selvatico, *Cento Note*, 39–62.

23. This painting has been variously attributed to Antonio Guardi and to his younger brother Francesco. Recently, Filippo Pedrocco has assigned the authorship to Francesco, and this has been generally accepted. See Pedrocco, *Ca' Rezzonico: Museum of 18th Century Venice* (Venice: Marsilio, 2012), 65. For nuns in Venice, see Mary Laven, *Virgins of Venice: Enclosed Lives and Broken Vows in the Renaissance Convent* (London: Viking, 2002), and Isabella Campagnol, *Forbidden Fashions: Invisible Luxuries in Early Venetian Convents* (Lubbock: Texas Tech University Press, 2014).

24. Pompeo Molmenti, *Venice: Its Individual Growth from the Earliest Beginnings to the Fall of the Republic*, trans. Horatio F. Brown (Chicago: McClurg, 1908), part III, vol. 2, 84–86. The story of the nun and the French ambassador is recounted in n. 3 on p. 84, where it is argued this story inspired Casanova.

25. Campagnol, *Forbidden Fashions.*

26. See Agnes Husslein-Arco and Georg Lechner, eds., *Martin van Meytens der Jüngere*, exh. cat. (Vienna: Österreichische Galerie Belvedere, 2014), 110–13.

27. A love affair between two members of Casanova's social circle that featured

passionate letters is recounted in Andrea di Robilant, *A Venetian Affair* (New York: Knopf, 2003). Casanova knew both parties of this relationship well, and Andrea Memmo and Giustiniana Wynne crop up frequently in his memoirs. Andrea's mother took a strong dislike to Casanova and seems to have tipped off influential nobles about his dissolute behavior (H 4:191).

28. A *casino* could also be a site for voyeurism. M.M.'s *casino* included a compartment entered through the back of a cupboard and equipped with "everything needed by a curious voluptuary one of whose principal pleasures must have been to remain there as the unknown spectator of others' pleasures" (H 4:103).

29. See the report of Manuzzi, filed July 17, 1755 (H 4:355–58). According to Philippe Monnier, *Venise au XIIIe siècle* (Paris: Perrin, 1907), 28n2, "al Rinaldo Trionfante" was one of twelve bars on the Procuratie Nuove (south) arcade of Piazza San Marco. Kelly, *Casanova*, 175–79, summarizes the misbehavior that pushed Venetian authorities to arrest Casanova.

30. Casanova's own account of his arrest, imprisonment, and escape, published in 1787 as *Histoire de ma fuite des prisons de la République de Venise*, largely supplies the account in the memoirs, beginning at H 4:190.

31. See Umberto Franzoi, *The Prisons of the Doge's Palace in Venice* (Milan: Electa, 1997).

32. See Louis Marchesano, "*Invenzioni capric di carceri*: The *Prisons* of Giovanni Battista Piranesi (1720–1778)," *Getty Research Journal* 2 (2010): 151–60.

33. Steffi Röttgen in *Clemente XIII Rezzonico: Un papa Veneto nella Roma di metà Settecento*, ed. Andrea Nante, Carlo Cavalli, and Susanna Pasquali, exh. cat. (Cinisello Balsamo, Milan: Silvana Editoriale, 2008), nos. 69, 70. Röttgen assigns the painting to the circle of Mengs. See also Francesco Petrucci in *Papi in posa: Five Hundred Years of Papal Portraiture*, ed. Francesco Petrucci, exh. cat. (Rome: Gangemi, 2005), 148. The evident quality of the portrait, both in its overall coherent impression and in specific details of fabric textures, suggests it is worth considering reassigning it to Mengs and workshop, if not the master himself.

34. His last position, as librarian to Count Waldstein at Duchcov, came about because his then-employer, the Venetian ambassador in Vienna, brought Casanova to a dinner attended by the count in 1784. See Kelly, *Casanova*, 338–39.

35. Elio Bartolini, *Lettere a Casanova: Trentatrè lettere di Francesca Buschini l'ultima amante veneziana* (Udine: Casamassima, 1986).

36. Kelly, *Casanova*, 327–31.

THE THEATER OF IDENTITY

1. Pierre Choderlos de Laclos, *Les liaisons dangereuses*, in *Oeuvres complètes* (Paris: Gallimard, 1979), 173, 174.

2. Louis de Rouvroy, duc de Saint-Simon, *Mémoires suivi d'additions au journal de Dangeau*, 8 vols. (Paris: Gallimard, 1983–88), 3:17.

3. Jean-Jacques Rousseau, *Émile, ou De l'éducation* (Paris: Gallimard, 1969), 515.

4. See Volker Hunecke, *Il patriziato veneziano alla fine della Repubblica, 1646–1797: Demografia, famiglia, ménage*, trans. Benedetta Heinemann Campana (Rome: Jouvence, 1997), 43–46, 165–72; Frederic C. Lane, *Venice: A Maritime Republic* (Baltimore: Johns Hopkins University Press, 1973), 331–34; and Dennis Romano, *Patricians and Popolani: The Social Foundations of the Renaissance Venetian State* (Baltimore: Johns Hopkins University Press, 1987), 149–55.

5. For reports filed by G. Manuzzi, Inquisitori di Stato, November 11, 1754, and March 22, 1755, see Giovanni Comisso, *Agenti segreti di Venezia, 1705–1797* (Milan: Longanesi, 1941), 64, 68; Pietro Chiari, *La commediante in fortuna*, 2 vols. (Venice: Angelo Pasinelli, 1755), 2:130–31.

6. Barbey d'Aurevilly is quoted in the introduction to Jacques Casanova, *Le messager de Thalie: Onze feuilletons inédits de critique dramatique* (Paris: Jean Fort, 1925), 33; Lawrence is quoted in J. Rives Childs, *Casanova: An Annotated World Bibliography of Jacques Casanova de Seingalt and of*

Works Concerning Him (Vienna: C. M. Nebehay, 1956), 300, 368, 297.

7. Stefan Zweig, *Adepts in Self-Portraiture: Casanova, Stendhal, Tolstoy*, trans. Eden Paul and Cedar Paul (New York: Viking, 1928), 43.

8. Franco Mancini et al., *I teatri del Veneto*, 4 vols. (Venice: Corbo e Fiori, 1995). Domenico Lovisa took Venice's strong associations with the theater to a logical conclusion when he published a collection of engravings of principal sights with the title *Il Gran Teatro di Venezia* (1717). The city itself was a vast stage.

9. For further information on the Capodimonte figures, see Angela Caròla-Perrotti, ed., *Le porcellane dei Borbone di Napoli: Capodimonte e real fabbrica Ferdinandea, 1743–1806*, exh. cat. (Naples: Museo Archeologico Nazionale, 1986); Hugo Morley-Fletcher, *Early European Porcelain and Faience: As Collected by Kiyi and Edward Pflueger*, vol. 2 (London: Christie, Manson & Woods, 1993), 8–16, 20–21, 26–27, 28–29; and Francesco Stazzi, *L'arte della ceramica Capodimonte* (Milan: Görlich Editore, 1972), 319–22.

10. On this drawing, see Colin B. Bailey, ed., *Gabriel de Saint-Aubin, 1724–1780*, exh. cat. (New York: Frick Collection, 2007), no. 58, ill. on p. 237; Daniel Rabreau, "Un contrepoint aux théâtre de la Cour: L'Opéra de Paris au XVIIIe siècle, ou L'Académie royale de musique et de danse privée de monument," in *Théâtre de Cour: Les spectacles à Fontainebleau au XVIIIe siècle*, ed. Vincent Droguet and Marc-Henri Jordan, exh. cat. (Paris: Réunion des musées nationaux and Musée et domaine nationaux du Château de Fontainebleau, 2005), 50–56, ill. on pp. 50, 53.

11. On this painting, see Leslie G. Hennessey, "Friends Serving Itinerant Muses: Jacopo Amigoni and Farinelli in Europe," in *Italian Culture in Northern Europe in the Eighteenth Century*, ed. Shearer West (Cambridge: Cambridge University Press, 1999), 20–45.

12. For a persuasive and detailed case that Henriette was Adélaïde de Gueidan, see Judith Summers, *Casanova's Women: The Great Seducer and the Women He Loved* (New York: Bloomsbury, 2006), 160–67.

13. On this painting, see ibid., 162–63.

14. On Nattier's painting of Madame Henriette, see Xavier Salmon, ed., *Jean-Marc Nattier, 1685–1766*, exh. cat. (Versailles: Musée national des châteaux de Versailles et de Trianon, 1999), 251–55, no. 71, ill. on p. 253.

15. See Paul Nettl, *The Other Casanova: A Contribution to Eighteenth-Century Music and Manners* (New York: Philosophical Library, 1950); Giacomo Casanova, *Le Polémoscope, ou Le calomnie démasquée par la présence d'esprit* (Alessandria, Italy: Edizioni dell'Orso, 2003); Casanova, *Le messager de Thalie: Onze feuilletons inédits de critique dramatique* (1780; Paris, Jean Foit, 1925).

16. *Codice Cicogna*, n.d., 2991-II, 55, Biblioteca del Museo Civico Correr, Venice.

17. On *The Minuet*, see Jane Martineau and Andrew Robinson, eds., *The Glory of Venice: Art in the Eighteenth Century*, exh. cat. (Washington, D.C.: National Gallery of Art, 1994), 328, 504; no. 222.

18. On *The Charlatan*, see Adriano Mariuz, *Giandomenico Tiepolo* (Venice: Alfieri, 1971), 111–12, no. 88.

19. On this painting, see Adriano Mariuz, *Pietro Longhi*, exh. cat. (Venice: Museo Correr, 1993), 141–42, no. 67; Terisio Pignatti, *L'opera completa di Pietro Longhi* (Milan: Rizzoli Editore, 1974), 95n119.

20. Edward Wright, *Some Observations Made in Travelling through France, Italy, &c. in the Years 1720, 1721, and 1722*, 2 vols. (London: Tho. Ward and E. Wicksteed, 1730), 1:87.

21. See James H. Johnson, *Venice Incognito: Masks in the Serene Republic* (Berkeley: University of California Press, 2011).

22. Jean de La Bruyère, *Oeuvres complètes* (Paris: Gallimard, 1951), 215.

23. For a full description of the ball, see Charles-Philippe d'Albert, duc de Luynes, *Mémoires du duc de Luynes sur la cour de Louis XV (1735–1758)*, 17 vols. (Paris: Didot Frères, 1860–65), 6:321–25.

24. On *Thalia*, see Xavier Salmon, *Jean-Marc Nattier*, 115–19, no. 23.

25. See Terry Castle, *Masquerade and Civilization: The Carnivalesque in Eighteenth-Century English Culture and Fiction* (Stanford, Cal.: Stanford University Press, 1986).

26. On this painting, see Brian Allen, *Francis Hayman*, exh. cat. (New Haven: Yale Center for British Art, 1987), 115, no. 39, ill. on p. 121.

27. *Mist's Weekly Journal*, February 15, 1718, and *A Seasonable Apology for Mr. H* (1724), quoted in Philip H. Highfill et al., *A Biographical Dictionary of Actors, Actresses, Musicians, Dancers, Managers, and Other Stage Personnel in London, 1660–1800*, 16 vols. (Carbondale: Southern Illinois University Press, 1973–93), 7:235, 237.

28. Jerry White, *A Great and Monstrous Thing: London in the Eighteenth Century* (Cambridge, Mass.: Harvard University Press, 2013), 297–98; H 5:134–39.

PLEASURES OF THE ROAD

This essay is dedicated to my mother, with whom I've shared so many pleasant journeys.

1. Evliya Efendi [Çelebi], *Narrative of Travels in Europe, Asia, and Africa in the Seventeenth Century*, trans. Joseph, Freiherr von Hammer-Purgstall, 2 vols. (London: Oriental Translation Fund of Great Britain and Ireland, 1834–50), 2:2.

2. See Marie-Laure Prévost and Chantal Thomas, eds., *Casanova: La passion de la liberté* (Paris: Bibliothèque nationale de France, 2011), 44.

3. See, for instance, John Brewer, "Whose Grand Tour?" in *The English Prize: The Capture of the "Westmorland," an Episode of the Grand Tour* (New Haven: Yale Center for British Art, 2012), 45–61.

4. On the constitutive role of travel to the *History*'s structure and development, see Giuseppe Marci, *Il viaggio di Casanova* (Cagliari: C.U.E.C., 1998), esp. chap. 8.

5. A virtually identical trunk by Selby includes the owner's initials and the date 1740; see Harold D. Eberlein, "Furniture with Decorative Coverings of Leather or Fabrics," *Good Furniture: The Magazine of Decoration* (November 1917): 325–31, figs. 1, 2, 2a.

6. "A twenty-four-sou piece graciously proffered made them human" (H 5:91); the fine was ultimately dismissed after a full day lost.

7. H 1:200, 202; 2:53, 60, 66, 100, 178.

8. H 3:75, 77; see also 309n2. At 6,800 feet, Mont Cenis was the preferred pass between Piedmont and Savoy before the construction of carriage roads in the late eighteenth century.

9. H 3:22. Such luxury was restricted to the wealthiest travelers, including the British, who often purchased carriages upon arrival in Calais.

10. H 10:98–99, 346n28.

11. Casanova's account of this six-day journey (H 1:248–57) chronicles the stages of seduction, culminating in the failed attempt at Sermoneta. The affair was finally consummated—hastily, and in a carriage—during a subsequent outing to Testaccio (H 1:270).

12. H 3:118. On the use and construction of diligences, see André-Jacob Roubo, *L'art du menuisier* ([Paris], 1769–75), pt. 3, sec. 1, titled "L'art du menuisier-carrossier," 548–53, 569–73 (noting that the Paris-Lyon diligence was both the speediest in the kingdom and the only one with springs, and describing a twelve-seater *gondole*), and plates 196–98, 205–7.

13. Tobias Smollett, *Travels through France and Italy* (London: Folio Society, 1979), 197–98 (letter 29, Nice, February 20, 1765).

14. Olivier Lefeuvre, "Les 'Quatre accidents' de musée de Rennes: Loutherbourg ou Casanova?" *Revue de l'art* 136, no. 2 (2002): 63–66; see also Mylène Allano, *La collection des peintures italiennes du Musée des Beaux-Arts de Rennes* (Paris: Somogy, 2004), 34–39.

15. H 1:153. On Francesco, see Fabrizio Magani, "Giacomo e i suoi fratelli Francesco e Giovanni Alvise Casanova, una famiglia d'artisti," in *Giacomo Casanova tra Venezia e l'Europa*, ed. Gilberto Pizzamiglio (Florence:

Olschki, 2001), 201–19, and Roland Kanz, *Die Brüder Casanova: Künstler und Abenteurer* (Berlin: Deutsche Kunstverlag, 2013). Francesco ended his career under the protection of the prince of Kaunitz in Vienna, where he executed notable commissions from Catherine the Great.

16. Horace Walpole to Richard West, September 28, 1739, in *The Letters of Horace Walpole*, ed. Peter Cunningham (Edinburgh: John Grant, 1906), 1:26 (letter 17, "From a Hamlet among the Mountains of Savoy," n.s.). Francesco had already been favorably compared to Rosa by Denis Diderot in the *Salon of 1761*, and his interest in bandits and brigands may derive from Rosa's example.

17. H 3:19; for Spain, compare 10:306, where it is explained to Casanova that "the Holy Inquisition must always be able to send to see what foreigners might be doing at night in their rooms."

18. See H 10:101, 311, where Casanova, then lodging at a "coffeehouse" recommended to him in Bordeaux (the Hôtel garni du Café français, 10:389n36), notes that "the workman, proud of having succeeded, made me pay a great deal for his trial piece."

19. H 6:123ff. On the house's possible identification as the château of Riemberg, demolished in 1798, see 6:303n2, and Pierre Grelet, *Les aventures de Casanova en Suisse* (Lausanne: Éditions Spes, 1919), 40.

20. Charles de Brosses to MM de Tournay et de Neuilly, in Romain Colomb, ed., *Le président de Brosses en Italie: Lettres familières écrites d'Italie en 1739 et 1740*, 3rd ed. (Paris: P. Didier, 1869), 2:90, letter 40.

21. H 3:116. Casanova was initiated as a Freemason in Lyon and achieved the rank of master in Paris.

22. Compare the prince de Ligne, who knew Casanova in Duchcov: "He played the seigneur in a coat of gray lutestring flowered in silver, a very large collar of Spanish point, a plumed hat, a yellow waistcoat, and breeches of crimson silk." *The Prince de Ligne: His Memoirs, Letters, and Miscellaneous Papers*, trans. Katharine Prescott Wormeley, 2 vols. (Boston, 1899), 2:160.

23. Richard Lassels, preface to *The Voyage of Italy* (Paris, 1670), sec. 5, "What Is to Be Learned in France and What Not," unpaginated.

24. H 2:68–100. On discrepancies regarding dates and circumstances, see Marie-Françoise Luna, "Le voyage au Levant," in Prévost and Thomas, *Casanova: La passion de la liberté*, 38–42; Casanova evidently conflated two trips, in 1741–42 (when he would have met Ismail at age sixteen) and 1744–45 or 1746.

25. One of five autograph versions of the painting is shown here. See Marcel Roethlisberger and Renée Loche, *Liotard: Catalogue, sources et correspondance*, 2 vols. (Doornspijk: Davaco, 2008), 1:275–76, nos. 67–69; vol. 2, plates 86–88; Kristel Smentek, "Looking East: Jean-Étienne Liotard, the Turkish Painter," *Ars Orientalis* 39 (2010): 84–112; Aileen Ribeiro, "The Beauty of the Particular: Dress in Liotard's Images of Women," in *Jean-Étienne Liotard, 1702–1789* (London: Royal Academy of Arts, 2015), 35–41.

26. Ribeiro, "Beauty of the Particular," 38.

27. On Bonneval, to whom Casanova also refers as the Pasha of Karamania, see Julia Landweber, "Fashioning Nationality and Identity in the Eighteenth Century: The Comte de Bonneval in the Ottoman Empire," *The International History Review* 30, no. 1 (March 2008): 1–31.

28. H 2:74, 87. Though Casanova attributes the motto to the Stoics, he may also have been reluctant, as he expressed to Yusuf, "to renounce the religion of my dear father" (H 2:80).

29. "In Praise of Travel in Germany, another oration made by the foresaid Hermannus Kirchnerus... pronounced in the noble University of Marpurg," in Thomas Coryat, *Coryat's Crudities, hastily gobbled up in five moneth's travells in France, Savoy, Italy* [1611] (Glasgow: James MacLehose and Sons, 1905), 2:71–86, quoted at 73–74. Coryat had presumably encountered Kirchner at Marburg, where he was professor of history, poetry, oratory, and rhetoric.

30. See Gino Benzoni, "In viaggio per l'Europa," in Pizzamiglio, *Giacomo Casanova tra Venezia e l'Europa*, 35–65, esp. 60.

31. *Prince de Ligne*, 2:169.

32. H 1:31–32, 157–58, 162, 318; 2:53; 3:3; 5:17.

33. See Chantal Thomas, "La passion de la liberté," in Prévost and Thomas, *Casanova: La passion de la liberté*, 10–15, and idem, *Casanova: Un voyage libertin* (Paris: Denoël, 1985).

34. Jerome Nadal, about 1565, translated by John W. O'Malley, S.J., in "To Travel to Any Part of the World: Jerónimo Nadal and the Jesuit Vocation," *Studies in the Spirituality of Jesuits* 16, no. 2 (March 1984): 8. I thank James Clifton for drawing my attention to this passage.

PARIS

1. Daniel Roche cites the city's population as 700,000 by 1780, in *France in the Enlightenment*, trans. Arthur Goldhammer (Cambridge, Mass.: Harvard University Press, 1998), 643.

2. See Alvin L. Clark, with Esther Bell and Françoise Joulie, *Genius and Grace: François Boucher and the Generation of 1700*, exh. cat. (Boston: The Horvitz Collection, 2014).

3. See Xavier Salmon, ed., *Jean-Marc Nattier, 1685–1766*, exh. cat. (Versailles: Musée national des châteaux de Versailles et de Trianon, 1999), 271–74, no. 78; on Casanova's description of Silvia, see H 3:124–25.

4. Luigi Riccoboni was married to Helena Balletti (Flaminia), the sister of Giuseppe Balletti (Mario), who was Silvia's husband.

5. On Luigi Riccoboni and the Théâtre-Italien, see Ola Forsans, *Le Théâtre de Lélio: Étude du répertoire du Nouveau Théâtre italien de 1716 à 1729*, Studies on Voltaire and the Eighteenth Century, vol. 8 (Oxford: Voltaire Foundation, 2006).

6. See Jeffrey S. Ravel, *The Contested Parterre: Public Theater and French Political Culture, 1680–1791* (Ithaca, N.Y.: Cornell University Press, 1999).

7. Mary Taverner Holmes, *Nicolas Lancret, 1690–1743*, exh. cat. (New York: The Frick Collection, 1999), 67, no. 5, plate 9.

8. Henry Carrington Lancaster, *French Tragedy in the Time of Louis XV and Voltaire, 1715–1774* (Baltimore: Johns Hopkins University Press, 1950); John Lough, *Paris Theatre Audiences in the Seventeenth and Eighteenth Centuries* (London: Oxford University Press, 1965); Henry Lagrave, *Le théâtre et le public à Paris de 1715 à 1750* (Paris: Librairie C. Klincksiek, 1972).

9. Lough, *Paris Theatre Audiences*, 56.

10. On the Salon, see Thomas E. Crow, *Painters and Public Life in Eighteenth Century Paris* (New Haven: Yale University Press, 1985).

11. See Perrin Stein in *Gabriel de Saint-Aubin, 1724–1780*, ed. Colin B. Bailey, exh. cat. (New York: Frick Collection, 2007), no. 69.

12. *Explication des peintures, sculptures, et autres ouvrages de messieurs de l'Académie Royale* (Paris: Jacques-François Collombat, 1750).

13. Francesco would later become the teacher of Philippe-Jacques de Loutherbourg (1740–1812); on Francesco Casanova, see H. Leporini, "Francesco Casanova," *Pantheon* 22 (1964): 173–83; Brigitte Kuhn, "Der Landschafts- und Schlachtenmaler Francesco Casanova (1727–1803)," *Wiener Jahrbuch für Kunstgeschichte* 37 (1984): 89–118, 223–36.

14. For select readings from the extensive literature on Pompadour, see Émile Campardon, *Madame de Pompadour et la cour de Louis XV au milieu du dix-huitième siècle* (Paris: Plon, 1867); Xavier Salmon, *Madame de Pompadour et les arts*, exh. cat. (Versailles: Musée national des châteaux de Versailles et de Trianon, 2002); Elise Goodman, *The Portraits of Madame de Pompadour: Celebrating the Femme Savante* (Berkeley: University of California Press, 2002); for a bibliography of the literature post-2000, see Alden R. Gordon, "Searching for the Elusive Madame de Pompadour," *Eighteenth-Century Studies* 37, no. 1 (Fall 2003): 91–92.

15. See Kimberly Chrisman Campbell, "Dressing to Impress: The Morning Toilette and the Fabrication of Femininity," in *Paris: Life and Luxury*, ed. Charissa Bremer-David, exh. cat. (Los Angeles: The J. Paul Getty Museum), 53–73.

16. See Melissa Hyde's excellent analysis of the painting in "The 'Makeup' of the Marquise: Boucher's Portrait of Pompadour at Her Toilette," *The Art Bulletin* 82, no. 3 (September 2000): 453–75; and Melissa Hyde, *Making Up the Rococo: François Boucher and His Critics* (Los Angeles: Getty Research Institute, 2006).

17. H 3:200; on the problematic identity of Boucher's sitter, see *François Boucher, 1703–1770*, exh. cat. (New York: Metropolitan Museum of Art, 1986), no. 61.

18. There is no evidence that Marigny had much personal interest in Francesco Casanova; his posthumous inventories reveal no paintings or drawings by him. See Alden Gordon, *The Houses and Collections of the Marquis de Marigny* (Los Angeles: Provenance Index of the Getty Research Institute, 2003).

19. See Ian Kelly, *Casanova: Actor, Lover, Priest, Spy* (New York: Penguin, 2008), 201.

20. On the Silvestre family, see Dena Goodman and Emily Talbot, "Documenting Art, Writing Biography: Construction of the Silvestre Family, 1660–1868," *Journal of Family History* 40, no. 3 (2015): 277–304.

21. On this drawing, see *The Arts of France from François Ier to Napoléon Ier*, ed. Joseph Baillio, exh. cat. (New York: Wildenstein, 2005), no. 75.

22. Casanova erroneously refers to her age as fifteen; in fact she was baptized on April 4, 1740.

23. See Salmon, *Jean-Marc Nattier*, no. 79.

24. Jacques-François Blondel was the father of Georges-François Blondel (1730–about 1790), an engraver.

25. See Rochelle Ziskin, *Sheltering Art: Collecting and Social Identity in Early Eighteenth-Century Paris* (University Park: Pennsylvania State University Press, 2012).

26. Cited in Katie Scott, *The Rococo Interior: Decoration and Social Spaces in Eighteenth-Century Paris* (New Haven: Yale University Press, 1995), 109–17.

27. Bremer-David, *Paris: Life and Luxury*, 36–39.

28. Scott, *The Rococo Interior*, 204; see also *François Boucher*, nos. 84, 85.

29. H 5:57; on Casanova and the French Revolution, see Jaroslav Jírů, "Casanova observateur de la Révolution française," *Annales historiques de la Révolution française* 31, no. 157 (July–September 1959): 227–39.

AMOROUS PURSUITS

1. Lawrence Stone, *The Family, Sex and Marriage in England 1500–1800* (New York: Harper & Row, 1977), 149–64, 217–53, 326–38; Allan H. Pasco, *Revolutionary Love in Eighteenth- and Early Nineteenth-Century France* (Farnham: Ashgate, 2009), 33–62; Faramerz Dabhoiwala, *The Origins of Sex* (New York: Oxford University Press, 2012), 80–140.

2. H 1:28. See also Jay Caplan, "Vicarious *Jouissances*: Or Reading Casanova," *MLN* 100, no. 4 (Sep. 1985): 803–4.

3. See Thomas M. Kavanagh, *Esthetics of the Moment: Literature and Art in the French Enlightenment* (Philadelphia: University of Pennsylvania Press, 1996), 101–25.

4. See Guillaume Faroult, *Fragonard amoureux: Galant et libertin*, exh. cat. (Paris: Réunion des musées nationaux, 2015), no. 41; Astrid Reuter et al., eds., *Fragonard, Poesie und Leidenschaft*, exh. cat. (Berlin: Deutscher Kunstverlag, 2013), no. 28; Mary D. Sheriff, *Fragonard: Art and Eroticism* (Chicago: University of Chicago Press, 1990), 185–206.

5. The significance of the scale of the blank canvas has been overlooked in scholarship on *The New Model*. Mary Sheriff writes that the blankness of the canvas invites the viewer to imagine what the painting will look like and that "it would be difficult... to imagine a moral scene... and easy to conjure an explicitly sexual one" (*Fragonard*, 201). Martin Schieder argues that "the model will become a work of art—the very painting at which the viewer

is looking," in *The Age of Watteau, Chardin, and Fragonard: Masterpieces of French Genre Painting*, ed. Colin B. Bailey, exh. cat. (New Haven: Yale University Press, 2003), no. 85, 294. Pierre-Antoine Baudouin's 1769 painting *The Honest Model* (National Gallery of Art, Washington, D.C.) depicts a similar subject, and the two works are often discussed together. The large canvas in Baudouin's work is a mythological painting.

6. See Colin B. Bailey, ed., *The Loves of the Gods: Mythological Painting from Watteau to David*, exh. cat. (New York: Rizzoli, 1992), no. 59; Jean-Pierre Cuzin, *Jean-Honoré Fragonard, Life and Work: Complete Catalogue of the Oil Paintings* (New York: Abrams, 1988), no. 55.

7. In his *Mémoires secrets sur le règne de Louis XIV, la régence et le règne de Louis XV* (Paris, 1808), Charles Pinot Duclos writes that the regent was always in need of "dissipation, noise, and debauchery," that he surrounded himself with a group he called "his roués," and that license in this inner circle was pushed to an extreme (1:219).

8. Louis-Sébastien Mercier, *Tableau de Paris* (Hamburg and Neuchatel, 1781), 2:22.

9. See Katie Scott, "D'un siècle à l'autre: History, Mythology, and Decoration in Early Eighteenth-Century Paris," in Bailey, *Loves of the Gods*, 32–59.

10. See Else Marie Bukdahl, *Diderot, critique d'art* (Copenhagen: Rosenkilde et Bagger, 1980), 95, 385; Marc Sandoz, *Les Lagrenée* (Paris: Éditart Les Quatre-Chemins, 1983), no. 215.

11. Denis Diderot, "Salon de 1771," in *Diderot, Salons*, ed. Jean Seznec (Oxford: The Clarendon Press, 1967), 4:170. The attribution of the "Salon of 1771" to Diderot has been questioned.

12. Denis Diderot, "Pensées détachées sur la peinture," in *Oeuvres de Denis Diderot*, ed. Jacques-André Naigeon (Paris, 1800), 15:162.

13. See Katie Scott, *The Rococo Interior: Decoration and Social Spaces in Early Eighteenth-Century Paris* (New Haven: Yale University Press, 1995); Joan DeJean, *The Age of Comfort: When Paris Discovered Casual—and the Modern Home Began* (New York: Bloomsbury, 2009).

14. See Mary Salzman, "Decoration and Enlightened Spectatorship," in *Furnishing the Eighteenth Century: What Furniture Can Tell Us about the European and American Past*, ed. Dena Goodman and Kathryn Norberg (New York: Routledge, 2007), 155–65.

15. J. F. Bastide, *La petite maison* (Paris, 1879), 12–13.

16. The 1694 edition of the *Dictionnaire de l'Académie Française* defined *galant* as "honest, civil, sociable, of good company, agreeable conversation." See also Guillaume Faroult, "Le berger galant," in Faroult, *Fragonard amoureux*, 64.

17. See Cuzin, *Jean-Honoré Fragonard*, no. 43; Richard Rand, *Intimate Encounters: Love and Domesticity in Eighteenth-Century France*, exh. cat. (Hanover, N.H.: Hood Museum of Art, 1997), 135–36; Marie-Anne Dupuy-Vachey, *Fragonard* (Paris: Terrail, 2006), 16.

18. Fragonard makes a similar allusion in his 1767 painting *The Swing* (The Wallace Collection, London). See Donald Posner, "The Swinging Women of Watteau and Fragonard," *The Art Bulletin* 64, no. 1 (March 1982): 75–88.

19. See Alastair Laing et al., *François Boucher, 1703–1770*, exh. cat. (New York: Metropolitan Museum of Art, 1986), 67–72, 233–37; Bailey, *Age of Watteau*, no. 55.

20. Cross-dressing, which features in several of Casanova's adventures was common in eighteenth-century mondaine culture. See Melissa Hyde, *Making Up the Rococo: François Boucher and His Critics* (Los Angeles: Getty Research Institute, 2006), 145–77.

21. See Jenny Uglow, *Hogarth, A Life and a World* (New York: Farrar, Straus, & Giroux, 1997), 178–82; David Bindman, *Hogarth* (London: Thames and Hudson, 1981), no. 37 and no. 38; Ronald Paulson, *Hogarth: His Life, Art, and Times* (New Haven: Yale University Press, 1971), no. 87 and no. 88.

22. Prior to the eighteenth century in France, *libertine* referred to a group of skeptics; it developed its purely erotic definition under the Regency of Philippe d'Orléans. See

Michel Feher, "Libertinisms," in *The Libertine Reader: Eroticism and Enlightenment in Eighteenth-Century France* (New York: Zone Books, 1997), 10–47.

23. Denis Diderot and Jean Le Rond d'Alembert, *Encyclopédie ou Dictionnaire raisonné des sciences, des arts et des métiers*. Available online, *ARTFL Encyclopédie Project*, ed. Robert Morrissey and Glenn Roe (University of Chicago), http://encyclopedie.uchicago.edu/.

24. Stone, *Family, Sex, and Marriage*, 266.

25. See Robin Simon in *Johann Zoffany RA: Society Observed*, ed. Martin Postle, exh. cat. (New Haven: Yale Center for British Art, 2011), no. 60; Mary Webster, *Johann Zoffany, 1733–1810* (New Haven: Yale University Press, 2011), 367–69; William L. Pressly, "Genius Unveiled: The Self-Portraits of Johann Zoffany," *The Art Bulletin* 69, no. 1 (March 1987): 88–101.

26. Pierre-Jean-Baptiste Nougaret, *Suzette et Pierrin, ou Les dangers du libertinage* (London and Paris, 1780), part II, 37.

27. Jean Astruc, *Traité des maladies vénériennes* (Paris, 1755), 3:115–16.

28. See Cuzin, *Jean-Honoré Fragonard*, no. 284; Rand, *Intimate Encounters*, no. 24; Faroult, *Fragonard amoureux*, no. 39.

29. See Robert Darnton, *The Forbidden Best-Sellers of Pre-Revolutionary France* (New York: W. W. Norton, 1996).

30. See Pierre Rosenberg, *Fragonard*, exh. cat. (New York: Metropolitan Museum of Art, 1988), no. 218; Annie Le Brun in *Sade: Attaquer le soleil*, exh. cat. (Paris: Musée d'Orsay, 2014), no. 140; Faroult, *Fragonard amoureux*, no. 58.

31. On *The Desired Moment*, see Rosenberg, *Fragonard*, no. 147; Andrei Molotiu, *Fragonard's Allegories of Love* (Los Angeles: J. Paul Getty Museum, 2007), 65–66; Faroult, *Fragonard amoureux*, no. 55.

32. Faroult, *Fragonard amoureux*, no. 54.

33. See Stone, *Family, Sex, and Marriage*, 326–39; Pasco, *Revolutionary Love*, 149–64.

34. Pierre Rousseau, ed., *Journal encyclopédique ou universel*, vol. 7 (Bouillon, 1775), 497.

35. Alexandre-Balthazar-Laurent Grimod de la Reynière, *Réflexions philosophiques sur le plaisir; par un célibataire* (Neufchatel, 1783), 65.

36. *Mercure de France*, Jan. 3, 1784, p. 184.

37. Philogamus, *The Present State of Matrimony; or, The Real Causes of Conjugal Infidelity and Unhappy Marriages* (London, 1739), 13. See also Stone, *Family, Sex, and Marriage*, 329–31.

38. Dabhoiwala, *Origins*, 77.

39. Louis-Sébastien Mercier, *Tableau de Paris: Nouvelle Édition* (Amsterdam, 1782), 3:327, 329; edition of 1781, 2:205.

40. See Rand, *Intimate Encounters*, no. 34.

41. Kristel Smentek, "Sex, Sentiment, and Speculation: The Market for Genre Prints on the Eve of the French Revolution," in *French Genre Painting in the Eighteenth Century*, ed. Philip Conisbee (Washington, D.C.: National Gallery of Art, 2007), 234–35.

42. See Dabhoiwala, *Origins*, 153–60; Stone, *Family, Sex, and Marriage*, 40, 391.

43. Grimod de la Reynière, *Réflexions*, 67.

44. Pasco, *Revolutionary Love*, 160–61.

45. See Christophe Leribault in Bailey, *Age of Watteau*, no. 46.

46. See Faroult, *Fragonard amoureux*, no. 56; Bernard N. Jazzar and J. Patrice Marandel, *Eye for the Sensual: Selections from the Resnick Collection*, exh. cat. (Stuttgart: Dr. Cantz'sche Druckerei, 2010), no. 14; Cuzin, *Jean-Honoré Fragonard*, no. 202.

47. H 1:139. See also Chantal Thomas and Noah Guynn, "The Role of Female Homosexuality in Casanova's Memoirs," *Yale French Studies* 94 (1998): 179–81.

48. See Satish Padiyar, "Menacing Cupid in the Art of Rococo," in *The Triumph of Eros: Art and Seduction in 18th-century France*, exh. cat. (London: Fontanka, 2006), 21.

49. François de la Rochefoucauld, *A Frenchman's Year in Suffolk, 1984*, trans. Norman Scarfe

(Woodbridge: Boydell, 2011), 36.

50. Faroult, *Fragonard amoureux*, no. 76. An early print reproduction of *The Contract* identifies Fragonard as the sole creator of the original painting, but Guillaume Faroux asserts that it was a collaboration between Fragonard and his sister-in-law, Marguerite Gérard.

51. See Chantal Thomas, *Casanova: Un voyage libertin* (Paris: Éditions Denoël, 1985), 232.

CLOTHES MAKE THE MAN

1. See Peter Thornton, *Baroque and Rococo Silks* (London: Faber and Faber, 1965), 80; Aileen Ribeiro, *Dress in Eighteenth-Century Europe* (New Haven: Yale University Press, 2002), 57.

2. *The Fable of the Bees: or, Private Vices, Publick Benefits* (London, 1714), cited in Ribeiro, *Dress in Eighteenth-Century Europe*, 51. See also Beverly Lemire, *Dress, Culture and Commerce* (London: Macmillan, 1997), 126.

3. "À l'age de seize ans on m'a fait docteur, et on m'a donné l'habit de prêtre pour aller faire ma fortune à Rome" (At the age of sixteen, I earned my doctorate and was given the habit of a preacher so that I could go to Rome and make my fortune). Giacomo Casanova, "Précis de ma vie," November 2, 1797, original manuscript from the State Archives Prague, online at http://expositions.bnf.fr/casanova/arret/01.htm.

4. See manuscript of *Histoire de ma vie*, vol. 1, chap. 8, p. 187r; online at http://gallica.bnf.fr.

5. Ibid., vol. 2, chap. 9, p. 124r. The original manuscript identifies his suit as being made of velvet.

6. Santina Levey, *Lace: A History* (London: Victoria & Albert Museum and W. S. Maney and Son, 1983), 53.

7. Madeleine Delpierre, *Se vêtir au XVIIIe siècle* (Paris: Adam Biro, 1996), 171–72.

8. Manuscript of *Histoire de ma vie*, vol. 7, chap. 8, p. 188v; http://gallica.bnf.fr.

9. Daniel Roche, *The Culture of Clothing: Dress and Fashion in the Ancien Regime*, trans. Jean Birrell (Cambridge, England: Cambridge University Press, 1996), 96.

LONDON

1. See Judith Summers, *Casanova's Women: The Great Seducer and the Women He Loved* (London: Bloomsbury, 2006), 281, 284.

2. Modern historians generally estimate London's population at around 750,000, twice the size of Naples and rivaled only by Paris. See Jerry White, *A Great and Monstrous Thing: London in the Eighteenth Century* (Cambridge, Mass.: Harvard University Press, 2013), 3. See also John Brewer, *The Pleasures of the Imagination: English Culture in the Eighteenth Century* (New York: Farrar, Straus & Giroux, 1997), 28.

3. White, *A Great and Monstrous Thing*, 77–78. See also Roy Porter, "The Wonderful Extent and Variety of London," in *London 1753*, ed. Sheila O'Connell (London: British Museum Press, 2003), 9–17.

4. Marcia Pointon, "The Lives of Kitty Fisher," *British Journal for Eighteenth-Century Studies* 27 (2004): 88.

5. Ronald Paulson, *The Art of Hogarth* (London: Phaidon, 1975), 21. Until 2014, this painting was attributed to Hogarth, but is now regarded as the earliest and best copy after a lost original. Correspondence from Matthew Hargraves, Yale Center for British Art.

6. While Casanova was in London, the Howdalians met weekly at Munday's coffeehouse in Maiden Lane, as they sought to establish public art exhibitions. See Matthew Hargraves, *Candidates for Fame: The Society of Artists of Great Britain, 1760–1791* (New Haven: Yale University Press for the Paul Mellon Centre for Studies in British Art, 2009), 66–68.

7. Brewer, *Pleasures of the Imagination*, 3.

8. Chippendale was one of the principal creditors of Mrs. Cornelys's estate, but no furniture by him is known to survive from Carlisle House. See Christopher Gilbert, *The Life and Works of Thomas Chippendale*, 2 vols. (London: Cassell, 1978), 1:160–61. For a detailed description of Carlisle House and its interiors, see

Summers, *Casanova's Women*, 311–14.

9. Pat Kirkham, "Samuel Norman: A Study of an Eighteenth-Century Craftsman," *The Burlington Magazine* 111, no. 797 (August 1969): 504.

10. Quoted in Oliver Brackett, *Thomas Chippendale: A Study of His Life, Work and Influence* (Boston: Houghton Mifflin, 1925), 83; see also 84–87.

11. Quoted in White, *A Great and Monstrous Thing*, 335; see also 336–43.

12. Judy Egerton, "Lord Charlemont and William Hogarth," in *Lord Charlemont and His Circle*, ed. Michael McCarthy (Dublin: Four Courts Press, 2001), 93. See also Ronald Paulson, *Hogarth*, vol. 3, *Art and Politics, 1750–1764* (New Brunswick: Rutgers University Press, 1993), 218–23.

13. See John Harris, *The Palladian Revival: Lord Burlington, His Villa and Garden at Chiswick* (New Haven: Yale University Press, 1994).

14. According to Casanova's memoirs, the event took place in June, although it is more likely that it occurred in October. See Horace Bleackley, ed., *Casanova in England* (New York: Knopf, 1925), 140–41.

15. As early as 1728, one French visitor advised, "One must here disengage from the idea of Versailles and the grand palaces of kings." Parliamentary oversight of royal income made it politically unfeasible for the Hanoverians to erect grand palaces. See Desmond Shawe-Taylor, ed., *The First Georgians: Art and Monarchy, 1714–1760* (London: Royal Collection Trust, 2014), 53.

16. *The London Magazine* 32 (April 1763): 225.

17. See Charles Beddington, *Canaletto in England: A Venetian Artist Abroad, 1746–1755* (New Haven: Yale University Press, 2006), nos. 23, 54.

18. Bleackley speculates that the "Star" tavern may be a mistranslation of a manuscript abbreviation for the better-known "Shakespeare's Head," an error repeated in subsequent editions of the memoirs. See Bleackley, *Casanova in England*, 47n. For an account of London's various forms and locations of prostitution, see Fergus Linnane, *Madams: Bawds and Brothel-Keepers of London* (Stroud: Sutton, 2005), and White, *A Great and Monstrous Thing*, chap. 9.

19. Quoted in Warwick Wroth, *The London Pleasure Gardens of the Eighteenth Century* (London: Macmillan, 1896), 204–5. See also Melanie Doderer-Winkler, *Magnificent Entertainments: Temporary Architecture of Georgian Festivals* (New Haven: Yale University Press for the Paul Mellon Centre for Studies in British Art, 2013), 83–85.

20. Quoted in White, *A Great and Monstrous Thing*, 47.

21. Quoted in Rosamond Bayne-Powell, *Eighteenth-Century London Life* (London: John Murray, 1937), 148. See also Doderer-Winkler, *Magnificent Entertainments*, 79–83.

22. Doderer-Winkler, *Magnificent Entertainments*, chap. 2.

23. Quoted in Edwin Beresford Chancellor, *The Pleasure Haunts of London* (London: Constable, 1925), 197.

24. H 9:197. For a comprehensive history of Vauxhall Gardens and its patronage of painters and sculptors, see David Coke and Alan Borg, *Vauxhall Gardens: A History* (New Haven: Yale University Press for the Paul Mellon Centre for Studies in British Art, 2011).

CHAMPAGNE AND OYSTERS

The author wishes to thank Thomas Chilton; The Arthur and Elizabeth Schlesinger Library on the History of Women in America, Radcliffe Institute for Advanced Studies, Harvard University; and Rosemary Shipton.

1. H 1:6. Trask notes that this lifestyle was ingrained by the time Casanova was twenty-four years old.

2. Tobias Smollett, *Travels through France and Italy*, ed. Frank Felsenstein (Peterborough, Ont.: Broadview Press, 2011), 34. Smollett was writing of his experiences in England, before crossing the Channel in 1763. He thought no better of inns in France or Italy.

3. James Boswell, *Boswell on the Grand Tour: Germany and Switzerland 1764*, ed. Frederick A. Pottle, 1st ed. (New York: McGraw-Hill, 1953), 145–46.

4. H 6:51. Maraschino was a distilled wine from Dalmatia made from sour Marasca cherries, a rarity popular with the nobility in the late eighteenth century.

5. Menon, *The Art of Modern Cookery Displayed... Translated from Les Soupers de La Cour*, trans. R. Davis (London, 1767), 1:222.

6. A larger version of Lancret's painting, titled *Ham Luncheon* (Musée de Chantilly), was originally paired with De Troy's *Oyster Luncheon* in the first dining room in the private Petits Cabinets of Louis XV at Versailles, where the king dined with friends after hunting. See Béatrix Saule, "Tables royales à Versailles 1682–1789," in *Versailles et les tables royales en Europe, XVIIème–XIXème siècles*, exh. cat. (Paris: Réunion des musées nationaux, 1993), 58; and Colin B. Bailey, ed., *The Age of Watteau, Chardin, and Fragonard: Masterpieces of French Genre Painting*, exh. cat. (New Haven: Yale University Press, 2003), 146.

7. The Rev. Dr. John Trusler, *The Honours of the Table, or, Rules for Behaviour During Meals...*, 2nd ed. (London: Literary Press, 1791), 3–4.

8. H 5:229–30. Macaroni *al sughillo* is with sauce; rice *in cagnoni* is similar to risotto Milanese; and *olla podrida* is a rich stew composed of many different types of meat, fowl, and vegetables.

9. François-Pierre La Varenne instructs in a later edition of his *Vrai cuisinier françois, le maitre d'hôtel et le grand ecuyer-tranchant* (Brussels: George de Backer, 1698) that there are no fewer than twenty-four named cuts to be made when carving fowl. His instructions and the accompanying diagrams for carving were copied by many subsequent authors.

10. Hannah Glasse, *The Art of Cookery Made Plain and Simple* (London, 1763), 32. The recipe "To Roast a Turkey the Genteel Way" describes such a procedure.

11. James Boswell, *Boswell on the Grand Tour: Italy, Corsica, and France, 1765–1766*, ed. Frank Brady and Frederick A. Pottle, 1st ed. (New York: McGraw-Hill, 1955), 155. Boswell was presented with "no less than twelve well-dressed dishes, served on Dresden china, with a dessert" when dining on Corsica in 1765, an illustration of the availability of Meissen in far-flung locations. Casanova mentions that he could rent silver tableware for one sou per ounce (H 5:180).

12. Carolin C. Young, *Apples of Gold in Settings of Silver: Stories of Dinner as a Work of Art* (New York: Simon & Schuster, 2002), 174.

13. Meredith Chilton, in *Daily Pleasures: French Ceramics from the Mary Lou Boone Collection*, ed. Elizabeth Ann Williams and Meredith Chilton (Los Angeles: Los Angeles County Museum of Art, 2012), 28.

14. H 4:72–73. Her lover was the abbé François-Joachim de Pierre de Bernis, the French ambassador and a close friend of Madame de Pompadour; he later became a cardinal. He was perfectly aware that M.M. was sharing her favors with Casanova.

15. Béatrix Saule, in *Versailles et les tables royales*, 58.

16. Anne Willan, *Great Cooks and Their Recipes from Taillevent to Escoffier* (Maidenhead, U.K.: McGraw-Hill, 1977); Prince de Dombes (attrib.), *Le cuisinier gascon*, new ed. (Amsterdam, 1747).

17. Silvano Serventi and Françoise Sabban, *Pasta: The Story of a Universal Food* (New York: Columbia University Press, 2002), 84. Macaroni and vermicelli appear on lists of essential ingredients for transporting to an English country house in the summer by Mrs. Pennington, the author of *The Royal Cook, or The Modern Etiquette of the Table, Displayed with Accuracy, Elegance and Taste* (London: Richard Snagg, 1774), 116.

DRESDEN TO DUCHCOV

1. Scholarly interest in Casanova's eastern travels has paled in comparison to the abundant examination of his pursuits in Venice, Rome, Paris, and London. On Casanova's final two decades, see Mitchell S. Buck, *The Life of Casanova*

from 1774 to 1798: A Supplement to the Memoirs (New York: Nicholas L. Brown, 1924); J. Rives Childs, *Casanova: A New Perspective* (New York: Paragon, 1988), chaps. 12, 13, and 17; Enrico Straub, "Casanova e la Boemia," *L'intermédiaire des Casanovistes* 7 (1990): 1–17.

2. See Tristan Weddingen, "The Picture Galleries of Dresden, Düsseldorf, and Kassel: Princely Collections in Eighteenth-Century Germany," in *The First Modern Museums of Art: The Birth of an Institution in Eighteenth- and Early Nineteenth-Century Europe*, ed. Carole Paul (Los Angeles: Getty Publications, 2012), 149; Harald Marx, ed., *Dresden in the Ages of Splendor and Enlightenment: Eighteenth-Century Paintings from the Old Masters Picture Gallery* (Columbus, Ohio: Columbus Museum of Art, 1999); and Gregor J. M. Weber, "The Princely Gallery of Augustus III: An Artwork in Itself," in *The Glory of Baroque Dresden* (Jackson, Miss. : Mississippi Arts Pavilion, 2004), 77–97.

3. Michael Levey, "Two Paintings by Tiepolo from the Algarotti Collection," *The Burlington Magazine* 102 (June 1960): 250–57; and Keith Christiansen, ed. , *Giambattista Tiepolo 1696–1770* (New York: Metropolitan Museum of Art, 1996), 31–32.

4. The fountain still exists in the courtyard of the Palais Brühl-Marcolini, in the Dresden district of Friedrichstadt.

5. Bellotto's work was part of a larger pictorial tradition. See for example Harald Marx, *Die schönsten Ansichten aus Sachsen: Johann Alexander Thiele (1685–1752)* (Dresden: Staatliche Kunstsammlungen Dresden, 2002), 57–60.

6. William Barcham, "Two Views by Bernardo Bellotto: *View of Dresden with the Frauenkirche at Left* and *View of Dresden with the Hofkirche at Right*," *North Carolina Museum of Art Bulletin* 15 (1991): 14–28; Gregor J. M. Weber, "The Freedom of a Vedute Painter: Bernardo Bellotto in Dresden," in *Bernardo Bellotto and the Capitals of Europe*, ed. Edgar Peters Bowron (New Haven: Yale University Press, 2001), 15–25; and idem, "Bernardo Bellotto in Dresden (1747–1758 und 1762–1766)," in *Bernardo Bellotto genannt Canaletto: Europäische Veduten*, ed. Wilfried Seipel (Vienna: Kunsthistorisches Museum, 2005), 81–99.

7. Bowron, *Bernardo Bellotto*, 150.

8. All these buildings were either damaged or destroyed in the Allied bombing of February 1945. For their prior appearance, see Fritz Löffler, *Das alte Dresden: Geschichte seiner Bauten* (Leipzig: E. A. Seemann, 1981), 195–210; on the Frauenkirche, see *George Bähr: Die Frauenkirche und das bürgerliche Bauen in Dresden* (Dresden: Staatliche Kunstsammlungen Dresden, 2000).

9. Barcham, "Two Views," 23.

10. A retelling of the Oedipus story, this work premiered in 1664 to mixed reviews. See Nicholas Cronk and Alain Viala, eds., *La réception de Racine à l'âge classique: De la scène au moment* (Oxford: Voltaire Foundation, 2005).

11. Ronald Taylor, *Berlin and Its Culture* (New Haven: Yale University Press, 1997), chap. 4.

12. Dimitri Shvidkovsky, *The Empress and the Architect: British Architecture and Gardens at the Court of Catherine the Great* (New Haven: Yale University Press, 1996), 167–72.

13. See Sergey Androsov, "Catherine II's Taste for Classicism," in *Catherine the Great: Art for Empire*, ed. Nathalie Bondil (Montreal: Montreal Museum of Fine Arts, 2005), 193–99.

14. Ian Kelly, *Casanova: Actor, Lover, Priest, Spy* (New York: Penguin, 2008), 280.

15. Asen Kirin, *Exuberance of Meaning: The Art Patronage of Catherine the Great (1762–1796)* (Athens: Georgia Museum of Art, 2013), 117.

16. Catherine's self-awareness was often interpreted as vanity. See Isabel de Madariaga, *Catherine the Great: A Short History* (New Haven: Yale University Press, 1990), 205–6.

17. Kelly, *Casanova*, 287, 291.

18. H 10:173–86. See also Casanova's 1780 account, *The Duel*, trans. J. G. Nichols (London: Hesperus Press,

2003); the exchange of insults is found on pp. 21–30 and the duel itself is recounted on pp. 35–41.

19. *Istoria delle turbolenze della Polonia dalla morte di Elisabetta Petrowna fino alla pace fra la Russia e la porta ottomana* (Gorizia, Italy, 1774).

20. Andrzej Rottermund, "Bellotto in Warsaw," in Bowron, *Bernardo Bellotto*, 33–39; and idem, *Bernardo Bellotto: A Venetian Painter in Warsaw* (Milan: 5 Continents, 2004).

21. Kelly, *Casanova*, 157.

22. Derek Parker, *Casanova* (Stroud: Sutton, 2002), 246.

23. Ibid., 247. On the castle, see Lubi Pořízka and Petr Kroupa, *Klenody hradů a zámků České republiky* (Brno: Barrister & Principal, 2004), 56–57; for how the estate came into Waldstein possession, see Thomas DaCosta Kaufmann, *Court, Cloister, and City: The Art and Culture of Central Europe, 1450–1800* (Chicago: University of Chicago Press, 1995), 250.

24. Parker, *Casanova*, 246.

25. Childs, *Casanova*, 288. It does not appear that Casanova and Goethe ever met.

26. Philip Mansel, *Prince of Europe: The Life of Charles-Joseph de Ligne 1735–1814* (London: Weidenfeld and Nicolson, 2003), 179–81.

27. H. E. Weidinger, "The 'Dux Drafts': Casanova's Contribution to Da Ponte's and Mozart's *Don Giovanni*," *Maske und Kothurn* 52, no. 4 (2006): 98.

28. *Icosameron, ou histoire d'Edouard et Elisabeth* (Prague, 1788); *Casanova's Icosameron, or The Story of Edward and Elizabeth*, trans. Rachel Zurer (New York: Jenna, 1986).

29. Mansel, *Prince of Europe*, 179–81.

30. Childs, *Casanova*, 283–84.

31. Ibid., 284–86; Kelly, *Casanova*, 332–37; Weidinger, "Dux Drafts," 122–30.

MAN OF NUMBERS

1. See Clare Haru Crowston, *Credit, Fashion, Sex: Economies of Regard in Old Regime France* (Durham, N.C.: Duke University Press, 2014), and Laurence Fontaine, *The Moral Economy: Poverty, Credit, and Trust in Early Modern Europe* (Cambridge, England: Cambridge University Press, 2014).

2. The phrase is used to mean *sans fondement* (without a foundation). Antoine Furetière, *Dictionnaire universel…*, 2nd ed., 3 vols. (The Hague and Rotterdam: Arnoud and Reinier Leers, 1701), vol. 1. See also Laurence Fontaine, "Antonio and Shylock: Credit and Trust in France, c. 1680–c. 1780," *The Economic History Review* 54 (Feb. 2001): 40.

3. H 1:26–27. A famous example of an assault on the insubstantiality of credit is Montesquieu's 1721 caricature of John Law as a propagator of illusions; see *The Persian Letters*, trans. Christopher Betts (London: Penguin, 1993), 256–58. See also Crowston, *Credit, Fashion, Sex*, esp. chaps. 2 and 5.

4. H 3:130. On his return trip to Paris, Casanova discovered that "my old acquaintances had different houses and different fortunes, I found the rich become poor, the poor rich" (H 10:290).

5. Louis-Sébastein Mercier, *Tableau de Paris*, new ed., 12 vols. (Amsterdam, 1782–88), vol. 2, chap. 191, p. 300. For a synopsis of eighteenth-century roguery see Stefan Zweig, *Casanova: A Study in Self-Portraiture* (1929; rept. London: Pushkin Press, 1998), 29–38.

6. For a discussion of this enigmatic drawing, whose attribution is not fully certain, see Marianne Roland Michel in *Mastery and Elegance: Two Centuries of French Drawings from the Collection of Jeffrey E. Horvitz*, ed. Alvin L. Clark, Jr., exh. cat. (Cambridge, Mass.: Harvard University Art Museums, 1998), 264, no. 76.

7. The bill of exchange was crucial to credit's expansion: it enabled commerce to take place in the absence of specie, facilitating international business transactions by permitting currency exchange. In a typical three-party transaction, the person drawing the bill of exchange would contract a second party (the drawee) to pay a third party. However, with the rising use of bills of

exchange, the drawee as a named individual (the person whose credit the bill was drawn against) disappeared: "Because an instrument could be endorsed multiple times before falling due, a large number of people could be held liable for it, even though many might be complete strangers to each other." Amalia D. Kessler, *A Revolution in Commerce: The Parisian Merchant Court and the Rise of Commercial Society in Eighteenth-Century France* (New Haven: Yale University Press, 2007), 204; see also 188–237.

8. H 1:237. For the episode in Grenoble, see 7:38–46.

9. Richard T. Gray, "Buying into Signs: Money and Semiosis in Eighteenth-Century German Language Theory," *The German Quarterly* 69, no. 1 (Winter 1996): 1–14.

10. Like money, names—Casanova goes on to assert—are devoid of inherent value, "for it is possible," he tells the official, "that you are not the son of the man whom you believe to be your father" (H 8:40).

11. Among his ill-advised business liaisons was one with P.C., a dissolute libertine whose sister had captured Casanova's heart. P.C. essentially endeavored to sell his sister to Casanova in exchange for an investment in his doomed business ventures. See H 3:240–301.

12. H 10:27–32. Casanova's experiences with fake bills of exchange illustrate the risks that accompanied their proliferation. Another example is the instrument brandished by the comte de l'Étoile, an actor posing as a wealthy aristocrat, who later winds up in prison (H 11:225–61).

13. The work featured among the illustrations in *Monument du costume physique et moral de la fin du dix-huitième siècle* (Neuwied: Société typographique, 1789), with text by Nicolas-Edme Rétif de la Bretonne and illustrations by Jean-Michel Moreau Le Jeune and Sigmund Freudeberg.

14. The recurrence of certain figures—including the hunchback at left—in Guardi's pictures of the ridotto has prompted one scholar to suggest as the basis for the subject a contemporaneous play, Carlo Goldoni's *Le donne gelose* (The Jealous Women, 1752). Alice Binion, *Antonio and Francesco Guardi: Their Life and Milieu with a Catalogue of Their Figure Drawings* (New York: Garland, 1976), 234.

15. Thomas M. Kavanagh, *Dice, Cards, Wheels: A Different History of French Culture* (Philadelphia: University of Pennsylvania Press, 2005), 94.

16. "Although Venice may have been the Las Vegas of the Enlightenment, gambling . . . was an all but universal passion." Thomas M. Kavanagh, *Esthetics of the Moment: Literature and Art in the French Enlightenment* (Philadelphia: University of Pennsylvania Press, 1996), 112; on Casanova as gambler, see also 101–25, and Kavanaugh, *Dice, Cards, Wheels*, 85–109.

17. H 3:245, 4:34, 1:27. Ian Kelly suggests that Casanova's "bedpost notches" numbered between 122 and 136, in *Casanova: Actor, Lover, Priest, Spy* (New York: Jeremy P. Tarcher/Penguin, 2008), 124.

18. When C.C. is sentenced by her father to a nunnery, Casanova gambles away all his money and then wins it back (H 3:277, 286–87). His subsequent romance with M.M. is marked similarly by winnings at the casino; see, for example, H 4:123–25.

19. A Dutch volume satirizing the financial disasters makes much of such iconography, from its title page featuring an image of Law as a male suitor to the recurrence in its prints of lascivious satyrs and bubble-blowing cupids. See William Goetzmann et al., eds., *The Great Mirror of Folly: Finance, Culture, and the Crash of 1720* (New Haven: Yale University Press, 2013).

MAN OF LETTERS

1. Translations from *Histoire de ma vie* are my own; citations of corresponding passages in the translation by Willard Trask are provided for reference.

2. Letter to the prince de Ligne, summer 1794, quoted in V 3:937.

3. *Histoire de ma fuite des prisons de la République de Venise qu'on appelle les Plombs, écrite à Dux en*

Bohême l'année 1787 (Leipzig [Prague], 1788).

4. Ian Kelly, *Casanova: Actor, Spy, Lover, Priest* (London: Hodder and Stoughton, 2008), 32.

5. J. Rives Childs, *Casanova: A Biography Based on New Documents* (London: George Allen and Unwin, 1961), 12.

6. V 2:589; H 7:187. The gift book was *Pandectarum liber unicus*, undoubtedly part of a collection of Roman legal decisions (*Pandectes*, or *Digestes*), established by order of the emperor Justinian in 530 and often republished. See editors' note, V 2:1239.

7. "Men of Letters," in Diderot and D'Alembert's *Encyclopédie ou Dictionnaire raisonné des sciences, des arts et des métiers* (1751–72).

8. At a masked ball at the court, Casanova was able to identify as an acquaintance a Parisian woman who imitated turns of phrase he had introduced in the circles he frequented: "Oh, the fancy event! The dear man!" (V 3:259; H 10:103).

9. Casanova reports that the abbé penned the play *Les Israélites à la montagne d'Horeb* in "charming free verse" after their discussion (V 1:641, 1069, 1288n192; H 3:177–78).

10. Casanova, *À Leonard Snetlage, Docteur en Droit de l'Université de Goettingue* (n.p., 1797), cited in Childs, *Casanova*, 283.

11. See C. W. Stollery, "Casanova's Meeting with Samuel Johnson," *Casanova Gleanings* 7 (1964): 1–4; also Casanova's anecdote of the encounter in *À Leonard Snetlage*, 53–55.

12. Giacomo Casanova, *Scrutinio del libro "Éloges de M. de Voltaire par différens auteurs"* (Venice, 1779).

13. Cited in Jean-Christophe Igalens, *L'écrivain en ses fictions* (Paris: Garnier, 2011), 167

14. *Les Thessaliennes, ou Arlequin au Sabbat*, Casanova's first play, cowritten with Le Prévost d'Exmes and staged at the Comédie-Italienne in Paris, has disappeared, as has *La Moluccheide*, a transposition of Racine's *Thebaid* into an Italian comedy.

15. *Zoroastro, tragedia tradotta del Francese, da rappresentarsi nel Reggio Elettoral Teatro di Dresda... nel Carnovale dell'anno 1752* (Dresden, 1752).

16. *Dell'Iliade di Omero, tradotta in ottava rima da Giacomo Casanova Viniziano*, 3 vols. (Venice, 1775–78); in Venetian dialect, ed. Carlo Odo Pavese (Venice, 2005). *Lettere della nobil Donna Silvia Belegno alla nobil Donzella Laura Gussoni* (Venice, 1780), and *Di aneddoti viniziani militari e damorosi del secolo decimo quarto...* (1782).

17. He asserted the importance of philology in a letter of January 10, 1791, to J. F. Opiz, cited in Igalens, *Casanova*, 142. Among Casanova's many pseudonyms were Eupolemo Pantaxeno (the brave warrior without a country) and Polutropos (the man with a thousand tricks), usually given to Ulysses (ibid., 144).

18. Giacomo Casanova, *Icosameron, ou Histoire d'Édouard, et d'Élizabeth qui passèrent quatre-vingts-un ans chez les Mégamicres habitans aborigènes du Protocosme dans l'intérieur de notre globe* (Prague: Schönfeld, 1787).

19. V 3:1061n31; H 11:42. See Furio Lucichenti, *Intermédiaire des Casanovistes* 27 (2010): 25–30. For the Sierra Morena project, see *Pages casanoviennes: Correspondance inédite de Jacques Casanova, 1767–1772* (Paris: Jean Fort, 1925),19–35, quoted in V 3:486n3. For the Gregorian calendar, see V 3:1031n8; H 10:357n6. See also Giacomo Casanova, *Prosopopea Ecaterina II und Istanza*, with excerpts from an unpublished memoir, *Rêveriessur la mesure moyenne de notre année sous la Reformation grégorienne par Jacques Casanova de Seingalt Docteur ès loix bibliothécaire de Monsieur le comte de Waldstein*, ed. Enrico Straub (Frankfurt am Main: Peter Lang, 1993).

20. Giacomo Casanova, *Lana caprina: Epistola di un licantropo* (Bologna, 1772).

21. Giacomo Casanova, *Solution du problème déliaque démontré par J. Casanova de Seingalt...* (Dresden, 1790).

22. Voltaire, "Men of Letters."

23. See Giacomo Casanova, *Soliloque d'un penseur* (Prague, 1786).

24. Quoted in *Mémoires et mélanges historiques et littéraires par Le Prince de Ligne* (Paris, 1828), 4:42.

25. Giacomo Casanova, *Confutazione della Storia del governo veneto d'Amelot de la Houssaie...*, 3 vols. (Amsterdam [Lugano]:Pietro Mortier, 1769).

26. In a rare moment of reflection, he asserted: "I see today that in order to be a true sage in the world, I would have needed only the smallest set of circumstances, for virtue always had for me more charms than vice" (V 3:217–18; H 10:53).

27. Casanova's discontent with his circumstances is expressed in nineteen insulting letters to the majordomo of the Count of Waldstein, Georg Feldkirchner, with whom he fought and whose name he altered disparagingly. For the text of these letters, see "Dix-neuf lettres adressées à Faulkurcher, maître d'hotel du comte de Waldstein seigneur de Dux par Jacques Casanova de Seingalt Vénitien," V 3:956–75. The quotation is from Letter 4 (V 3:959).

Select Bibliography

Baetjer, Katharine, and Joseph G. Links. *Canaletto*. Exh. cat. New York: Metropolitan Museum of Art, 1989.

Bailey, Colin B., ed. *The Age of Watteau, Chardin, and Fragonard: Masterpieces of French Genre Painting*. Exh. cat. New Haven: Yale University Press in association with the National Gallery of Canada, Ottawa, 2003.

Beddington, Charles. *Canaletto in England. A Venetian Artist Abroad, 1746–1755*. Exh. cat. New Haven: Yale University Press, 2006.

Binion, Alice. *Antonio and Francesco Guardi: Their Life and Milieu with a Catalogue of Their Figure Drawings*. New York: Garland, 1976.

Bleackley, Horace, ed. *Casanova in England*. New York: Knopf, 1925.

Bowron, Edgar Peters, ed. *Bernardo Bellotto and the Capitals of Europe*. New Haven: Yale University Press, 2001.

Bremer-David, Charissa, ed. *Paris: Life and Luxury in the Eighteenth Century*. Exh. cat. Los Angeles: J. Paul Getty Museum, 2011.

Breuinger, Scott, and David Burrow, eds. *Sociability and Cosmopolitanism: Social Bonds on the Fringes of the Enlightenment*. London: Routledge, 2012.

Brewer, John. *The Pleasures of the Imagination: English Culture in the Eighteenth Century*. New York: Farrar, Straus & Giroux, 1997.

Brown, Beverly Louise, ed. *Giambattista Tiepolo: Master of the Oil Sketch*. Exh. cat. New York: Abbeville, 1993.

Buck, Mitchell S. *The Life of Casanova from 1774 to 1798: A Supplement to the Memoirs*. New York: Nicholas L. Brown, 1924.

Campagnol, Isabella. *Forbidden Fashions. Invisible Luxuries in Early Venetian Convents*. Lubbock: Texas Tech University Press, 2014.

Castle, Terry. *Masquerade and Civilization: The Carnivalesque in Eighteenth-Century English Culture and Fiction*. Stanford, Cal.: Stanford University Press, 1986.

Childs, J. Rives. *Casanova: A Biography Based on New Documents*. London: George Allen and Unwin, 1961.

——. *Casanova: A New Perspective*. New York: Paragon House, 1988.

——. *Casanova: An Annotated World Bibliography of Jacques Casanova de Seingalt and of Works Concerning Him*. Vienna: C. M. Nebehay, 1956.

Clark, Alvin L., Jr., ed. *Mastery and Elegance: Two Centuries of French Drawings from the Collection of Jeffrey E. Horvitz*. Exh. cat. Cambridge, Mass.: Harvard University Art Museums, 1998.

Clark, Alvin L., et al. *Genius and Grace: François Boucher and the Generation of 1700*. Exh. cat. Boston: The Horvitz Collection, 2014.

Christiansen, Keith, ed. *Giambattista Tiepolo 1696–1770*. Exh. cat. New York: Metropolitan Museum of Art, 1996.

Constable, William George, and Joseph G. Links. *Canaletto: Giovanni Antonio Canal, 1697–1768*. 2 vols. Oxford: Clarendon Press, 1989.

Crow, Thomas E. *Painters and Public Life in Eighteenth-Century Paris*. New Haven: Yale University Press, 1985.

Faroult, Guillaume. *Fragonard amoureux: Galant et libertin*. Exh. cat. Paris: Réunion des musées nationaux, 2015.

Fontaine, Laurence. *The Moral Economy: Poverty, Credit, and Trust in Early Modern Europe*. Cambridge, England: Cambridge University Press, 2014.

Goodman, Elise. *The Portraits of Madame de Pompadour: Celebrating the Femme Savant*. Exh. cat. Berkeley: University of California Press, 2002.

González, Kathleen Ann. *Casanova's Venice: A Walking Guide*. Venice: Supernova, 2013.

Haskell, Francis. *Patrons and Painters: A Study in the Relations between Italian Art and Society in the Age of the Baroque*, rev. ed. New Haven: Yale University Press, 1980.

Howard, Deborah. *The Architectural History of Venice*, rev. ed. New Haven: Yale University Press, 2002.

Hyde, Melissa. *Making Up the Rococo: François Boucher and His Critics*. Los Angeles: Getty Research Institute, 2006.

Il mondo di Giacomo Casanova: Un veneziano in Europa, 1725–1798. Exh. cat. Venice: Marsilio, 1998.

Jazzar, Bernard N., and J. Patrice Marandel. *Eye for the Sensual: Selections from the Resnick Collection*. Exh. cat. Stuttgart: Dr. Cantz'sche Druckerei, 2010.

Johnson, James H. *Venice Incognito: Masks in the Serene Republic*. Berkeley: University of California Press, 2011.

Kanz, Roland. *Die Brüder Casanova: Künstler und Abenteurer*. Berlin: Deutsche Kunstverlag, 2013.

Kavanagh, Thomas M. *Esthetics of the Moment: Literature and Art in the French Enlightenment*. Philadelphia: University of Pennsylvania Press, 1996.

Kelly, Ian. *Casanova: Actor, Lover, Priest, Spy*. New York: Penguin, 2008.

Kessler, Amalia D. *A Revolution in Commerce: The Parisian Merchant Court and the Rise of Commercial Society in Eighteenth-Century France*. New Haven: Yale University Press, 2007.

Laing, Alastair, et al. *François Boucher, 1703–1770*. Exh. cat. New York: Metropolitan Museum of Art, 1986.

Lane, Frederic C. *Venice: A Maritime Republic*. Baltimore: Johns Hopkins University Press, 1973.

Laven, Mary. *Virgins of Venice: Enclosed Lives and Broken Vows in the Renaissance Convent*. London: Viking, 2002.

Lemire, Beverly. *Dress, Culture and Commerce*. London: Macmillan, 1997.

Levey, Michael. *Painting in Eighteenth-Century Venice*, 2nd ed. Ithaca, N.Y.: Cornell University Press, 1980.

Maczak, Antoni. *Travel in Early Modern Europe*. Translated by Ursula Phillips. Cambridge, England: Polity, 1995.

Mariuz, Adriano, Giuseppe Pavanello, and Giandomenico Romanelli. *Pietro Longhi*. Exh. cat. Milan: Electa, 1993.

Martineau, Jane, and Andrew Robinson, eds. *The Glory of Venice: Art in the Eighteenth Century*. Exh. cat. Washington, D.C.: National Gallery of Art, 1994.

Muldrew, Craig. *The Economy of Obligation: The Culture of Credit and Social Relations in Early Modern England*. London: Palgrave Macmillan, 1998.

Nettl, Paul. *The Other Casanova: A Contribution to Eighteenth-Century Music and Manners*. New York: Philosophical Library, 1950.

Norwich, John Julius. *A History of Venice*. New York: Knopf, 1982.

Parker, Derek. *Casanova*. Stroud, England: Sutton, 2002.

Pieri, Piero. *Casanova: L'eroe libertino e il teatro dell'autobiografia*. Ravenna: Giorgio Pozzi, 2015.

Prévost, Marie-Laure, and Chantal Thomas, eds. *Casanova: La passion de la liberté*. Exh. cat. Paris: Bibliothèque nationale de France/ Seuil, 2011.

Rand, Richard with Juliette M. Bianco and Mark Ledbury. *Intimate Encounters: Love and Domesticity in Eighteenth-Century France*. Exh. cat. Hanover, N.H.: Hood Museum of Art; Princeton: Princeton University Press, 1997.

Redford, Bruce. *Venice and the Grand Tour*. New Haven: Yale University Press, 1996.

Ribeiro, Aileen. *Dress in Eighteenth-Century Europe*. New Haven: Yale University Press, 2002.

Roche, Daniel. *The Culture of Clothing: Dress and Fashion in the Ancien Regime*. Translated by Jean Birrell. Cambridge, England: Cambridge University Press, 1996.

——. *France in the Enlightenment*. Translated by Arthur Goldhammer. Cambridge, Mass.: Harvard University Press, 1998.

Romano, Dennis. *Patricians and Populani: The Social Foundations of the Renaissance Venetian State*. Baltimore: Johns Hopkins University Press, 1987.

Rosenberg, Pierre. *Fragonard*. Exh. cat. New York: Metropolitan Museum of Art, 1988.

Rossi, Toto Bergamo. *Inside Venice: A Private View of the City's Most Beautiful Interiors*. New York: Rizzoli, 2015.

Rottermund, Andrzej. *Bernardo Bellotto: A Venetian Painter in Warsaw*. Exh. cat. Milan: 5 Continents, 2004.

Salmon, Xavier, ed. *Jean-Marc Nattier 1685–1766*. Exh. cat. Versailles: Musée national des châteaux de Versailles et de Trianon, 1999.

——. *Madame de Pompadour et les arts*. Exh. cat. Versailles: Musée national des châteaux de Versailles et de Trianon, 2002.

Scott, Katie. *The Rococo Interior: Decoration and Social Spaces in Eighteenth-Century Paris*. New Haven: Yale University Press, 1995.

Selvatico, Riccardo. *Cento note per Casanova a Venezia (1753–1756)*. Vicenza: Neri Pozza, 1997.

Shawe-Taylor, Desmond, ed. *The First Georgians. Art and Monarchy, 1714–1760*. Exh. cat. London: Royal Collection Trust, 2014.

Sheriff, Mary D. *J. H. Fragonard. Art and Eroticism*. Chicago: University of Chicago Press, 1990.

——. *Moved by Love: Inspired Artists and Deviant Women in Eighteenth-Century France*. Chicago: University of Chicago Press, 2004.

Summers, Judith. *Casanova's Women: The Great Seducer and the Women He Loved*. New York: Bloomsbury, 2006.

Thomas, Chantal. *Casanova: Un voyage libertine*. Paris: Denoël, 1985.

Thornton, Peter. *Baroque and Rococo Silks*. London: Faber and Faber, 1965.

White, Jerry. *A Great and Monstrous Thing: London in the Eighteenth Century*. Cambridge, Mass.: Harvard University Press, 2013.

Ziskin, Rochelle. *Sheltering Art: Collection and Social Identity in Early Eighteenth-Century Paris*. University Park: Pennsylvania State University Press, 2012.

Zweig, Stefan. *Casanova: A Study in Self-Portraiture*. Translated by Eden Paul and Cedar Paul. London: Pushkin Press, 1998

List of Illustrations

Exhibition venues are indicated as follows: *FW*, Kimbell Art Museum, Fort Worth; *SF*, Fine Arts Museums of San Francisco; *B*, Museum of Fine Arts, Boston

THE ART OF DISPLAY

1

Giovanni Antonio Canal, called Canaletto (Italian, 1697–1768)
The Square of Saint Mark's and the Piazzetta, about 1731
Oil on canvas
66 × 102.9 cm (26 × 40 ½ in.)
Wadsworth Atheneum Museum of Art, Hartford, Connecticut
The Ella Gallup Sumner and Mary Catlin Sumner Collection Fund, 1947.2
Photograph: Allen Phillips/Wadsworth Atheneum

SF, B

2

Giovanni Antonio Canal, called Canaletto (Italian, 1697–1768)
Saint Mark's Basin, about 1738
Oil on canvas
124.5 × 204.5 cm (49 × 80 ½ in.)
Museum of Fine Arts, Boston
Abbott Lawrence Fund, Seth K. Sweetser Fund, and Charles Edward French Fund, 39.290

FW, SF, B

3

Francesco Narice (Italian, about 1722–1785)
Giacomo Casanova (?), about 1767–70
Oil on canvas
152 × 130 cm (59 ⅞ × 51 ⅛ in.)
Collezione Bignami, Genoa
Photograph: Andrea Sorgoli, Genoa

4

Jean-Honoré Fragonard (French, 1732–1806)
The Bolt, about 1777
Oil on canvas
73 × 93 cm (28 ¾ × 36 ⅝ in.)
Musée du Louvre, R.F. 1974-2
Image © RMN-Grand Palais/Art Resource, NY

5

Console table, Italian (Venice), about 1725–50
Carved and gilded wood
80.6 × 124.5 × 62.2 cm (31 ¾ × 49 × 24 ½ in.)
Collection of The John and Mable Ringling Museum of Art, the State Art Museum of

Florida, Florida State University, Sarasota, Florida
Museum Purchase, 1949, SN1531

FW, SF, B

6

Armchair, Italian (Venice), about 1750
Walnut
96 × 60 × 50 cm (37 3/4 × 23 5/8 × 19 5/8 in.)
Isabella Stewart Gardner Museum, F19e5.1

FW, SF, B

7

Pair of wall lights, 1750–60
Possibly by Jean-Claude Duplessis (French, 1699–1774), François-Thomas Germain (French, 1726–1791), or Jacques Caffieri (French, 1678–1755)
Gilded bronze
Each: 88.9 × 61 × 30.5 cm (35 × 24 × 12 in.)
Museum of Fine Arts, Boston
Museum purchase with funds donated anonymously and the John H. and Ernestine A. Payne Fund, Mary S. and Edward J. Holmes Fund, Frank B. Bemis Fund, Arthur Tracy Cabot Fund, Helen and Alice Colburn Fund, Edwin E. Jack Fund, Elizabeth M. and John F. Paramino Fund in memory of John F. Paramino, Boston Sculptor, Harriet Otis Cruft Fund, Frederick Brown Fund, Seth K. Sweetser Fund, Helen B. Sweeney Fund, Susan Cornelia Warren Fund, Samuel Putnam Avery Fund, Jane Marsland and Judith A. Marsland Fund, Alice M. Bartlett Fund, and Mary E. Moore Gift, 2017.83.1-2

FW, SF, B

8

Giovanni Antonio Canal, called Canaletto (Italian, 1697–1768)
View of the Molo, about 1730–35
Oil on canvas
113 × 160.7 cm (44 1/2 × 63 1/4 in.)
El Paso Museum of Art
Gift of the Samuel H. Kress Foundation, 1961.1.49

FW, SF, B

9

Jean-Marc Nattier (French, 1685–1766)
Manon Balletti, 1757
Oil on canvas
54 × 47.5 cm (21 1/4 × 18 3/4 in.)
National Gallery, London
Bequeathed by Emilie Yznaga, 1945, NG5586
Image © National Gallery, London/Art Resource, NY

FW, SF, B

10

Snuffbox, German (probably Dresden), about 1760–65
Gold, agate, enamel; miniature on inside of lid
5.1 × 9.4 cm (2 × 3 3/4 in.)
Museum of Fine Arts, Boston
Gift of Mrs. Albert J. Beveridge in memory of Delia Spencer Field, 48.1333

FW, SF, B

11

Snuffbox, English, about 1750–60
Gold, gray agate, diamonds, rubies, enamel
4 × 6 × 6.2 cm (1 5/8 × 2 3/8 × 2 1/2 in.)
Museum of Fine Arts, Boston
Gift of the heirs of Bettina Looram de Rothschild, 2013.1751

FW, SF, B

12

François Boucher (French, 1703–1770)
Resting Girl or *Blond Odalisque*, 1751
Oil on canvas
59.5 × 73.5 cm (23 3/8 × 28 7/8 in.)
Wallraf-Richartz Museum & Fondation Corboud, Cologne, WRM 2639
Image © Rheinisches Bildarchiv

FW, SF, B

13

Anton Raphael Mengs (German, 1728–1779)
Self-Portrait, 1776
Oil on canvas
90 × 65.5 cm (35 1/2 × 25 7/8 in.)
The Metropolitan Museum of Art, New York
Harris Brisbane Dick Fund, 2010, 2010.445
www.metmuseum.org

FW, SF, B

14

Francesco Casanova (Italian, 1727–1803)
Giacomo Casanova, about 1751
Red chalk on paper
20 × 15 cm (7 7/8 × 5 7/8 in.)
State Historical Museum, Moscow
Photograph © State Historical Museum, Moscow

15

Pietro Longhi (Italian, 1701–1785)
Abate François-Joachim de Pierre de Bernis, French Ambassador to Venice, 1753–55
Oil on canvas
46.6 × 38.5 cm (18 3/8×15 1/8 in.)
Private collection
Photograph: Arte fotografica, Rome

VENICE

16

Giovanni Antonio Canal, called Canaletto (Italian, 1697–1768)
Entrance to the Grand Canal, about 1730
Oil on canvas
49.6 × 73.6 cm (19 1/2 × 29 in.)
The Museum of Fine Arts, Houston
The Robert Lee Blaffer Memorial Collection, gift of Sarah Campbell Blaffer, 56.2

FW, SF, B

17

Giovanni Antonio Canal, called Canaletto (Italian, 1697–1768)
The Grand Canal Near the Rialto Bridge, about 1730
Oil on canvas
49.7 × 73 cm (19 5/8 × 28 3/4 in.)
The Museum of Fine Arts, Houston
The Robert Lee Blaffer Memorial Collection, gift of Sarah Campbell Blaffer, 55.103

FW, SF, B

18

Giovanni Antonio Canal, called Canaletto (Italian, 1697–1768)
The Grand Canal from Campo San Vio, 1730–35
Oil on canvas
114 × 161.3 cm (44 7/8 × 63 1/2 in.)
Memphis Brooks Museum of Art, Memphis, Tennessee
Gift of the Samuel H. Kress Foundation, 61.216

FW, SF, B

19

Giovanni Battista Tiepolo (Italian, 1696–1770)
Apollo and the Continents, about 1739
Oil on canvas
99.1 × 63.5 cm (39 × 25 in.)
Kimbell Art Museum, Fort Worth, Texas, AP 1985.04

FW, SF, B

20

Giovanni Battista Tiepolo (Italian, 1696–1770)
Time Unveiling Truth, about 1758
Oil on canvas
231.1 × 167 cm (91 × 65 3/4 in.)
Museum of Fine Arts, Boston
Charles Potter Kling Fund, 61.1200

FW, SF, B

21

Giovanni Battista Tiepolo (Italian, 1696–1770)
The Empire of Flora, about 1743

Oil on canvas
71.8 × 88.9 cm (28 ¼ × 35 in.)
Fine Arts Museums of San Francisco
Gift of the Samuel H. Kress Foundation, 61.44.19

FW, SF, B

22

Pietro Longhi (Italian, 1702–1785)
The Music Lesson (The Bird Cage), about 1740–45
Oil on canvas
56.5 × 43.8 cm (22 ¼ × 17 ¼ in.)
Fine Arts Museums of San Francisco
Gift of Mortimer Leventritt, 1952.83

FW, SF, B

23

Pietro Longhi (Italian, 1702–1785)
The Concert (The Mandolin Recital), about 1760
Oil on canvas
58.4 × 47.6 cm (23 × 18 ¾ in.)
Fine Arts Museums of San Francisco
Gift of Kathryn Bache Miller, 1964.71

FW, SF, B

24

Pietro Longhi (Italian, 1702–1785)
The Temptation, about 1745
Oil on canvas
49.5 × 61 cm (19 ½ × 24 in.)
Wadsworth Atheneum Museum of Art, Hartford, Connecticut
The Ella Gallup Sumner and Mary Catlin Sumner Collection Fund, 1931.188
Photograph: Allen Phillips/Wadsworth Atheneum

FW, SF, B

25

Giovanni Antonio Canal, called Canaletto (Italian, 1697–1768)
San Cristoforo, San Michele, and Murano from the Fondamenta Nuove, 1722–23
Oil on canvas
143.5 × 151.1 cm (56 ½ × 59 ½ in.)
Dallas Museum of Art
Foundation for the Arts Collection, Mrs. John B. O'Hara Fund, 1984.51.FA

FW, SF, B

26

Francesco Guardi (Italian, 1712–1793)
The Parlatorio, 1746
Oil on canvas
108 × 208 cm (42 ½ × 81 ⅞ in.)
Ca' Rezzonico, Venice, inv. Cl. I n. 0125
2016 © Photo Archive–Fondazione Musei Civici di Venezia

FW, SF, B

27

Martin van Meytens (Swedish, 1695–1770)
Kneeling Nun, about 1731
Oil on copper, painted on recto and verso
28 × 21 cm (11 × 8 ¼ in.)
Nationalmuseum, Stockholm
Photograph: front, Cecilia Hesser/Nationalmuseum; back, Erik Cornelius/Nationalmuseum

B

28

Angelo Gambini (Italian, 19th century)
Cross Section of the Prisons of the Palazzo Ducale
From Francesco Zanotto, *Il Palazzo Ducale di Venezia*, 4 vols. (Venice, 1842–60)
Harvard University Fine Arts Library, FA2185.219

29

Giovanni Battista Piranesi (Italian, 1720–1778)
The Well, plate XIII of the second edition, second issue, of the *Carceri*, 1761
Etching and engraving
Platemark: 40.9 × 55.5 cm (16 ⅛ × 21 ⅞ in.)
Museum of Fine Arts, Boston
Gift of Miss Ellen T. Bullard, 21.11686

FW, SF, B

30

Anton Raphael Mengs (German, 1728–1779) and studio
Pope Clement XIII, 1758 or later
Oil on canvas
137.6 × 98.3 cm (54 1/8 × 38 3/4 in.)
Ca' Rezzonico, Venice, inv. Cl. I n. 2373
2016 © Photo Archive–Fondazione Musei Civici di Venezia

FW, SF, B

THE THEATER OF IDENTITY

31

Jan Berka (Czech, 1759–1838)
Portrait of the author, frontispiece to Giacomo Casanova, *Icosameron* (Prague, 1787)
Engraving
General Collection, Beinecke Rare Book and Manuscript Library, Yale University, Hfd35 57x

32

Commedia dell'arte figures
Capodimonte manufactory, Italian (near Naples), active 1743–59
Modeled by Giuseppe Gricci (Italian, about 1700–1770)
Soft-paste porcelain with colored enamel and gilded decoration
Museum of Fine Arts, Boston

FW, SF, B

The Doctor and Isabella, about 1750
H. 14.6 cm (5 3/4 in.)
Kiyi and Edward M. Pflueger Collection. Bequest of Edward M. Pflueger and Gift of Kiyi Powers Pflueger, William Francis Warden Fund, and John H. and Ernestine A. Payne Fund, 2002.121

The Minuet, about 1750
H. 19.7 cm (7 3/4 in.)
Kiyi and Edward M. Pflueger Collection. Bequest of Edward M. Pflueger and Gift of Kiyi Powers Pflueger, 2006.953

Mezzetin, about 1750
H. 14.9 cm (5 7/8 in.)
Kiyi and Edward M. Pflueger Collection. Bequest of Edward M. Pflueger and Gift of Kiyi Powers Pflueger, 2006.943

Pantaloon, about 1745
H. 20.3 cm (8 in.)
Kiyi and Edward M. Pflueger Collection. Bequest of Edward M. Pflueger and Gift of Kiyi Powers Pflueger, 2006.962

The Doctor, Harlequin, and Colombine, about 1750
H. 16.5 cm (6 1/2 in.)
Kiyi and Edward M. Pflueger Collection. Bequest of Edward M. Pflueger and Gift of Kiyi Powers Pflueger, William Francis Warden Fund, and John H. and Ernestine A. Payne Fund, 2002.123

33

Gabriel de Saint-Aubin (French, 1724–1780)
Quinault and Lully's Opera "Armide" Performed at the Palais-Royal Opera House, 1761
Pen and brown ink, watercolor and gouache over graphite pencil on paper
31.1 × 50.2 cm (12 1/4 × 19 3/4 in.)
Museum of Fine Arts, Boston
Gift of Elizabeth Paine Card, in memory of her father, Robert Treat Paine 2nd, 1970.36

B

34

Jacopo Amigoni (Italian, about 1685–1752)
Carlo Maria Michelangelo Nicola Broschi, called Farinelli, about 1752
Oil on canvas
125.2 × 104.5 cm (49 1/4 × 41 1/8 in.)
Staatsgalerie Stuttgart, 3163

FW, SF

35

Claude Arnulphy (French, 1697–1786)
Adélaïde de Gueidan and Her Sister at the Harpsichord, about 1735–40

Oil on canvas
162 × 130 cm (63 ¾ × 51 ⅛ in.)
Musée Granet
Gueidan bequest, 1880, Inv. 880.1.7
Photograph: Hugo Maertens–Fondation BNP Paribas

FW, SF, B

36

Jean-Marc Nattier (French, 1685–1766)
Anne-Henriette de Bourbon, 1754
Oil on canvas
246 × 185 cm (96 ⅞ × 72 ⅞ in.)
Chateaux de Versailles et de Trianon, Versailles, France, Inv. no. MV3800
Image © RMN-Grand Palais/Art Resource, NY
Photograph: Daniel Arnaudet

37

Giovanni Domenico Tiepolo (Italian, 1727–1804)
The Minuet, 1756
Oil on canvas
80.7 × 109.3 cm (31 ¾ × 43 in.)
Museu Nacional d'Art de Catalunya, 064989-000
Image © Museu Nacional d'Art de Catalunya, Barcelona

38

Giovanni Domenico Tiepolo (Italian, 1727–1804)
The Charlatan, 1756
Oil on canvas
80.5 × 109 cm (31 ¾ × 43 in.)
Museu Nacional d'Art de Catalunya, 064988-000
Image © Museu Nacional d'Art de Catalunya

FW, SF, B

39

Pietro Longhi (Italian, 1702–1785)
The Perfume Seller, about 1757
Oil on canvas
61 × 51 cm (24 × 20 ⅛ in.)
Ca' Rezzonico, Venice, inv. Cl. I n. 0127
2016 © Photo Archive–Fondazione Musei Civici di Venezia

40

Gaetano Gherardo Zompini (Italian, 1700–1778)
Keeper of Theater Boxes, from *Le arti che vanno per via nella città di Venezia* (1785)
Illustrated book with 63 etchings
Closed: 52.8 × 37 × 2.5 cm (20 ¾ × 14 ⅗ × 1 in.)
Museum of Fine Arts, Boston
The Gift of Philip and Frances Hofer, 55.515

FW, SF, B

41

Nicolas Guérard (French, about 1648–1719)
The Perpetual Carnival–Universal Masquerade, 17th century
Etching
Bibliothèque nationale de France, Département des estampes et de la photographie, Reserve FCL-QB-201 (75)

42

Jean-Baptiste Henri Deshays (French, 1729–1765)
Bust of a Lady Holding a Mask, 1760
Oil on canvas
52 × 42 cm (20 ½ × 16 ½ in.)
Private collection
Photograph: Michael Gould

B

43

Jean-Marc Nattier (French, 1685–1766)
Thalia, Muse of Comedy, 1739
Oil on canvas
135.9 × 124.5 cm (53 ½ × 49 in.)
Fine Arts Museums of San Francisco
Museum purchase, Mildred Anna Williams Collection, 1954.59

FW, SF, B

44

Francis Hayman (English, about 1708–1776)
David Garrick and Mrs. Pritchard in Benjamin Hoadly's "The Suspicious Husband," 1747
Oil on canvas laid to board
71.4 × 91.8 cm (28 1/8 × 36 1/8 in.)
Yale Center for British Art
Paul Mellon Collection, B1976.7.35

FW, SF

PLEASURES OF THE ROAD

45

Trunk, mid-18th century
Labeled by John Selby (English, active in London about 1730–60)
Leather on wood studded with brass
54.6 × 109.9 × 58.4 cm (21 1/2 × 43 1/4 × 23 in.)
Museum of Fine Arts, Boston
Gift of Mary Adelaide Sargent Poor in memory of Adelaide Joanna Sargent, 47.1360

FW, SF, B

46

Giovanni Domenico Tiepolo (Italian, 1727–1804)
The Burchiello, about 1765
Oil on canvas
38 × 78.3 cm (15 × 30 7/8 in.)
Kunsthistorisches Museum, Vienna, GG6424
Photograph: KHM-Museumsverband

47

George Keate (English, 1729–1850)
The Manner of Passing Mount Cenis, August 1755, 1755
Gray wash with pen and black ink on paper
24.4 × 31.6 cm (9 5/8 × 12 1/2 in.)
British Museum, London, 209.304

48

Francesco Casanova (Italian, 1727–1803)
Collapse of the Bridge, about 1770
Oil on canvas
226 × 282 cm (89 3/8 × 111 3/8 in.)
Musée des Beaux-Arts, Rennes
Image © RMN-Grand Palais/Art Resource, NY
Photograph: Patrick Merret

FW, SF, B

49

Francesco Casanova (Italian, 1727–1803)
Travelers in a Storm, about 1770
Oil on canvas
229.5 × 286 cm (90 3/8 × 112 5/8 in.)
Musée des Beaux-Arts, Rennes
Image © RMN-Grand Palais/Art Resource, NY
Photograph: Patrick Merret

FW, SF, B

50

Unknown artist
What Is This My Son Tom?, 1774
Published by R. Sayer and J. Bennett, no. 53 Fleet Street, London
Mezzotint
35 × 25 cm (13 3/4 × 9 7/8 in.)
Library of Congress, 7081.1.1436

51

Jean-Étienne Liotard (Swiss, 1702–1789)
A Frankish Woman and Her Servant, about 1750
Oil on canvas
72.4 × 57.2 cm (28 1/2 × 22 1/2 in.)
The Nelson-Atkins Museum of Art, Kansas City, Missouri
Purchase: William Rockhill Nelson Trust, 56.3

FW, SF, B

PARIS

52

Jean-Marc Nattier (French, 1685–1766)
Zanetta Balletti, called Mademoiselle Silvia, 1750–58

Oil on canvas
48 × 42.5 cm (18 7/8 × 16 3/4 in.)
Private collection
Photograph © Private collection. All rights reserved

FW, SF, B

53

Nicolas Lancret (French, 1690–1743)
La Camargo Dancing, about 1730
Oil on canvas
76.2 × 106.7 cm (30 × 42 in.)
National Gallery of Art, Washington
Andrew W. Mellon Collection, 1937.1.89
Photograph courtesy of National Gallery of Art, Washington

54

Gabriel de Saint-Aubin (French, 1724–1780)
View of the Salon of 1753, 1753
Etching
Image: 14.8 × 18.1 cm (5 7/8 × 7 1/8 in.)
The Metropolitan Museum of Art, New York
Wrightsman Fund, 2006, 2006.84
www.metmuseum.org

55

François Boucher (French, 1703–1770)
Jeanne-Antoinette Poisson, marquise de Pompadour, 1750, with later additions
Oil on canvas
81.2 × 64.9 cm (32 × 25 1/2 in.)
Harvard Art Museums/Fogg Museum
Bequest of Charles E. Dunlap, 1966.47
Photograph: Imaging Department © President and Fellows of Harvard College

B

56

Toilette service of the duchesse de Cadaval, 1738–39
Étienne Pollet (French, active 1715–51)
Silver, glass, hair
Mirror h. 66 cm (26 in.)
Detroit Institute of Arts
Founders Society Purchase, Elizabeth Parke Firestone Collection of Early French Silver Fund, 53.177-192
Image © Detroit Institute of Arts, USA/ Bridgeman Images

57

Jean-Baptiste Lemoyne the younger (French, 1704–1778)
Louis XV, 1757
White marble
77.5 × 64.1 × 41.6 cm (30 1/2 × 25 1/4 × 16 3/8 in.)
The Metropolitan Museum of Art, New York
Gift of George Blumenthal, 1941, 41.100.244
www.metmuseum.org
FW

58

Charles-Nicolas Cochin the younger (French, 1715–1790)
Marquise de Pompadour in a Scene from "Acis and Galatea," 1749
Gouache over graphite with traces of pen and brown ink on ivory laid paper, with gold-leaf paper borders
16.5 × 41 cm (6 1/2 × 16 1/8 in.)
National Gallery of Canada, Ottawa
Purchased 2006, 41953
Image © National Gallery of Canada

SF

59

François Boucher (French, 1703–1770)
Venus at Vulcan's Forge, 1769
Oil on canvas
273.5 × 204.7 cm (107 5/8 × 80 5/8 in.)
Kimbell Art Museum, Fort Worth, Texas, AP 1972.09

FW, SF, B

60

François Boucher (French, 1703–1770)
Aurora and Cephalus, 1769
Oil on canvas
265 × 86 cm (104 3/8 × 33 7/8 in.)

The J. Paul Getty Museum, Los Angeles, 71. PA.55
Digital image courtesy of the Getty's Open Content Program

FW, SF, B

61

François Boucher (French, 1703–1770)
Mercury Confiding the Infant Bacchus to the Nymphs of Nysa, 1769
Oil on canvas
272.5 × 201.6 cm (107 1/4 × 79 3/8 in.)
Kimbell Art Museum, Fort Worth, Texas, AP 1972.07

FW, SF, B

62

François Boucher (French, 1703–1770)
Boreas Abducting Oreithyia, 1769
Oil on canvas
273.3 × 205 cm (107 5/8 × 80 3/4 in.)
Kimbell Art Museum, Fort Worth, Texas, AP 1972.10

FW, SF, B

63

François Boucher (French, 1703–1770)
Venus on the Waves, 1769
Oil on canvas
265.7 × 76.5 cm (104 5/8 × 30 1/8 in.)
The J. Paul Getty Museum, Los Angeles, 71. PA.54
Digital image courtesy of the Getty's Open Content Program

FW, SF, B

64

François Boucher (French, 1703–1770)
Juno Asking Aeolus to Release the Winds, 1769
Oil on canvas
278.2 × 203.2 cm (109 1/2 × 80 in.)
Kimbell Art Museum, Fort Worth, Texas, AP 1972.08

FW, SF, B

65

Writing table, about 1750
Marked by Pierre Macret (French, 1727–about 1796)
European red, black, and gold lacquer on beech; interior veneered with tulipwood on oak; fruitwood drawer linings; modern green leather writing surface; gilt-bronze mounts
83.3 × 82.2 × 44.3 cm (32 3/4 × 32 3/8 × 17 1/2 in.)
Museum of Fine Arts, Boston
Bequest of Forsyth Wickes—The Forsyth Wickes Collection, 65.2506

FW, SF, B

66

Harpsichord, probably 1736
Henri Hemsch (French, born in Germany, 1700–1769)
Painted poplar, carved and gilded oak, fir, ebony, ivory
238 × 89 × 92.5 cm (93 3/4 × 35 × 36 3/8 in.)
Museum of Fine Arts, Boston
The Edward F. Searles Musical Instrument Collection; Gift of Edward S. Rowland, Benjamin A. Rowland, Jr., George B. Rowland, Daniel B. Rowland, Rodney D. Rowland and M. A. Swedlund in memory of their father, Benjamin Allen Rowland, 1981.747

B

67

Charles-Antoine Coypel (French, 1694–1752)
Portrait of a Nobleman as Daphnis, about 1738–40
Pastel on paper adhered to canvas
81.2 × 64.5 cm (32 × 25 3/8 in.)
Private collection
Photograph: Michael Gould

B

AMOROUS PURSUITS

68

Jean-Honoré Fragonard (French, 1732–1806)
The New Model, about 1770–73
Oil on canvas
52 × 64 cm (20 ½ × 25 ¼ in.)
Musée Jacquemart-André, Paris
Image © RMN-Grand Palais/Art Resource, NY
Photograph: Jean Schormans

B

69

Jean-Honoré Fragonard (French, 1732–1806)
Aurora Triumphing over Night, about 1755–56
Oil on canvas
95.3 × 131.4 cm (37 ½ × 51 ¾ in.)
Museum of Fine Arts, Boston
Museum purchase with funds by exchange by contribution, and by exchange from a Gift of Laurence K. and Lorna J. Marshall, 2013.62

B

70

Louis Jean François Lagrenée (French, 1725–1805)
Mars and Venus, Allegory of Peace, 1770
Oil on canvas
64.8 × 53.8 cm (25 ½ × 21 ⅛ in.)
The J. Paul Getty Museum, Los Angeles, 97.PA.65
Digital image courtesy of the Getty's Open Content Program

FW, SF, B

71

Jean-François de Troy (French, 1679–1752)
The Declaration of Love, 1724
Oil on canvas
65.1 × 53.3 cm (25 × 21 in.)
The Wrightsman Collection
Photograph courtesy of the Metropolitan Museum of Art, New York

72

Jean-Honoré Fragonard (French, 1732–1806)
The Seesaw, about 1750–52
Oil on canvas
120 × 94.5 cm (47 ¼ × 37 ¼ in.)
Museo Thyssen-Bornemisza, Madrid, inv. no. 148 (1956.13)
Image © Museo Thyssen-Bornemisza/Scala/Art Resource, NY

FW, SF

73

François Boucher (French, 1703–1770)
Are They Thinking about the Grape?, 1747
Oil on canvas
80.8 × 68.5 cm (31 ¾ × 27 in.)
Art Institute of Chicago
Martha E. Leverone Endowment, 1973.304

B

74

William Hogarth (English, 1697–1764)
Before, 1730–31
Oil on canvas
37.2 × 44.7 cm (14 ⅝ × 17 ⅝ in.)
Fitzwilliam Museum, Cambridge, PD.11-1964

FW, SF

75

William Hogarth (English, 1697–1764)
After, 1731
Oil on canvas
37.2 × 45.1 cm (14 ⅝ × 17 ¾ in.)
Fitzwilliam Museum, Cambridge, PD.12-1964

FW, SF

76

Johann Zoffany (German, 1733–1810)
Self-Portrait, 1770s
Oil on canvas, painted on recto and verso

43 × 39 cm (16 7/8 × 15 3/8 in.)
Galleria Nazionale di Parma

FW, SF, B

77

Jean-Honoré Fragonard (French, 1732–1806)
Useless Resistance, about 1770–73
Oil on canvas
45 × 60.5 cm (17 3/4 × 23 7/8 in.)
Nationalmuseum, Stockholm, NM5415
Photograph: Nationalmuseum

B

78

Jean-Honoré Fragonard (French, 1732–1806)
Curiosity, about 1775–80
Oil on panel
16.5 × 12.5 cm (6 1/2 × 4 7/8 in.)
Musée du Louvre, M.I. 860
Image © RMN-Grand Palais/Art Resource, NY
Photograph: Stéphane Maréchaile

FW, SF, B

79

Jean-Honoré Fragonard (French, 1732–1806)
The Desired Moment, about 1770
Oil on canvas
50 × 61 cm (19 5/8 × 24 in.)
Collection George Ortiz, Switzerland
Image © Scala/White Images/Art Resource, NY

FW, SF, B

80

Jean-Baptiste Le Prince (French, 1734–1781)
Fear, 1769
Oil on canvas
50 × 64 cm (19 3/4 × 25 1/4 in.)
Toledo Museum of Art, 1970.444

FW, SF, B

81

Pierre Subleyras (French, 1699–1749)
The Amorous Courtesan, 1735
Oil on canvas
30.5 × 23.5 cm (12 × 9 1/4 in.)
Musée du Louvre, RF 1985-80
Image © RMN-Grand Palais/Art Resource, NY
Photograph: Franck Raux

FW, SF, B

82

Jean-Honoré Fragonard (French, 1732–1806)
Two Girls Playing on a Bed with Their Dogs, about 1770
Oil on canvas
74.3 × 59.3 cm (29 1/4 × 23 3/8 in.)
Collection of Lynda & Stewart Resnick, Los Angeles

FW, SF, B

83

Maurice Blot (French, 1753–1818), after Jean-Honoré Fragonard (French, 1732–1806) and Marguerite Gérard (French, 1761–1837)
The Contract, 1792
Engraving
37 × 46 cm (14 5/8 × 18 1/8 in.)
National Gallery of Art, Washington
Widener Collection, 1942.9.2178
Photograph courtesy of the National Gallery of Art, Washington

CLOTHES MAKE THE MAN

84

Suit
French or Italian, about 1750
Silk; polychrome velvet with supplementary patterning wefts
Jacket center back length: 95 cm (37 3/8 in.); breeches length: 80 cm (31 1/2 in.); waistcoat center back length: 83.8 cm (33 in.)
Museum of Fine Arts, Boston

William Francis Warden Fund and funds donated by Doris May 2016.489.1-3

B

85

Pietro Longhi (Italian, 1702–1785)
The Letter, 1746
Oil on canvas
61 × 49.5 cm (24 × 19 ½ in.)
The Metropolitan Museum of Art, New York
Frederick C. Hewitt Fund, 1912, 14.32.1
www.metmuseum.org

86

Cloth of gold (detail)
French (Lyon), about 1760
Silk plain weave with supplementary silk and metallic patterning wefts
Overall: 68.5 × 47 cm (27 × 18 ½ in.)
Museum of Fine Arts, Boston
Denman Waldo Ross Collection, 00.467

87

Lace border (detail)
French (Argentan), about 1760
Linen needlelace
Overall: 257.8 × 9.2 cm (101 ½ × 3 ⅝ in.)
Museum of Fine Arts, Boston
Gift of Mrs. Paul G. Pennoyer in memory of her mother Jane North Morgan, 51.1382

88

Francesco Guardi, *The Parlatorio* (detail, fig. 26)

89

William Hogarth (English, 1697–1764)
A Rake's Progress, Plate 1, *The Heir*, 1735
Engraving
Platemark: 35.4 × 40.6 cm (13 ⅞ × 16 in.)
Museum of Fine Arts, Boston
Harvey D. Parker Collection–Harvey Drury Parker Fund, 97.1198

90

Pietro Longhi (Italian, 1702–1785)
Lady at the Dressmaker's, 1760
Oil on canvas
61 × 52 cm (24 × 20 ½ in.)
Ca' Rezzonico, Venice, inv. Cl. I n. 1310
2016 © Photo Archive–Fondazione Musei Civici di Venezia

91

Capelet with hood (detail)
Probably French, about 1770
Silk plain weave with warp stripe, hand painted
Overall: 66.7 × 76.2 cm (26 ¼ × 30 in.)
Museum of Fine Arts, Boston
The Elizabeth Day McCormick Collection 43.696a

92

François-Hubert Drouais (French, 1727–1775)
Madame de Pompadour at Her Tambour Frame, 1763–64
Oil on canvas
217 × 156.8 cm (85 ⅜ × 61 ¾ in.)
The National Gallery, London, NG6440
Image © National Gallery, London/Art Resource, NY

93

Suit
French, about 1780
Silk voided velvet embroidered with silk and gold paillettes, glass and metallic thread
Jacket center back length: 110.5 cm (43 ½ in.); breeches length: 67.3 cm (26 ½ in.); waistcoat center back length: 60 cm (23 ⅝ in.)
Museum of Fine Arts, Boston
The Elizabeth Day McCormick Collection 43.644a–c

FW, SF, B

LONDON

94

Nathaniel Hone (Irish, 1718–1784)
Kitty Fisher, 1765
Oil on canvas
74.9 × 62.2 cm (29 ½ × 24 ½ in.)
National Portrait Gallery, London, NPG 2354
Image © National Portrait Gallery, London

FW, SF, B

95

Unknown artist, after William Hogarth (English, 1697–1764)
A Midnight Modern Conversation, about 1732
Oil on canvas
76.2 × 163.8 cm (30 × 64 ½ in.)
Yale Center for British Art
Paul Mellon Collection, B1981.25.351

SF, B

96

John Hamilton Mortimer (English, 1740–1779)
A Caricature Group, about 1766
Oil on canvas
83.8 × 106.7 cm (33 × 42 in.)
Yale Center for British Art
Paul Mellon Collection, B1981.25.467

FW, SF

97

Covered vase
Chinese, Qing dynasty, Kangxi period (1662–1722)
Porcelain with blue underglaze decoration
51.5 × 20.3 cm (20 ¼ × 8 in.)
Museum of Fine Arts, Boston, 95.577a–b

FW, SF, B

Vase stand
English (London), about 1755
Mahogany
45.7 × 27 cm (18 × 10 ⅝ in.)
Museum of Fine Arts, Boston
Gift of Horace Wood Brock, 2010.1034.1

FW, SF, B

98

William Hogarth (English, 1697–1764)
The Lady's Last Stake, 1759
Oil on canvas
91.4 × 105.4 cm (36 × 41 ½ in.)
Albright-Knox Art Gallery, Buffalo, New York
Gift of Seymour H. Knox, Jr., 1945, 1.35071875
Image © Albright-Knox Art Gallery/Art Resource, NY

FW, SF, B

99

Benjamin West (American, 1738–1820)
George III, 1783
Oil on canvas
126.5 × 101 cm (49 ¾ × 39 ¾ in.)
Cleveland Museum of Art
Gift of Mr. and Mrs. Lawrence S. Robbins, 1952.17

100

Giovanni Antonio Canal, called Canaletto (Italian, 1697–1768)
Westminster Bridge with the Lord Mayor's Procession on the Thames, 1747
Oil on canvas
95.9 × 127.6 cm (37 ¾ × 50 ¼ in.)
Yale Center for British Art
Paul Mellon Collection, B1976.7.94

SF, B

101

Giovanni Antonio Canal, called Canaletto (Italian, 1697–1768)
Ranelagh Rotunda, about 1751
Oil on canvas
51 × 76 cm (20 ⅛ × 29 ⅞ in.)
Compton Verney, Warwickshire, CVCSC: 0356.S
Image © Compton Verney, Warwickshire

102

Giovanni Antonio Canal, called Canaletto (Italian, 1697–1768)
The Grand Walk–Vauxhall Gardens, about 1751
Oil on canvas
51 × 76 cm (20 1/8 × 29 7/8 in.)
Compton Verney, Warwickshire, CVCSC: 0355.S
Image © Compton Verney, Warwickshire

CHAMPAGNE AND OYSTERS

103

Jean-Baptiste Pater (French, 1695–1736)
The Pyramid of Chicken Wings and Thighs Elevated on a Plate of Destiny by Madame Bouvillon, before 1733
Oil on canvas
29 × 38 cm (11 3/8 × 15 in.)
Neues Palais, Potsdam, Germany, GKI 5061
Image © Stiftung Preussische Schlösser & Gärten Berlin-Brandenburg
Photograph: Jörg P. Anders

104

Sauceboat and stand, 1756–59
Marked by François-Thomas Germain (French, 1726–1791)
Silver
Overall: 13.8 × 39 × 22.6 cm (5 3/8 × 15 3/8 × 8 7/8 in.)
Museum of Fine Arts, Boston
Elizabeth Parke Firestone and Harvey S. Firestone, Jr. Collection, 1993.515.2

FW, SF, B

105

Nicolas Lancret (French, 1690–1743)
Luncheon Party in a Park, about 1735
Oil on canvas
54.1 × 46 cm (21 1/4 × 18 1/8 in.)
Museum of Fine Arts, Boston
Bequest of Forsyth Wickes–The Forsyth Wickes Collection, 65.2649

FW, SF

106

Jean-François de Troy (French, 1679–1752)
The Oyster Luncheon, 1735
Oil on canvas
180 × 126 cm (70 7/8 × 49 5/8 in.)
Musée Condé, Chantilly, France
Photograph © RMN-Grand Palais/Art Resource, NY

107

Tureen in the form of a turkey, about 1760
Made by the Holitsch Manufactory (Hungarian, founded in 1743)
Tin-glazed earthenware
H. 39.4 cm (15 1/2 in.)
Museum of Fine Arts, Boston
Kiyi and Edward M. Pflueger Collection. Bequest of Edward M. Pflueger and Gift of Kiyi Powers Pflueger, 2006.890a–b

B

108

Tureen in the form of a boar's head, about 1750
Made by the Holitsch Manufactory (Hungarian, founded in 1743)
Tin-glazed earthenware, enamel decoration
Overall: 35.56 cm (14 in.)
Helen and Alice Colburn Fund, 57.169a–b

FW, SF, B

109

Jean-Baptiste Pater (French, 1695–1736)
Madame Bouvillon, Who, in Order to Tempt Destiny, Asks Him to Look for Lice, before 1733
Oil on canvas
29 × 38 cm (11 3/8 × 15 in.)
Neues Palais, Potsdam, Germany, GKI 5073
Image © Stiftung Preussische Schlösser & Gärten Berlin-Brandenburg
Photograph: Wolfgang Pfauder

110

Tureen with lid and stand, about 1760
Made at the Meissen manufactory (German, founded in 1710)

Hard-paste porcelain with polychrome enamel decoration and gilding
Tureen: 30.6 × 37.2 cm (12 × 14 5/8 in.); stand: 43.4 × 30.1 cm (17 1/8 × 11 7/8 in.)
Museum of Fine Arts, Boston
Bequest of William A. Coolidge, 1993.59.1a–c

FW, SF, B

111

Joseph Heinz the younger (Swiss, active in Italy, about 1600–1678)
View of a Kitchen, before 1678
Oil on canvas
153 × 134 cm (60 1/4 × 52 3/4 in.)
Museo Davia Bargellini, Bologna, Italy, inv. 44
Photograph: Archivio Fotografico Musei Civici d'Arte Antica i Istituzione Bologna Musei

DRESDEN TO DUCHCOV

112

Jean-Étienne Liotard (Swiss, 1702–1789)
Francesco Algarotti, 1745
Pastel on parchment
42 × 32.5 cm (16 1/2 × 12 3/4 in.)
Rijksmuseum, Amsterdam
M. A. Liotard Bequest, SK-A-234

113

Bernardo Bellotto (Italian, 1721–1780)
View of Dresden with the Frauenkirche at Left, 1747
Oil on canvas
130.8 × 232.4 cm (51 1/2 × 91 1/2 in.)
North Carolina Museum of Art, Raleigh
Purchased with funds from the State of North Carolina, 52.9.145

FW, SF, B

114

Bernardo Bellotto (Italian, 1721–1780)
View of Dresden with the Hofkirche at Right, 1748
Oil on canvas
135.9 × 233.7 cm (53 1/2 × 92 in.)
North Carolina Museum of Art, Raleigh
Purchased with funds from the State of North Carolina, 52.9.146

FW, SF, B

115

Johann Georg Ziesenis (German, 1716–1776)
Frederick II of Prussia, 1763
Oil on panel
142 × 98 cm (16 1/2 × 38 1/2 in.)
Stiftung Preussische Schlösser & Gärten Berlin-Brandenburg
Image © Erich Lessing/Art Resource, NY

116

Louis-Nicolas Lespinasse (French, 1734–1808)
View of the Oranienbaum, St. Petersburg, about 1783
Watercolor, pen with brown ink, brush with gray wash, and graphite on cream laid paper
21.8 × 65.3 cm (8 5/8 × 25 3/4 in.)
Private collection

B

117

Pierre-Étienne Falconet (French, 1741–1791)
Catherine the Great, 1773
Oil on canvas
68.6 × 55.9 cm (27 × 22 in.)
Hillwood House and Gardens, Washington, D.C., 51.60
Photograph: Edward Owen

FW, SF, B

118

Bernardo Bellotto (Italian, 1721–1780)
View of Krakowski Street, 1778
Oil on canvas
107.5 × 83.5 cm (42 3/8 × 32 7/8 in.)
National Museum, Warsaw, Poland
Image © Scala/White Images/Art Resource, NY

119

Snuffbox showing the view over Duchcov Castle with French garden and Baroque hospital, 18th century
Copper, enamel, glaze
4.5 × 10 × 7 cm (1 3/4 × 3 7/8 × 2 3/4 in.)
National Heritage Institute of Czech Republic, no. DH 8229
Photograph: Marta Pavlikova

MAN OF NUMBERS

120

Jean-Honoré Fragonard (French, 1732–1806)
The Charlatans, about 1775–76
Oil on canvas
49.5 × 38.7 cm (19 1/4 × 15 1/4 in.)
Private collection
Photograph © Private collection. All rights reserved

121

Pietro Longhi (Italian, 1702–1785)
The Fortune Teller, 1752
Oil on canvas
59.1 × 48.6 cm (23 1/4 × 19 1/8 in.)
Ca' Rezzonico, Venice, Cl. I n. 1309
2016 © Photo Archive–Fondazione Musei Civici di Venezia

FW, SF, B

122

Pietro Longhi (Italian, 1702–1785)
The Alchemists, 1752
Oil on canvas
61 × 50 cm (24 × 19 5/8 in.)
Ca' Rezzonico, Venice, Cl. I n. 1299
2016 © Photo Archive–Fondazione Musei Civici di Venezia

FW, SF, B

123

Antoine-Jean Duclos (French, 1742–1795) and François-Robert Ingouf (French, 1747–1812), after Sigmund Freudeberg (Swiss, 1745–1801)
The Event at the Ball, 1775
Etching and engraving
Sheet: 40.8 × 29.3 cm (16 1/8 × 11 1/2 in.)
National Gallery of Art, Washington
Rosenwald Collection, 1943.3.4370
Photograph courtesy of the National Gallery of Art, Washington

124

Francesco Guardi (Italian, 1712–1793)
The Ridotto of Palazzo Dandolo at San Moisè with Masked Figures Conversing, about 1750
Oil on canvas
76.2 × 104.7 cm (30 × 41 1/4 in.)
Private collection

FW, SF, B

125

Card table
English, about 1715
Laburnum, laburnum veneer, oak; brass and iron hardware; modern velvet playing surface
72.6 × 86.7 × 43.3 cm (28 5/8 × 34 1/8 × 17 in.)
Museum of Fine Arts, Boston
Bequest of Herbert Heidelberger in honor of Frederick and Minna Heidelberger, 1984.116

FW, SF, B

Pair of wine glasses
English, about 1750
Glass
Each: h. 16.9 cm (6 5/8 in.)
Museum of Fine Arts, Boston
Bequest of Forsyth Wickes–The Forsyth Wickes Collection, 65.2341-42

FW, SF, B

Pair of candlesticks
English (London), 1743–44
Silver
21 × 11.6 × 11.7 cm (8 1/4 × 4 1/2 × 4 5/8 in.);
20.6 × 11.8 × 11.8 cm (8 1/8 × 4 5/8 × 4 5/8 in.)

Museum of Fine Arts, Boston
Anonymous gift in memory of Charlotte Beebe Wilbour (1833–1914), 33.144, 33.146

FW, SF, B

126

Counting boxes with counters, about 1750–70
Made by Mariaval Le Jeune (French, active by 1746)
Painted ivory, gilt-metal
Each box: 2.2 × 8.5 × 6 cm (7/8 × 3 3/8 × 2 3/8 in.); baton counter: 6.7 × 1 cm (2 5/8 × 3/8 in.); circular counter: diam. 2.5 cm (1 in.); rectangular counter: 3.5 × 2 cm (1 3/8 × 3/4 in.)
Museum of Fine Arts, Boston
Gift of Stella Champollion Trafford, 2001.238.1–4

FW, SF, B

127

Jacques-Philippe Le Bas (French, 1707–1783), after Charles Eisen (French, 1720–1778)
A Game of Tric-Trac, about 1740–80
Engraving
Platemark: 38 × 27.3 cm (15 × 10 3/4 in.)
Museum of Fine Arts, Boston
Arthur and Charlotte Vershbow Fund, 2016.59

FW, SF, B

128

Jacques-Philippe Le Bas (French, 1707–1783), after Charles Eisen (French, 1720–1778)
A Game of Comet, about 1740–80
Engraving
Platemark: 38.8 × 27 cm (15 1/4 × 10 5/8 in.)
Museum of Fine Arts, Boston
Arthur and Charlotte Vershbow Fund, 2016.60

FW, SF, B

MAN OF LETTERS

129

Illustration from Giacomo Casanova, *Histoire de ma fuite* (Prague, 1787), page 212
Engraving
Houghton Library, Harvard University, *IC7.C2633.787h

SF, B

130

Giovanni Antonio Canal, called Canaletto (Italian, 1697–1768)
The Porta Portello, Padua, about 1741–42
Oil on canvas
62 × 109 cm (24 3/4 × 42 7/8 in.)
National Gallery of Art, Washington
Samuel H. Kress Collection, 1961.9.53
Photograph courtesy of the National Gallery of Art, Washington

FW, SF, B

131

Pierre Subleyras (French, 1699–1749)
Pope Benedict XIV, 1746
Oil on canvas
64.1 × 48.9 cm (25 1/4 × 19 1/4 in.)
The Metropolitan Museum of Art, New York
Purchase, Friends of European Paintings Gifts, Bequest of Joan Whitney Payson, by exchange, Gwynne Andrews Fund, Charles and Jessie Price Gift, and Valerie Delacorte Fund Gift, in memory of George T. Delacorte, 2009, 2009.145
www.metmuseum.org

B

132

Jean-Antoine Houdon (French, 1741–1828)
Jean Le Rond d'Alembert, about 1802
Marble
Overall with base: 52.5 × 28.4 × 23.5 cm (20 5/8 × 11 1/8 × 9 1/4 in.)
Yale University Art Gallery

Gift of McA. Donald Ryan, B.A. 1934, and William H. Ryan, class of 1921s, 1957.47.1

FW, SF, B

133

Joseph Siffred Duplessis (French, 1725–1802)
Benjamin Franklin, 1779
Oil on canvas
74.3 × 59.7 cm (29 ¼ × 23 ½ in.)
Courtesy of the Trustees of the Boston Public Library

FW, SF, B

134

Joshua Reynolds (English, 1723–1792)
Samuel Johnson, 1756–57
Oil on canvas
127.6 × 101.6 cm (50 ¼ × 40 in.)
National Portrait Gallery, London, NPG 1597
Image © National Portrait Gallery, London

FW, SF, B

135

Jean-Antoine Houdon (French, 1741–1828)
Voltaire, 1778
Marble
36.5 × 21.3 × 21.3 cm (14 ⅜ × 8 ⅜ × 8 ⅜ in.)
National Gallery of Art, Washington 1963.10.240
Photograph courtesy of the National Gallery of Art, Washington

FW, SF, B

136

Allan Ramsay (Scottish, 1713–1794)
Jean-Jacques Rousseau, 1766
Oil on canvas
74.9 × 64.8 cm (29 ½ × 25 ½ in.)
Scottish National Gallery, NG 820

FW, SF, B

DETAILS

pp. 2–3: fig. 37; p. 4: fig. 55; p. 15: fig. 4; pp. 18–19: fig. 2; pp. 30–31: fig. 8; p. 35: fig. 7; p. 43: fig. 24; pp. 64–65: fig. 26; p. 75: fig. 44; pp. 88–89: fig. 38; p. 99: fig. 51; p. 104: fig. 46; p. 117: fig. 61; p. 130: fig. 64; p. 135: fig. 64; p. 143: fig. 70; p. 158: fig. 79; p. 167: fig. 85; p. 181: fig. 93; p. 185: fig. 98; p. 188: fig. 94; p. 205: fig. 106; p. 221: fig. 118; p. 239: fig. 124; p. 257: fig. 3; p. 266: fig. 136

Pattern on chapter openings adapted from: Cravat end, Flemish (Brussels), mid-18th century, linen bobbin lace. Metropolitan Museum of Art, Gift of Mrs. Edward S. Harkness, 1948, 48.41.1, www.metmuseum.org

APPENDIX

Additional Exhibited Objects

Unless otherwise stated, objects are from the collection of the Museum of Fine Arts, Boston. Where a single dimension is given, it represents the largest dimension of the object, whether height, length, or width/diameter.

VENETIAN CONVENT TABLEAU

Suit in three pieces, French, late 18th century
Jacket and breeches of cut and uncut voided velvet embroidered with gilt silver wire, sequins, and glass; vest of silk satin, embroidered with silver-metallic yarns
The Elizabeth Day McCormick Collection, 43.644a–c

FW, SF, B

Dress with panniers, French or Italian, 1740–1750; textile about 1720
Silk lampas
The Elizabeth Day McCormick Collection, 43.695

FW, SF, B

Tricorne hat, French, 18th century
Retailed by Babin (French, 18th century)
Beaverfelt trimmed with ostrich feathers, paste brooch, and gold galloon; 33 cm (13 in.)
The Elizabeth Day McCormick Collection, 43.1844

FW, SF, B

Pair of woman's shoes, probably Italian, 1690–1720
Silk velvet, embroidered with metallic yarn, leather sole and wood heel; 15.3 cm (6 in.)
The Elizabeth Day McCormick Collection, 44.491a–b

FW, SF, B

Stomacher, possibly French, early 18th century
Silk compound weave brocaded with silver metallic patterning wefts; trimmed with silver and silk braid; 34.6 cm (13 5/8 in.)
Gift of Emily Welles Robbins (Mrs. Harry Pelham Robbins) and the Hon. Sumner Welles, in memory of Georgiana Welles Sargent, 49.917

FW, SF, B

Dress, English, 1740–50
Silk plain weave brocaded with silk and metallic threads
The Elizabeth Day McCormick Collection, 43.1642a

B

Stomacher, Italian, 1740–50
Silk plain weave embroidered with silk and metallic thread; 29.9cm (11 3/4 in.)
The Elizabeth Day McCormick Collection, 43.1905

B

Pair of woman's buckle shoes, European, 1760s
Silk damask; leather sole and heel; 22 cm (8 5/8 in.)
The Elizabeth Day McCormick Collection, 44.536a–b

B

Fan, Italian (Venice), 1730s
Double paper leaf painted in gouache; ivory sticks, lacquered and gilded; mother of pearl; 53 cm (20 7/8 in.)
Oldham Collection, 1976.190

FW, SF, B

Dress, English or Dutch, 1740–50
Silk plain weave, self-patterned and brocaded
The Elizabeth Day McCormick Collection, 43.1641

FW, SF

Petticoat, probably French, mid-18th century
Silk matelassé; 102 cm (40 1/8 in.)
Gift of Miss Helen F. Pettes, 42.434

FW, SF

Stomacher, French or Italian, 1740–50
Silk passementerie; 32.7 cm (12 7/8 in.)
The Elizabeth Day McCormick Collection, 43.1923

FW, SF

Pair of woman's mules, European, about 1770
Silk damask embroidered with silvered metallic yarn and fringe; leather lining, heel and sole; 22.5 cm (8 7/8 in.)
The Elizabeth Day McCormick Collection, 43.1721a–b

FW, SF

PARISIAN MORNING TOILETTE TABLEAU

Dress in two parts, French, 1760s
Silk satin patterned with weft floats
John H. and Ernestine A. Payne Fund, 2010.589.1–2

FW, SF, B

Pair of woman's buckle shoes
European, 1770s–80s
Printed leather; 10.2 cm (4 in.)
The Elizabeth Day McCormick Collection, 44.490a–b

FW, SF, B

Dress, French, 1775
Cotton plain weave, block printed and glazed
Gift of Mrs. Samuel Cabot, 55.1006

FW, SF, B

Apron, American, late 18th to early 19th century
Cotton plain weave with warp stripes; 94 cm (37 in.)
Gift of Miss Ellen A. Stone, 99.664.21

FW, SF, B

Pair of sleeve ruffles (engageantes), possibly Flemish, third quarter of the 18th century
Cotton plain weave embroidered with cotton; 40.6 cm (16 in.)
The Elizabeth Day McCormick Collection, 43.2549a–b

FW, SF, B

Pair of woman's buckle shoes, European, 1780s
Leather and silk ribbon; 22.7 cm (8 7/8 in.)

Gift of Prince Serge Belosselsky, 1970.340a–b

FW, SF, B

Suit in three parts, probably English or American, 1770–80
Silk voided velvet with uncut pile
Gift of the Misses Sara, Elizabeth Gaskell and Margaret Norton, 17.1441a–c

FW, SF

Armchair, French, about 1730–40
Beechwood; 18th-century tapestry woven upholstery; 102.7 cm (40 3/8 in.)
Bequest of Forsyth Wickes–The Forsyth Wickes Collection, 65.2494

FW, SF, B

Guéridon, French, about 1775
Kingwood and tulipwood veneers, gilded bronze; 75.2 cm (29 5/8 in.)
Bequest of Forsyth Wickes–The Forsyth Wickes Collection, 65.2503

FW, SF, B

Teapot, sugar bowl, cup, and saucer, French, 1760
Made at Sèvres Manufactory, France
Soft-paste porcelain, colored enamels, gilding; teapot: 12.2 cm (4 3/3 in.)
Bequest of R. Thornton Wilson in memory of Joan Bergere Drayton, 1983.111a–b to 113a–b

FW, SF, B

LONDON CARD PARTY TABLEAU

Suit in three pieces, French, late 18th century
Jacket and breeches of silk velvet embroidered with pailettes and metallic thread; vest of silk plain weave with supplementary wefts of silver metallic thread
The Elizabeth Day McCormick Collection, 43.639a–c

FW, SF, B

Suit in three pieces, British or French, 1770s
Silk plain weave
The Elizabeth Day McCormick Collection, 43.611a–c

FW, SF, B

Dress in two parts, English, about 1745, dress restyled about 1760
Silk plain weave, self patterned and brocaded
The Elizabeth Day McCormick Collection, 43.1639a–b

FW, SF, B

Stomacher, English, early 18th century
Silk and linen embroidered with silk and metallic thread; 34.5 cm (13 5/8 in.)
The Elizabeth Day McCormick Collection, 43.1911

FW, SF, B

Pair of sleeve ruffles (engageantes), French, about 1750–75
Silk bobbin lace; 45.7 cm (18 in.)
The Elizabeth Day McCormick Collection, 43.2548a–b

FW, SF, B

Pair of woman's buckle shoes, possibly English, 1770s
Silk plain weave embroidered with silk; leather sole and lining; 26.4 cm (10 3/8 in.)
The Elizabeth Day McCormick Collection, 44.505a–b

FW, SF, B

Side chair, English, about 1750–65
Mahogany, beech; 93.5 cm (36 3/4 in.)
Bequest of Forsyth Wickes–The Forsyth Wickes Collection, 65.2523

FW, SF, B

Side chair, English, about 1750–65
Mahogany; 94 cm (37 in.)
Bequest of Janet H. Stevens, 1978.181

FW, SF, B

Pair of wine glasses, English, 18th century
Glass; 14 cm (5 1/2 in.)
Gift of the Estate of Frank C. Doble, 1972.1177–78

FW, SF, B

Pair of card tables, English, about 1715
Laburnum, laburnum veneer, oak; each: about 72.5 cm (28 1/2 in.)
Bequest of Herbert Heidelberger in honor of Frederick and Minna Heidelberger, 1984.115-16

FW, SF, B

Ladle, English (London), about 1750
Marked by Isaac Callard
Silver; 27.7 cm (10 7/8 in.)
Samuel Putnam Avery Fund, 20.1626

FW, SF, B

Punch bowl, English, mid-18th century
Tin glazed earthenware, enamel decoration; 25.4 cm (10 in.)
Gift of the Bragg family, 2011.211

FW, SF, B

WORKS ON PAPER AND BOOKS

Giovanni Battista Albrizzi (Italian, 1698–1777), *Forestiere illuminato intorno le cose più rare, e curiose, antiche, e moderne della città di Venezia, e dell' isole circonvicine: Con la descrizione delle chiese, monisteri, ospedali, tesoro di S. Marco, fabbriche pubbliche, pitture celebri, e di quanto v'è di più riguardevole* (Venice, 1740)
Printed book, 17 cm (6 3/4 in.)
Museum of Fine Arts Library, Special Collections, 262.01

FW, SF, B

Giovanni Battista Albrizzi (Italian, 1698–1777), *Forestiere illuminato intorno le cose più rare, e curiose, antiche, e moderne della città di Venezia, e dell' isole circonvicine: con la descrizione delle chiese, monisteri, ospedali, tesoro di S. Marco, fabbriche pubbliche, pitture celebri, e di quanto v'è di più riguardevole* (Venice, 1765)
Printed book, 17 cm (6 3/4 in.)
Museum of Fine Arts Library, Special Collections, 262.01a

FW, SF, B

Georges François Blondel (French, 1730–after 1799)
A View of the Inside of the New Prison at Rome, 1765
Mezzotint; platemark: 56.4 × 40.5 cm (22 1/4 × 15 7/8 in.)
Stephen Bullard Memorial Fund, by exchange, 66.341

FW, SF, B

Georges François Blondel (French, 1730–after 1799)
A View of a Prison of the Composition of Mr. Blondel Done at Rome, 1765
Mezzotint; sheet: 57.1 × 41.5 cm (22 1/2 × 16 1/4 in.)
Stephen Bullard Memorial Fund, by exchange, 66.342

FW, SF, B

Rosalba Giovanna Carriera (Italian [Venetian], 1675–1757)
Portrait of a Woman Dressed with Jewels (Personification of Fire), about 1724
Pastel on paper, 63.5 × 50.8 cm (25 × 20 in.)
Gift of Mrs. Albert J. Beveridge, 53.942

B

Rosalba Giovanna Carriera (Italian [Venetian], 1675–1757)
Portrait of a Woman Wearing a Laurel Wreath (Personification of Poetry), about 1724
Pastel on paper; 63.5 × 50.8 cm (25 × 20 in.)
Gift of Mrs. Albert J. Beveridge, 53.943

B

Giacomo Casanova, *Histoire de ma fuite des prisons de la république de Venise, qu'on appelle les Plombs* (Leipzig: Schönefeld, 1788 [Prague, 1787])
Houghton Library, Harvard University, Cambridge, Massachusetts, *IC7 C2633 787h

Giacomo Casanova, *Icosameron, ou Histoire d'Édouard, et d'Élisabeth qui passèrent quatre vingts un ans chez les Mégamicres habitans aborigènes du Protocosme dans l'intérieur de notre globe* (Prague, 1788)
Houghton Library, Harvard University, *IC7 C2633 788j

Giacomo Casanova, *Scrutinio del libro Eloges de M. Voltaire par differens auteurs* (Venice, 1779)
Houghton Library, Harvard University, *IC7 C2633 779s

The Gentleman's Pocket Companion, for Travelling into Foreign Parts (London: Thomas Taylor, 1722)
Houghton Library, Harvard University *EC7.A100.722g2

Giacomo Casanova, *Exposition raisonnée du différent, qui subsiste entre les deux republiques de Venise et d'Hollande* (Venice, 1785)
Houghton Library, Harvard University *IC7 C2633 784ℓb

Giacomo Casanova, *Confutazione della Storia del governo veneto d'Amelot de La Houssaie* (Amsterdam, 1769)
Houghton Library, Harvard University, *IC7 C2633 769c)

Charles Nicolas Cochin, père (French, 1688–1754), and Charles Nicolas Cochin le fils (French, 1715–1790), after François-Nicolas Martinet (French, 1739–1796)
Décoration de la salle de spectacle, from *Recueil des festes, feux d'artifice, et pompes funebres, ordonées pour le roi par MM. les premiers gentilshommes de sa chambre*, 1756
Etching; sheet: 91.7 × 58 cm (36 1/8 × 22 7/8 in.)
Gift of William H. Schab and Frederick G. Schab, in honor of Mr. Henry P. Rossiter, 67.993

FW, SF, B

Charles Nicolas Cochin, père (French, 1688–1754), and Charles Nicolas Cochin le fils (French, 1715–1790), after François-Nicolas Martinet (French, 1739–1796)
Décoration du bal masqué donné par le roy, from *Recueil des festes, feux d'artifice, et pompes funebres, ordonées pour le roi par MM. les premiers gentilshommes de sa chambre*, 1756
Etching; sheet: 58 × 92.8 cm (22 3/4 × 36 1/2 in.)
Gift of William H. Schab and Frederick G. Schab, in honor of Mr. Henry P. Rossiter, 67.995

FW, SF, B

Thomas Chippendale, *The Gentleman and Cabinet Maker's Director: Being a Large Collection of the Most Elegant and Useful Designs of Household Furniture, in the Most Fashionable Taste*, London, 1762)
Illustrated book with 199 engravings
Gift of Maxim Karolik, 31.995

B

Giovanni Maria De Pian (Venetian, 1764–1800)
Prigioni dette Forni dove si facevano rinchiudere quelli che non volevano palesare i loro delitti, late 18th century
Engraving, 24.3 × 30.3 cm (9 5/8 × 11 7/8 in.)
Museo Correr, Venice

FW, SF, B

William Hogarth (English, 1697–1764), engraved by Simon François Ravenet, l'aîné (French, 1706–1774)
Marriage a la Mode, Plate 5, 1745

Etching and engraving; platemark: 38.7 × 46.4 cm (15 1/4 × 18 1/4 in.)
Katherine E. Bullard Fund in memory of Francis Bullard, 62.707

FW, SF, B

William Hogarth (English, 1697–1764)
A Rake's Progress, Plate 2, 1735
Engraving; platemark: 35.4 × 40.6 cm (13 7/8 × 16 in.)
Harvey D. Parker Collection–Harvey Drury Parker Fund, 97.1198

FW, SF, B

John S. Muller (German, active in Britain, ca. 1715–1792), after Samuel Wale RA (British, 1721–1786)
Vauxhall Gardens Shewing the Grand Walk at the Entrance of the Garden and the Orchestra with the Music Playing, after 1751
Etching and engraving, hand-colored, 25.6 × 40 cm (10 1/8 × 15 3/4 in.)
Yale Center for British Art, Paul Mellon Collection, B1977.14.18699

FW, SF, B

Henry Overton (British; 1676–1751)
A Pocket Map of London, Westminster, and Southwark, 1741
25 × 50 cm (9 7/8 × 19 5/8 in.)
Pusey Library, Harvard University, G5754. L7 1741.O8

Nathaniel Parr (English, active 1742–1751), after Canaletto (Italian, 1697–1768)
An Inside View of the Rotundo in Ranelagh Gardens, 1740s
Hand-colored engraving, 23.2 × 39.1 cm (9 1/8 × 15 3/8 in.)
Yale Center for British Art, Paul Mellon Collection, B1977.14.17973

FW, SF, B

Giovanni Battista Piranesi (Italian, 1720–1778)
Five plates from the *Carceri* (second edition, second issue), 1761
Etching and engraving
The Grand Piazza (Plate IV), platemark: 54.8 × 41.5 cm (21 5/8 × 16 3/8 in.)
The Staircase with Trophies (Plate VIII), platemark: 55.1 × 40.4 cm (21 6/8 × 15 7/8 in.)
Prisoners on a Projecting Platform (Plate X), platemark: 41.5 × 54.9 cm (16 3/8 × 21 5/8 in.)
The Gothic Arch (Plate XIV), platemark: 41.8 × 55 cm (16 1/2 × 21 5/8 in.)
The Pier with Chains (Plate XVI), platemark: 40.8 × 55.5 cm (16 1/8 × 21 7/8 in.)
Gift of Miss Ellen T. Bullard, 21.11675, 21.11679, 21.11681, 21.11687, 21.11690

FW, SF, B

Matthaeus Seutter (German, 1678–1757)
Provincia Austriaca Societatis Iesu, between 1730 and 1760 (?)
Hand-colored map, 37 × 54 cm (14 5/8 × 21 1/4 in.)
Pusey Library, Harvard University, G6481. E423 1730 S4

Matthaeus Seutter (German, 1678–1757)
Dresden an der Elb, eine Haupt-Stadt des Obern Sachsen, und höchst vortreffliche Residentz des dasigen Churfürsten und Konigs in Pohlen, 1740
Hand-colored map, 48 × 56 cm (18 7/8 × 22 in.)
Pusey Library, Harvard University, G6299. D7 1740 S4

William Sharp (English, 1749–1824)
Carlisle House Masque Ball Ticket, 1760s–70s
Engraving; sheet: 11 × 14.1 cm (4 3/8 × 5 1/2 in.)
Harvey D. Parker Collection–Harvey Drury Parker Fund, P9925

B

Currus civilis; or Genteel designs, for coaches, chariots, post-chaises, vis a vis, road and park phaetons, whiskeys, single-horse chaises, &c.: in the most fashionable taste, engraved on thirty plates, 1787–97

Printed by I. and J. Taylor's Architectural Library, London, England
Bound album, 20 × 29 cm (7 7/8 × 11 3/4 in.)
Redwood Library and Athenaeum, TS 2025 .C87 1787 quarto

FW, SF, B

Claude-Louis Desrais (French, 1746–1816)
Suite of twelve amorous drawings, about 1790
Variable media
Variable dimensions
Private collection

FW, SF, B

DECORATIVE ARTS

Pair of brackets, English or possibly French, about 1745
Gilded wood; each about 23.5 cm (9 1/4 in.)
Bequest of Herbert Heidelberger in honor of Frederick and Minna Heidelberger. Purchased by Decorative Arts Special Fund, 1984.123–24

FW, SF, B

Mirror, English, about 1760–65
Carved and gilded wood, 130.8 cm (51 1/2 in.)
Bequest of Herbert Heidelberger in honor of Frederick and Minna Heidelberger, 1984.133

FW, SF, B

Pair of armchairs, English, about 1755
Mahogany, mahogany veneer, deal; each about 101.5 cm (40 in.)
Bequest of George Nixon Black, 29.743-44

FW, SF, B

Pair of vases, about 1760
Made by Derby Manufactory, England (active about 1750–1848)
Soft-paste porcelain, enamel decoration; each about 38 cm (15 in.)
Gift of Mrs. Thomas Lindall Winthrop in memory of Mr. Winthrop, 21.1184–85

FW, SF, B

Epergne, English (London), 1755-56
Marked by Edward Wakelin (active after 1748, died in 1784)
Silver, 29.4 cm (11 5/8 in.)
Theodora Wilbour Fund in memory of Charlotte Beebe Wilbour, 1986.241a-j

FW, SF, B

Snuffbox mounted with a timepiece, English, about 1765
Probably by John and George Hannett (English, active in London, about 1730–90)
Agate and gold, 6.3 cm (2 1/2 in.)
Gift of the heirs of Bettina Looram de Rothschild, 2013.1746

FW, SF, B

Sauceboat, stand and ladle, English (London), 1746–47
Marked by Nicholas Sprimont (born in Liège, active in London, 1716–1771)
Silver; sauceboat: 20.3 cm (8 in.)
Gift of Alan and Simone Hartman and Harriet J. Bradbury Fund, 2001.68.2a–c

FW, SF, B

Telescoping spyglass and timepiece, English, mid-18th century
Gold, agate, diamonds, emeralds, rubies, 7.9 cm (3 1/8 in.)
Gift of the heirs of Bettina Looram de Rothschild, 2013.1747a–b

FW, SF, B

Toilette service, probably English, about 1750
Looking glass, ewer, basin, glove trays, scent bottles, bowls and boxes with covers, pin cushion
Gilded silver, cut glass, silk, walnut; looking glass: 69 cm (27 1/8 in.)
Gift of Alan and Simone Hartman and Harriet J. Bradbury Fund, 2001.132.1–14

FW, SF, B

Pair of wall lights, French, about 1750
Gilt bronze; each about 59.8 cm (23 ½ in.)
Helen and Alice Colburn Fund and Harriet Otis Cruft Fund, 1983.405-6

FW, SF, B

Pedal harp, French, about 1785
Godefroi Holtzman (French, active 1780–94)
Maple, spruce; 156.8 cm (61 ¾ in.)
Leslie Lindsey Mason Collection, 18.30

B

Snuffbox, French (Paris), about 1740
Gold, mother of pearl, 8.3 cm (3 ¼ in.)
Gift of the heirs of Bettina Looram de Rothschild, 2015.99

FW, SF, B

Clock, French (Paris), mid-18th century
Made at Meissen Manufactory, Germany, and Vincennes Manufactory, France
Gilt bronze, enameled metal, hard paste porcelain, soft paste porcelain, polychrome enamel decoration, gilding; 72.4 cm (28 ½ in.)
Bequest of William A. Coolidge, 1993.54

B

Folding fan, 1760s, French or English
Skin leaf painted in gouache and gilded; pierced and carved ivory sticks with applied mother of pearl; 54 cm (21 ¼)
Gift of Miss Annie Jewett, 13.586f

SF

Wine cooler from the Prince de Rohan service, about 1771
Made at Sèvres Manufactory, France
Painted by Étienne Evans (French, born 1733, active 1752–1806)
Soft paste porcelain, overglaze enamels, gilding; 17.4 cm (6 ⅞ in.)
Gift of John Fox, 46.8

FW, SF, B

Covered bowl and stand, 1759–60
Made at Sèvres Manufactory, France
Soft paste porcelain decorated in polychrome enamels and gold; bowl with cover: 17 cm (6 ¾ in.)
Bequest of Forsyth Wickes—The Forsyth Wickes Collection, 65.1785a–c

FW, SF, B

Covered tureen and stand, 1756
Made at Vincennes/Sèvres Manufactory, France
Probably painted by Charles Nicolas Dodin (French, 1734–1803)
Soft paste porcelain decorated in polychrome enamels and gold; tureen with lid: 33.8 cm (13 ¼ in.)
Bequest of Forsyth Wickes—The Forsyth Wickes Collection, 65.1885a–c

FW, SF, B

Snuffbox, French (Paris), about 1750–52
Probably by Gilles Langlois (French)
Gold, enamel; 7 cm (2 ¾ in.)
Anonymous gift, 1976.822

FW, SF, B

Chestnut bowl with cover and stand, 1766
Made at Sèvres Manufactory, France
Soft paste porcelain, colored enamels, gilding; 14 cm (5 ½ in.)
Gift of Michele Beiny in memory of her grandfather Hanns Weinberg, 1981.740a–b

FW, SF, B

Tureen in the form of a goose, 1775–80
Made at Niderviller Manufactory, France
Tin-glazed earthenware, 52.1 cm (20 ½ in.)
Bequest of R. Thornton Wilson in memory of Florence Ellsworth Wilson, 1983.101a–b

FW, SF

Tobacco box, French (Paris), 1756–62
Marble, silver mounts; 27.9 cm (11 in.)
Elizabeth Parke Firestone and Harvey S. Firestone, Jr. Collection, 1993.310

FW, SF, B

Sundial, French (Paris), about 1730–40
Mark of Macquart
Silver, enamel; 6.4 cm (2 ½ in.)
Elizabeth Parke Firestone and Harvey S. Firestone, Jr. Collection, 1993.313a

FW, SF, B

Hand candlestick, French (Paris), 1754–55
Silver, 23.1 cm (9 ⅛ in.)
Elizabeth Parke Firestone and Harvey S. Firestone, Jr. Collection, 1993.383

FW, SF, B

Shaving set, French (St. Omer) 1730
Henri-Louis Le Gaigneur
Silver; dish: 33.3 cm (13 ⅛ in.)
Elizabeth Parke Firestone and Harvey S. Firestone, Jr. Collection, 1993.387.1–4

FW, SF, B

Spittoon, French (Paris), 1772
Jean Francois Riel
Silver, 16.3 cm (6 ⅜ in.)
Elizabeth Parke Firestone and Harvey S. Firestone, Jr. Collection, 1993.468

FW, SF, B

Second course dish with cover, 1757
François-Thomas Germain (French, 1726–1791)
Silver, 30.5 cm (12 in.)
Elizabeth Parke Firestone and Harvey S. Firestone, Jr. Collection, 1993.495.1a–b

FW, SF, B

Pair of pigeon tureens with covers, about 1748
Made by Strasbourg Manufactory, France
Tin-glazed earthenware, 33 cm (13 in.)
Kiyi and Edward M. Pflueger Collection. Bequest of Edward M. Pflueger and Gift of Kiyi Powers Pflueger, 2006.913.1a–b, 2006.913.2a–b

FW, SF, B

Lidded tureen, liner, and stand, German (Dresden), 1768
Marked by Schrödel Brothers (German, active about 1767–72)
Silver with gilding; tureen with lid: 38.8cm (15 ¼ in.)
Bequest of William A. Coolidge, 1993.52a–e

FW, SF, B

Chest of drawers, Italian (Venice), about 1735–40
Gilded pine, gilt metal, marble top; 167.6 cm (66 in.)
Bequest of Susan Greene Dexter in memory of Charles and Martha Babcock Amory, 25.76

FW, SF, B

Pair of armchairs, Italian (Venice), about 1750
Carved, gessoed, and gilt wood; upholstered in period cut velvet; 129.5 cm (51 in.)
Toledo Museum of Art
Purchased with funds from the Florence Scott Libbey Bequest in Memory of her Father, Maurice A. Scott, 1977.32–33

FW, SF, B

Covered bowl and stand, 1770–80
Made at Cozzi Manufactory, Venice (active 1764–1812)
Hard paste porcelain with underglaze blue, colored enamel and gilded decoration; covered bowl: 17.4 cm (6 ⅞ in.)
Bequest of Forsyth Wickes–The Forsyth Wickes Collection, 65.2179a–c

FW, SF, B

Oval snuffbox with miniature of Catherine the Great, Swiss, about 1775
Gold and enamel, set with semiprecious gemstones; 8.3 cm (3 ¼ in.)
Gift of the heirs of Bettina Looram de Rothschild, 2013.1741

FW, SF, B

Snuffbox with portrait of Madame de Pompadour, Swiss or German, late 18th century
Portrait after François Hubert Drouais (French, 1727–1775)
Gold, enamel; 8.3 cm (3 ¼ in.)
Gift of the heirs of Bettina Looram de Rothschild, 2015.40

FW, SF, B

Fan, French, 1770–80
Skin/paper leaf painted in gouache; pierced, carved, painted and gilded ivory sticks; articulated medallion in ivory guards; 52 cm (20 ½ in.)
Oldham Collection, 1976.186

FW

Fan, French, 1750–60
Paper leaf painted in gouache; pierced, painted, and regilded ivory sticks; paste; 45 cm (17 ¾ in.)
Oldham Collection, 1976.226

B

Lenders to the Exhibition

Albright-Knox Gallery, Buffalo
Art Institute of Chicago
Boston Public Library
Ca' Rezzonico, Venice
Dallas Museum of Art
El Paso Museum of Art
Fitzwilliam Museum, Cambridge, England
Galleria Nazionale di Parma
Harvard Art Museums, Cambridge, Massachusetts
Harvard Map Collection, Pusey Library, Cambridge, Massachusetts
Hillwood House and Gardens, Washington, D.C.
Houghton Library, Harvard University, Cambridge, Massachusetts
Isabella Stewart Gardner Museum, Boston
J. Paul Getty Museum, Los Angeles
John and Mable Ringling Museum of Art, Sarasota
Memphis Brooks Museum of Art
Metropolitan Museum of Art, New York
Musée des Beaux-Arts, Rennes
Musée Granet, Aix-en-Provence
Musée Jacquemart-André, Paris
Musée du Louvre, Paris
Museo Correr, Venice
Museo Thyssen-Bornemisza, Madrid
Museu Nacional d'Art de Catalunya, Barcelona
Museum of Fine Arts, Houston
National Gallery of Art, Washington, D.C.
National Gallery of Canada, Ottawa
National Gallery, London
National Portrait Gallery, London
Nationalmuseum, Stockholm
Nelson-Atkins Museum of Art, Kansas City, Missouri
North Carolina Museum of Art, Raleigh
Redwood Library and Museum, Newport, Rhode Island
Scottish National Gallery, Edinburgh
Staatsgalerie Stuttgart
Toledo Museum of Art, Toledo, Ohio
Wadsworth Atheneum Museum of Art, Hartford, Connecticut
Wallraf-Richartz Museum & Fondation Corboud, Cologne
Yale Center for British Art, New Haven
Yale University Art Gallery, New Haven
Private collections

Acknowledgments

At the Museum of Fine Arts, Boston, we would like to thank Matthew Teitelbaum, Ann and Graham Gund Director, for his encouragement, and his predecessor, Malcolm Rogers, Ann and Graham Gund Director Emeritus, for endorsing this project from the outset. Special thanks are due to Maria Muller, Patrick McMahon, Edward Saywell, Mark Kerwin and his team, Chris Newth, and Benjamin Weiss, Director of Collections and Leonard A. Lauder Curator of Visual Culture, for their efforts on behalf of the exhibition. Colleagues past and present in the Art of Europe department who have contributed time and talent to this project are Courtney Leigh Harris; Marietta Cambareri, Senior Curator of European Sculpture and Jetskalina H. Phillips Curator of Judaica; Ronni Baer, William and Ann Elfers Senior Curator of Paintings, Art of Europe; Mary Feenan; Aleksandra Bursac; Adrien Enfedaque; Ashley Hannebrink; Rachel Kase; Caroline McCune; Samantha Muir; and Clelia Simpson. In MFA Publications, we thank Emiko Usui, Jennifer Snodgrass, Hope Stockton, and Terry McAweeney; and in the MFA Imaging Studios, photographers Michael Gould and John Woolf. We are grateful to Ryan Polich for the elegant layout and design of this volume; to Tomomi Itakura and Keith Crippen and his team for their exhibition and graphic design, and to the facilities, carpentry, and electrical teams for bringing them to life. Barbara Martin, Barbara and Theodore Alfond Curator of Education, and Adam Tessier have helped develop and shape the interpretive materials. Logistical support has been provided across several Museum departments by Jill Kennedy-Kernohan, Janet Moore, Gillian Fruh, and Anne Silk. Essential to a successful loan exhibition are the conservators of paintings, objects, furniture and frames, works on paper, and textiles: Rhona MacBeth, Eijk and Rose-Marie van Otterloo Conservator of Paintings and Head of Paintings Conservation; Pamela Hatchfield, Robert P. and Carol T. Henderson Head of Objects Conservation; Gerri Strickler, Gordon Hanlon, Christine Storti, Andrew Haines, Katrina Newbury, Saundra B. Lane Associate Conservator, Gail English, Claudia Iannuccilli, and Joel Thompson. For their ingenious display mounts, we thank Brett Angell, Steve Deane, and Kimberly McParland. Colleagues across curatorial departments and from the Museum's library who have assisted with object selection and loan negotiations include Pamela Parmal, Chair and David and Roberta Logie Curator of Textile and Fashion Arts; Meghan Melvin, Jean S. and Frederic A. Sharf Curator of Design; Darcy Kuronen, Department Head and Pappalardo Curator of Musical Instruments; Nancy Berliner, Wu Tung Curator of Chinese Art; Erica Hirshler, Croll Senior Curator of American Paintings; Victoria Reed, Monica S. Sadler Curator for Provenance; and Paul McAlpine. Finally, we thank Linda Chernoff, Patty Doyle, Karen Frascona, Dawn Griffin, Kristen Hoskins, Olga Khvan, and Gary Mak.

At the Kimbell Art Museum, we are grateful to the Board of Directors, led by Kay Fortson, for their support of the exhibition. In addition, thanks are due to our director, Eric M. Lee; deputy director George T. M. Shackelford; Brenda Cline, executive vice president and chief financial officer of the Kimbell Art Foundation; Susan Drake, deputy director of finance and administration; Claire Barry, director of conservation, with Rafael Barrientos; Patricia Decoster, head of collections management and registration, with Samantha Sizemore and Shelly Threadgill; Jessica Brandrup, head of marketing and public relations, with Claire Lukeman and Madison Ladd; Robert McAn, head of membership and special events, with Ann Huffman; Angie Bulaich, head of development; Larry Eubank, operations manager, with Jesse Hernandez, Bert Herrington, Cory Ottinger, and Rickey Honaker; Connie Hatchette-Barganier, education manager; Liz Johnson, executive assistant to the director; Robert LaPrelle, photographer; Gary Yawn, visitor services manager; Megan Smyth, manager of publications; Mark Krauter, designer; Regina Palm, curatorial assistant; and curators Jennifer Casler-Price and Nancy E. Edwards.

At the Fine Arts Museums of San Francisco, we would like to thank, above all, Max Hollein, Director and CEO, for his enthusiasm for this project, which was brought to the Museums originally by Colin B. Bailey, former Director of Museums, and shepherded by Richard Benefield, former acting director and chief operating officer. Our Board of Trustees, led by Diane B. Wilsey, has advocated for the exhibition since its inception. Heartfelt appreciation goes to Ed Prohaska, chief financial officer, and Julian Cox, chief curator and founding curator of photography, who have supported the presentation at the administrative level. A particular debt of gratitude must also be paid to our curators who have managed the program so aptly, including Martin Chapman, curator-in-charge of decorative arts and sculpture; Melissa Buron, associate curator of European paintings; and Kirk Nickel, assistant curator of European paintings. Further thanks are extended to the Museums' exhibitions team, including Krista Brugnara, director of exhibitions; Tomomi Itakura, director of exhibition design; and Hilary Magowan, senior exhibitions coordinator. Conservators across our Museums helped with the many objects featured in the presentation, including Elise Effmann Clifford, head paintings conservator; Tricia O'Reagan, paintings conservator; Sarah Kleiner, assistant paintings conservator; Natasa Morovic, frames and gilded surfaces conservator; Sarah Gates, head textiles conservator; Anne Getts, Andrew W. Mellon Assistant Textiles Conservator; and Emily Meyer, senior museum mountmaker. Throughout the Museums, further support was provided by Abigail Dansiger, research librarian; Leslie Dutcher, director of publications; Deanna Griffin, director of registration and collections management, and Kimberley Montgomery, associate registrar; Stuart Hata, director of retail operations, and Tim Niedert, book and media manager; Susan Klein, director of marketing and communications; Sheila Pressley, director of education; and Amanda Riley, director of development.

Many colleagues at museums around the world have collaborated by sharing works of art, information, ideas, and enthusiasm for the project.

Art Institute of Chicago: James Rondeau, Douglas Druick, Aimee Marshall, Christopher Monkhouse. Albright-Knox Art Gallery: Janne Sirén, Catherine Scrivo Baker. Bibliothèque nationale de France: Laurence Engel, Isabelle Le Masne de Chermont, Cyril Chazal, Gennaro Toscano. Boston Public Library: David Leonard, Eve Griffin, Laura Irmscher. Boston Athenaeum: David Dearinger. Dallas Museum of Art: Agustín Arteaga, Walter Elcock, Maxwell L. Anderson, Olivier Meslay. Detroit Institute of Arts: Salvador Salort-Pons, Stephen McLallen. El Paso

Museum of Art: Tracey B. Jerome, Christian Gerstheimer, Patrick Shaw Cable. Fitzwilliam Museum: Tim Knox, David Packer. Fondazione Musei Civici di Venezia: Gabriella Belli, Alberto Craievich, Monica Vianello. Galleria Nazionale di Parma: Sabina Magrini, Marina Gerra. Harvard Art Museums: Martha Tedeschi, Deborah Martin Kao, Maureen Donovan, Cassandra Albinson, Francine Flynn. Hillwood House and Gardens: Kate Markert, Liana Paredes, MJ Meredith Hagan. Houghton Library, Harvard University: Thomas Hyry, Carie McGinnis. Isabella Stewart Gardner Museum: Peggy Fogelman, Anne Hawley, Christina Nielsen, Amanda Venezia. J. Paul Getty Museum: Timothy Potts, Richard Rand, Davide Gasparotto, Anne Woollett, Betsy Severance. John and Mable Ringling Museum of Art: Steven High, Virginia Brilliant, Heidi Taylor. Memphis Brooks Museum of Art: Emily Ballew Neff, Stanton Thomas. Musée des Beaux-Arts, Rennes: Anne Dary, Guillaume Kazerouni. Musée du Louvre: Jean-Luc Martinez, Sebastien Allard, Guillaume Faroult, Martine Depagniat, Olivier Laville, Fanny Meurisse. Musée Granet: Bruno Ely, Stéphanie Lardez. Musée Jacquemart-André: Nicolas Sainte Fare Garnot, Pierre Curie. Museo Thyssen-Bornemisza: Guillermo Solana, Beatriz Blanco, Marian Aparicio. Museu Nacional d'Art de Catalunya: Josep Serra Villalba, Susana López, Ana Izquierdo Ramírez, Joan Yeguas. Museum of Fine Arts, Houston: Gary Tinterow, Maggie Williams, Helga Aurisch. Metropolitan Museum of Art, New York: Thomas P. Campbell, Keith Christiansen, Luke Syson, Denny Stone. National Gallery, London: Gabriele Finaldi, Letizia Treves, Caroline Campbell, Humphrey Wine, Naomi Lewis. National Gallery of Art, Washington, D.C.: Earl A. Powell III, David Alan Brown, C. D. Dickerson, Shannon Schuler. National Gallery of Canada: Marc Mayer, Sonia Del Re, Kate Beresford, Ceridwen Maycock. Nationalmuseum, Stockholm: Berndt Arell, Magnus Olausson, Per Hedström, Karin Sandstedt. National Portrait Gallery, London: Nicholas Cullinan, Lucy Peltz, David McNeff. Nelson-Atkins Museum of Art: Julián Zugazagoitia, Nicole Myers, Julie Mattsson. North Carolina Museum of Art: Lawrence J. Wheeler, David Steel. Pusey Library, Harvard University: David E. Weimer. Redwood Library and Museum: Benedict Leca. Scottish National Gallery: Michael Clarke, Luke Smithson. Staatsgalerie Stuttgart: Christiane Lange. Toledo Museum of Art: Brian Kennedy, Larry Nichols, Jutta Page, Elizabeth Spencer. Wadsworth Atheneum Museum of Art: Thomas J. Loughman, Oliver Tostmann, Linda

Roth, Mary Busick. Wallraf-Richartz-Museum & Fondation Corboud: Marcus Dekiert, Barbara Schaefer, Iris Schaefer, Roland Krischel. Yale Center for British Art: Amy Meyers, Matthew Hargraves, Gillian Forrester, Cory Myers. Yale University Art Gallery: Jock Reynolds, Pamela Franks, Laurence Kanter.

We are profoundly grateful to individual lenders and their support staff who have shared works of art from their private collections and facilitated loans: Lynda and Stewart Resnick, Bernard Jazzar, Jeffrey and Carol Horvitz, Alvin Clark, Mr. and Mrs. Randall Smith, Carolyn Thompson, the George Ortiz collection, and other lenders who wish to remain anonymous.

In the course of developing the exhibition and accompanying publication, many people have been generous with their help and advice: Christopher Apostle, Lorenzo Buonanno, Melissa Conn, Leslie Contarini, John Fiorilla, Alberto Franchetti, Andrea Chiari Gaggia, Giovanni Giol, William and Sandra Lobkowicz, Dulcia Meijers, Roger and Bikem de Montebello, Peter Nisbet, Liesl Odenweller, Lelia Passi, Francesca Bortolotto Possati, Bruce Redford, Andrea di Robilant,Toto Bergamo Rossi, Philip Rylands, Helmut Watzlawick, Alan Wintermute and Luca Zentilini. Generous support for initial research was provided by the Gladys Krieble Delmas Foundation and generous support for this publication was provided by the Andrew W. Mellon Publications Fund.

To those whose names we have inadvertently omitted, we offer our apology and extend our sincere thanks.

Frederick Ilchman
Chair and Mrs. Russell W. Baker Curator of Paintings, Art of Europe, Museum of Fine Arts, Boston

C. D. Dickerson III
Curator and Head of Sculpture and Decorative Arts, National Gallery of Art, Washington, D.C.

Thomas Michie
Russell B. and Andrée Beauchamp Stearns Senior Curator of Decorative Arts and Sculpture, Art of Europe, Museum of Fine Arts, Boston

Esther Bell
Robert and Martha Berman Lipp Senior Curator, Clark Art Institute

Contributors

ESTHER BELL, former Curator-in-Charge of European Paintings at the Fine Arts Museums of San Francisco, is Robert and Martha Berman Lipp Senior Curator, Clark Art Institute.

MEREDITH CHILTON is Chief Curator of the Gardiner Museum, Toronto.

JEFFREY L. COLLINS is Professor of Early Modern Art and Visual Culture at Bard Graduate Center.

C. D. DICKERSON III is Curator and Head of Sculpture and Decorative Arts, National Gallery of Art, Washington, D.C.

NINA L. DUBIN is Associate Professor of Art History at the University of Illinois at Chicago.

COURTNEY LEIGH HARRIS is Curatorial Research Fellow, Decorative Arts and Sculpture, Art of Europe, Museum of Fine Arts, Boston.

FREDERICK ILCHMAN is Chair and Mrs. Russell W. Baker Curator of Paintings, Art of Europe, Museum of Fine Arts, Boston.

JAMES H. JOHNSON is Professor of History at Boston University.

THOMAS MICHIE is Russell B. and Andrée Beauchamp Stearns Senior Curator of Decorative Arts and Sculpture, Art of Europe, Museum of Fine Arts, Boston.

PAMELA A. PARMAL is Chair and David and Roberta Logie Curator of Textile and Fashion Arts, Museum of Fine Arts, Boston.

MALINA STEFANOVSKA is Professor of French and Francophone Studies at the University of California, Los Angeles.

SUSAN M. WAGER is Assistant Professor of Art History at the University of New Hampshire.

MICHAEL YONAN is Associate Professor of Eighteenth- and Nineteenth-Century European Art and Director of Graduate Studies, Department of Art History and Archaeology, at the University of Missouri.

Index

Page numbers in *italics* refer to illustrations.

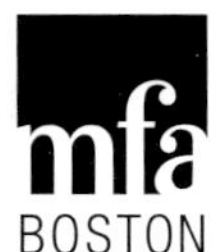

MFA Publications
Museum of Fine Arts, Boston
465 Huntington Avenue
Boston, Massachusetts 02115
www.mfa.org/publications

Published in conjunction with the exhibition *Casanova: The Seduction of Europe*, organized by Museum of Fine Arts, Boston; Kimbell Art Museum; and Fine Arts Museums of San Francisco

Kimbell Art Museum, Fort Worth: August 27–December 31, 2017

Fine Arts Museums of San Francisco, Legion of Honor: February 10–May 28, 2018

Museum of Fine Arts, Boston: July 1–October 8, 2018

Generous support for this publication was provided by the Andrew W. Mellon Publications Fund.

ISBN 978-0-87846-842-3

Library of Congress Control Number: 2017940415

All illustrations in this book were photographed by the Imaging Studios, Museum of Fine Arts, Boston, except where otherwise noted.

Edited by Jennifer Snodgrass
Copyedited by Dalia Geffen
Proofread by Fronia Simpson
Designed by Ryan Polich, Lucia | Marquand
Typeset in Ashbury and Cala by Tina Henderson
Production by Terry McAweeney
Production assistance by Hope Stockton
Printed on 150 gsm Perigord
Printed and bound at Verona Libri, Verona, Italy

Front cover: Jean-Marc Nattier, *Thalia, Muse of Comedy*, 1739 (detail, fig. 43)
Back cover: Canaletto, *Entrance to the Grand Canal*, about 1730 (detail, fig. 16)

Distributed in the United States of America and Canada by

ARTBOOK | D.A.P.
75 Broad Street, Suite 630
New York, New York 10004
www.artbook.com

Distributed outside the United States of America and Canada by

Thames & Hudson, Ltd.
181A High Holborn
London WC1V 7QX
www.thamesandhudson.com

FIRST EDITION
Printed and bound in Italy

This book was printed on acid-free paper.